MW01002438

BEYOND CALVIN:

ESSAYS ON THE DIVERSITY OF THE REFORMED TRADITION

Proceedings of the 4th Annual Convivium
Irenicum
Presented June 1–4, 2016

Edited by W. Bradford Littlejohn and Jonathan Tomes

Copyright © 2017 The Davenant Trust
All rights reserved.

ISBN: 0692890823
ISBN-13: 978-0692890820

Front cover image taken from John Rogers Herbert, *Assertion of Liberty of Conscience by the Independents of the Westminster Assembly of Divines* (1847; Palace of Westminster)

Cover design by Rachel Rosales, Orange Peal Design

"For just as the body is one and has many members, and all the members of the body, though many, are one body, so it is with Christ. For in one Spirit we were all baptized into one body—Jews or Greeks, slaves or free—and all were made to drink of one Spirit. For the body does not consist of one member but of many. If the foot should say, 'Because I am not a hand, I do not belong to the body,' that would not make it any less a part of the body. And if the ear should say, 'Because I am not an eye, I do not belong to the body,' that would not make it any less a part of the body. If the whole body were an eye, where would be the sense of hearing? If the whole body were an ear, where would be the sense of smell? But as it is, God arranged the members in the body, each one of them, as he chose. If all were a single member, where would the body be? As it is, there are many parts, yet one body."—1 Cor. 12:12–20

LIST OF CONTRIBUTORS

Jake Meador is the Vice President of the Davenant Trust and Editor-in-Chief of Mere Orthodoxy. He lives in Lincoln, NE with his wife and two children. His writing has appeared in *First Things*, *Books & Culture*, *Front Porch Republic*, *Christianity Today*, and *Fare Forward*.

Dr. E.J. Hutchinson is Assistant Professor of Classics at Hillsdale College (Hillsdale, Mich.), where he has taught since 2007. His research interests focus on the literature of Late Antiquity and the Neo-Latin literature of the Renaissance and Reformation, and he is translating Niels Hemmingsen's *De Lege Naturae* for the Sources in Early Modern Economics, Ethics, and Law series. He is a member of the Orthodox Presbyterian Church.

Dr. W. Bradford Littlejohn is the President of the Davenant Trust and teaches philosophy at Moody Bible Institute (Spokane). He is the author of three books, most recently *The Peril and Promise of Christian Liberty: Richard Hooker, the Puritans, and Protestant Political Theology* (Eerdmans, 2017), and has published numerous articles and book chapters in historical theology and Christian ethics. He also serves as an Associate Editor of *Political Theology*.

Dr. Andre Gazal teaches at Trinity Evangelical Divinity School, the University of Northwestern Ohio, and North Greenville University. He is the author of *Scripture and Royal Supremacy in Tudor England: The Use of Old Testament Historical Narrative*. He has also contributed to the *Encyclopedia of Christianity in the United States* (Rowman and Littlefield, 2016) and the *Encyclopedia of Martin Luther and Reformation* (Rowman and Littlefield, forthcoming 2017).

Michael J. Lynch is a Ph.D candidate at Calvin Theological Seminary, where he is researching the theology of John Davenant and early modern hypothetical universalism under Richard Muller. He is a Contributing Editor of the Acts of the Synod of Dordrecht Research Project, and is editing a translation of John Davenant's *De Praedestione et Reprobatione*.

Stephen Wolfe is a Ph.D student in the Department of Political Science at

Louisiana State University. His research interests include religion and the American founding, Reformed political theology, political economy, and the phenomenology of place. He is a graduate of West Point and is currently an Army officer in the Louisiana National Guard. He lives in Baton Rouge, LA with his wife and three children.

CONTENTS

FOREWORD

Carl Trueman, The Davenant Trust

THE *CONVIVIUM Irenicum* is an eclectic gathering of Reformed pastors and theologians which takes place annually in an idyllic location in South Carolina. For a couple of days, denominational rivalries are set aside in the interest of full and frank discussion of a range of theological topics. The purpose is to recapture some of the irenic discussions (and there were at least some irenic discussions) that characterized the Reformed world of earlier generations.

It was my pleasure and privilege to be the guest speaker at the Convivium in 2016 and this volume contains a number of the papers which were delivered at that gathering. The subjects reflect areas of historic importance to anyone thinking about Reformed theology and ecumenism.

The collection begins with a discussion of Martin Bucer, a man perhaps second only to Martin Luther in establishing the early impulses of Reformation theology, a profound influence on Calvin, and undoubtedly the most ecumenical of all the early Reformers. His emphasis upon love as a vital mark of the church captures a New Testament emphasis too often neglected in subsequent ecclesiology.

Beza's *Icones* may not be well-read today but many of the woodcuts it contained will be familiar, from its famous depiction of the long-bearded John Knox to the stern William Tyndale. Here the work is explored as offering an example of how the cultural ambitions of humanism and the theological concerns of the Reformation worked together to shape the sixteenth century.

Of course, no attempt to draw on Reformed irenicism could be complete without some reference to Richard Hooker, the great theorist of Elizabethan Anglicanism. Because of its aesthetically moderate approach to Protestantism, Anglicanism is often neglected as a positive voice in discussions of Reformed church life. Here his approach to that most divisive of ecumenical issues in the Reformation, Christology with reference to the eucharist, is addressed.

Church government was also an issue at the Reformation. A paper on George Carleton takes the reader to the heart of the issue as it fed into discussions at the Synod of Dordt. Again, that neglected part of the Reformed tradition, the Anglican/epsicopalian contribution, is used as a positive source.

Finally two papers address hardy perennials: the issue of the extent of the atonement and the confessional and historical status of hypothetical universalism; and the possibilities of pagan virtue as allowed by Francis Turretin.

These papers are all historical in their starting points and in their orientation. Yet their significance for today is obvious. Each addresses an issue with which Reformed Christians continue to wrestle today. In an age where we are witnessing a seismic shift in the social status of the church and of Christianity, clear thinking on topics such as ecclesiology is vital. In addition, we need to think carefully about the nature and limits of virtue within a secular context. And, of course, as our numbers decrease and our established denomination structures come under pressure, we need to think constantly about the nature of ecumenism, of confessional boundaries, and on those things which unite us and divide us from other Christians—Reformed and otherwise.

In such a context, we need to draw upon our history. We should not do this in an uncritical manner—the past is the past and has no intrinsic authority over the present. But the past is the church's past and something from which we need to draw help for the present in an appreciative, thoughtful and critical manner. These papers individually, and this collection as a whole, exemplify how this can be done.

Read, learn and go and do likewise.

Carl Trueman
Oreland, PA
April 2017

INTRODUCTION

W. Bradford Littlejohn, The Davenant Trust

THE VOLUME which you have before you, and the conference which produced it, and indeed the organization which put on that conference and published this book, grew out of a group of friends calling themselves the "Reformed irenicists." To the few Christians today who are even familiar with the term *irenic* ("aiming at peace"), such a moniker might well seem like an oxymoron. If Reformed theology is associated with anything nowadays, it is often with a factiousness and dogmaticism that seems ready to leave a church or denomination (or better yet, kick your opponents out of one) over almost any offense, real or imagined.

But it was not always so. Some of the great names of early modern Reformed theology adopted the term for themselves, or wrote books with the title *Irenicum*. Such authors include a Scots Episcopalian, John Forbes, an English Independent, Jeremiah Burroughs, an English Episcopalian, Edward Stillingfleet, and two of the giants of early Dutch Reformed theology, Franciscus Junius and David Pareus.[1] During the early 17th century, the Reformed world was the focal point for some of the most ambitious and sincerely meant initiatives for the healing of the divisions in Christendom. Perhaps the most comprehensive, worked out by French Huguenot leader Pierre du Moulin and King of England and Scotland, James VI and I, called for all the Reformed churches to unite in council and establish a common

---

[1] John Forbes, *Irenicum amatoribus veritatis et pacis in Ecclesia Scoticana* (Aberdeen: E. Rabanus, 1629); Jeremiah Burroughs, *Irenicum, to the lovers of truth and peace heart-divisions [...]* (London: Robert Dawlman, 1653); Edward Stillingfleet, *Irenicum, a weapon-salve for the churches wounds [...]* (London: Mortlock, 1662); Franciscus Junius, *Eirenicum de pace ecclesiae catholicae* (1593); and David Pareus, *Irenicum sive de Unione et Synodo Evangelicorum concilianda Liber Votivus [...]* (Johannes Lancellotus, 1615).

confession of faith, recognizing that they differed only in non-essential matters, and then to approach the Lutheran churches to work out their differences, before finally undertaking an ecumenical council between a united Protestantism and Rome.[2] Political developments, and the Arminian controversy, ultimately scuttled the scheme, but its mere existence puts the lie to popular perceptions of the Reformed as invariably spiteful, contentious hair-splitters interested only in comprehensive purity of doctrine, rather than unity.

But who were the Reformed? The names mentioned already suggest rather more diversity than is generally recognized, specifically the inclusion of the Anglican churches. We are so accustomed to the stubborn divisions over church government that have characterized Anglophone Protestantism for the past four centuries that is difficult for us to wrap our heads around the fact that both James (an episcopalian) and du Moulin (a presbyterian) considered the question a secondary one, and no bar to union. At the Synod of Dort, as you will read in this volume, Reformed episcopalians came together with presbyterians of various sorts to craft a common statement of soteriology, and showed in the process respect for one another's differing views on polity. Indeed, although there were by the time of James elements within the Church of England leaning away from the Reformed (or at least "Calvinist" self-identification, they were a decided minority, and would long remain so. The Reformed brotherhood of churches of course also included in its ranks the German Reformed, many of them Melanchthonian Lutherans more than Calvinists in their origins and emphases, not to mention the great forgotten Reformed church of Hungary. Indeed, the Reformed can lay some fair claim to being not the narrowest, but the broadest of the Reformation traditions.

But how does such breadth square with a commitment to confessions? Reformed churches are and always have been confessional churches, with the French Reformed drafting the Gallican Confession in 1559, the Scots the Scots Confession in 1560, the Dutch the Belgic Confession in 1562 and the Canons of Dort in 1619, the German Reformed the Heidelberg Catechism in 1563, the English the Thirty-Nine Articles in 1563, the Swiss the Second Helvetic Confession of 1566, and finally the British Presbyterians the Westminster Confession in 1647. Nowadays, many are prone

---

[2] See W. Brown Patterson, *King James VI and I and the Reunion of Christendom* (Cambridge: Cambridge University Press, 2000), ch. 5.

to think of confessionalism as a straitjacket, but few who make such complaints have bothered to familiarize themselves with many of these confessions. Most of them are far more capacious than we expect to find them, never even touching on many of the arcane doctrinal minutia that card-carrying contemporary confessionalists spill much of their ink upon. Even where they do pronounce decidedly on matters debated within the broader tradition, early modern Reformed theologians often emphasized that such points of difference were secondary and no bar to communion.

Still, what role ought confessions to have in the life of the church, especially today when we no longer think in terms of national churches, and no longer assume, as earlier confessionalists did, a godly magistrate to enforce the confessions? Today we find ourselves making common cause against militant secularism with low-church evangelicals of every stripe, not to mention often high-church Anglicans, Lutherans, and even Roman Catholics, and find that the theological and ethical issues that most divide us often go almost entirely unmentioned in the earlier documents. Moreover, vast new advances in biblical scholarship over the past century have shed new light on traditional doctrines, not necessarily invalidating them, but suggesting in some cases fresh, more biblically sound ways of articulating them.

At our 2016 Convivium Irenicum, dedicated to the theme of "Confessionalism and Diversity in the Reformed Tradition," we explored such questions at length with the aid of our esteemed guest Dr. Carl Trueman, together with Peter Escalante and Rev. Steven Wedgeworth. The panel discussions and perhaps even more valuable informal discussions that filled the gaps between the paper sessions cannot, alas, find their way into this volume. But what you will find here is a set of illuminating studies on just how rich, diverse, and frankly surprising the early centuries of the Reformed tradition were. How many card-carrying Reformed Christians today would be sympathetic to an argument for *jure divino* episcopacy in their tradition, as we see with George Carleton, or the hypothetical universalism articulated by John Davenant, or the robust account of unbelievers' ability to do virtuous acts and build relatively just societies that we find in Turretin? How many would have as broad a view of their fathers in the faith as did Theodore Beza, or address Anabaptists as irenically as did Bucer, or Lutherans as irenically as did Hooker? On all of these points and so many more, we have much to learn from our Reformed forebears, even where we may sometimes disagree with them. May our churches in the decades to come be enriched with the depth and breadth of these oft-forgotten giants of Reformed irenicism!

As always, we are profoundly grateful to each of the gentlemen who undertook the labor of revising and polishing their papers for publication in this volume, rather than taking them, as in many cases they could have, to a more prestigious academic journal. We also appreciate the fine contributions at last year's event by Matthew Bingham, Joel Carini, and Paul Nedelisky, even though they opted not to publish their essays at this time. Finally, we appreciate the tireless labors of Brian Marr in helping to prepare this manuscript for publication.

I:

"THAT NO ONE SHOULD LIVE FOR HIMSELF, BUT FOR OTHERS":
LOVE AND THE THIRD MARK OF THE CHURCH IN THE THEOLOGY OF MARTIN BUCER

Jake Meador, Mere Orthodoxy

INTRODUCTION

THE GREATEST difficulty one meets when attempting to understand the legacy of early Protestant reformer Martin Bucer is that the Strasbourg reformer doesn't have *a* legacy. Whereas Calvin and Luther both gave birth to movements that still, accurately or not, bear their name 500 years later, there is no Bucerian tradition that still plays a prominent role in the western church. He left behind no systematic theology, no educational institutions, and not even a distinct theological school. Great as he was in his own day, he was mostly neglected after his death. Bucer's work in Strasbourg would be largely forgotten after his exile following the end of the first Schmalkaldic War. His work in England, meanwhile, was doomed by both the short time in which he worked there and the reign of Bloody Mary, which began not long after his death in 1551. Indeed, as if attempting to guarantee Bucer's relegation to the dustbin of history, Mary ordered his remains to be exhumed, burned, and cast into the sea. For all these reasons, the influence and significance of Bucer was largely forgotten from the late 16th century until early in the 20th when a small group of scholars began to revisit the work of the neglected reformer.

Once this work began, however, they began to notice something: Even if Bucer's influence could not be identified with a *single* movement within the western church, his influence on a number of other movements was much more apparent. Indeed, the strangest thing about Bucer's neglect may not be that a major reformer was ignored for nearly 400 years, but that a reformer as concerned with building and promoting the reformation as a movement would be neglected for so long. Though he did not leave behind a single, easily discerned legacy, when you consider the early reformation more broadly you find that Bucer's fingerprints are everywhere. The most obvious example is of course Bucer's influence on Calvin, whom he mentored for three years during the latter's exile from Geneva when he served as a pastor at a church of French refugees in Strasbourg. Calvin's understanding of pastoral theology as well as his eucharistic theology were both deeply shaped by his time with Bucer and much of what he did in Geneva looks very like what Bucer *wanted* to accomplish in Strasbourg. Though the pupil's writing ability and clarity as a thinker explains much of why he overtook his master, the political conditions of their respective cities also played a part.

That said, there is a second stream in which Bucer's influence can be detected—the various churches descended from the Reformation that affirm a more disciplinarian approach to the Christian life and more rigid practices regarding church membership and discipline. The question of Christian discipline occupied Bucer for much of his ministry. Indeed, Bucer is one of the central figures in the oft-rehearsed debate amongst Protestants about the true marks of the church. This was a significant question for all Protestants as their movement by definition rejected Roman Catholic teachings on the nature of the church. Thus the marks of the true church were a central question for all Protestant reformers. All the Protestants agreed on two marks: the teaching of the Word and the administration of the Sacraments. The debate happened around a proposed third mark of the church: the practice of church discipline. Though he pre-dates the defining of the debate in these exact terms, Bucer's work nonetheless has a great deal to say about this question.

Why was Bucer so concerned with these questions? To understand why, we can simply start at the beginning of his pastoral ministry in Strasbourg. Bucer's first full-time pastoral job in Strasbourg was as the parish pastor of St Aurelia's Church, a parish dominated by a local craftsmen's group called the gardener's guild which was, in turn, dominated by Anabaptists.[1] The Anabaptists were amongst the first group to consider the question of a third mark. This is entirely to be expected since the discipline question flows naturally out of their sacramental theology: If baptism is only to be conferred upon those who have professed faith in Christ, how can the authenticity of that profession be discerned? In assuming the pastoral position at St. Aurelia's, Bucer was entering into a congregation where these sorts of questions were regularly being asked. Indeed, Strasbourg's first prominent native-born radical, Clement Ziegler, was a member of the gardeners' guild and thus almost certainly an attendee at St. Aurelia's. Later when Pilgrim Marpeck, who would come to be seen as something of a "safe" radical due to his comparatively moderate views, came to the city he would promptly begin working with this same gardeners' guild.[2] From his earliest days in pastoral ministry, Bucer was thus forced to confront these questions in ways that his peers, such as Luther, never quite had to due to their distance from the Anabaptists. This, then, was not simply an academic question for Bucer to be debated in pamphlets exchanged with elite Roman Catholic theologians. It was a deeply practical pastoral question as he sought to pastor a church full of congregants asking these questions.

In addition to the natural influence that arose from pastoring so many radicals, Bucer had a long-standing personal interest in the role of Christian discipline within the life of individual Christians and the broader life of the church. Like many reformers, Bucer was well-schooled in the humanism of Erasmus. This reform movement within the late medieval church sought to restore the right practice of simple Christian piety over and against the arcane and abstruse Christianity of the scholastics. However, while many reformers were in some measure influenced by this school, Bucer was especially shaped by it. Indeed, when Bucer first met Luther he wrote to his mentor (and later Erasmus's biographer) Beatus Rhenanus that Luther was simply making explicit what had been implied by Erasmus's work all along, "He agrees with Erasmus in all things, but with this difference in his favor, that what Erasmus only insinuates, he teaches openly and

---

[1] George H. Williams, *The Radical Reformation* (Ann Arbor, MI: Sixteenth Century Journal Publishers), 1992, 366–67.

[2] Stephen B. Boyd, *Pilgrim Marpeck: His Life and Social Theology* (Durham, NC: Duke University Press, 1992), 59.

freely."[3] Thus Bucer's embrace of the Lutheran teaching on justification, which he steadfastly held to, was always paired with a more Erasmian emphasis on the importance of simple Christian piety, which Bucer spoke of chiefly in terms of Christian discipline serving the goal of Christian love. This synthesis of Erasmian humanism and Lutheran soteriology would become a hallmark of the Strasbourg reformer's thought.

Multiple scholars, most notably Paul Avis and Torrance Kirby, have commented on this attribute of Bucer's thought, especially as it concerns the question of discipline and the third mark of the church. *If* a specific moral program is entailed within Bucer's understanding of Luther's teachings, does it not follow that the practice of such morality would be a necessary mark of the church? And does it not also follow that those who do not practice such morality or even affirm the necessity of it are outside the true church? Avis identifies Bucer as the *source* of what would become the third mark of the church—*discipline*, in addition to the Augsburg Confession's two, Word and sacrament. Writing in the *Scottish Journal of Theology*, Avis says,

> A tradition of ecclesiology from Bucer to the puritans attempted to avoid these anomalies, not by broadening, but by narrowing the definition of the church, tightening its circumference by making discipline essential to its very existence. The watchword of this school is found in Bucer's remark of 1538, 'There cannot be a church without *ein ban*'. The word alone is not enough; it must be heard with joy and obeyed with zeal. The quality of Christian discipleship becomes a mark of the church. Love and discipline must be added to word and sacrament.[4]

Avis would expand on this claim in his essential book *The Church in the Theology of the Reformers*.[5] Kirby agrees with this reading in his work *Richard Hooker's Doctrine of the Royal Supremacy*. To be sure, there is something to this claim, yet though it has a grain of truth to it, it also simplifies an aspect

[3] David Wright, ed., *Commonplaces of Martin Bucer* (Abingdon: Sutton Courtenay Press, 1972), 20.

[4] Paul D. L. Avis, "The True Church in the Theology of the Reformation," *Scottish Journal of Theology* 30 (1977): 336.

[5] Paul D. L. Avis, *The Church in the Theology of the Reformers* (London: Marshall, Morgan, and Scott, 1981).

of Bucer's theology that is far more complex than such a description would suggest. By describing Bucer as a partisan in a debate between those who affirm a third mark and those who do not, much of the complexity of Bucer's thought (as well as his context) is obscured or lost. It also raises a second question: how is it that a man once mocked by a dear friend as an "ecumaniac" would lay the foundation for the sort of ecclesiology that would become a significant part of many separatist movements in Protestant Europe?[6]

The answers to these difficult questions can be found by a closer examination of Bucer's pastoral ministry and how the ideas of Christian discipline and Christian love are woven together in Bucer's thinking. Amy Nelson Burnett has done the most important work of addressing Bucer's understanding of discipline in her monograph *The Yoke of Christ*,[7] but the way in which Bucer's understanding of discipline relates to Avis's and Kirby's argument in particular has not been discussed as much. Additionally, the relevance of Bucer's thought on this issue to the contemporary church has been, to the best of my knowledge, entirely unexplored.

In this paper, I will argue that Bucer's thoughts on discipline are actually more complex than simply affirming the idea of a third mark and are, in fact, more in line with those who hold to only *two* marks of the true church. I will then explain how Bucer's theology of discipline worked itself out in practice before concluding by commenting on the relevance of Bucer's thought to the contemporary church.

1. BUCER'S DISCIPLINE

To begin, we must consider Bucer's unique background prior to his work as a reformer. His work as a leader of the reformation will become far more sensible if we first understand his origins. We have already noted his fondness for Erasmus, but the humanist influence on Bucer runs far deeper than a mere affection for a single prominent reformer. Northern European humanism was, in many ways, the air Bucer grew up breathing. Born in the Alsatian town of Selestat, Bucer would have been familiar with the humanist ethos from his youngest days. The Selestat Latin school enjoyed a pres-

---

[6] Wright, *Commonplaces*, 50.

[7] Amy Nelson Burnett, *The Yoke of Christ: Martin Bucer and Christian Discipline* (Ann Arbor: Sixteenth Century Journal Publishers, 1994).

tigious reputation throughout Europe, as did its headmaster Jacob Wem-
pheling.[8] Bucer almost certainly studied there as a young man, but when he
reached age 15 the bookish Bucer faced a difficult choice: His family lacked
the means to pay for continued schooling and so the only way he could
continue his studies was to join the Dominican order. This he did and so in
1507 Bucer took the first steps to becoming a monk. It is perhaps worth
noting that what drove Bucer to the monastery, a thirst for greater
knowledge and a desire to study, is strikingly different from what had driv-
en Martin Luther to an Augustinian monastery two years prior.[9]

The irony of this move for Bucer, of course, is that he was now stud-
ying with Dominicans: the primary purveyors of the very sort of scholasticism that Bucer's humanist education treated with such disdain. Thus even
as he received a typical Dominican education in late medieval scholastic
theology and particularly the writings of Thomas Aquinas, Bucer maintained a strong personal interest in humanism. A widely cited list of books
he owned while still in his mid 20s and in the Dominican order reveals that
the young Bucer owned not only the sort of books one would expect a
young Dominican to own, the works of Thomas Aquinas most obviously,
but also every book of Erasmus's that he could find.[10] It did not take long
for Bucer to ally himself with Luther, given this background.

That said, as Bucer emerged as a more independent thinker and less
an acolyte of Luther's, the differences between the two quickly began to
bubble to the surface. Their disagreements on the question of eucharistic
presence are well known and documented. Luther also had little regard for
Bucer's ecumenical work, seeing the Strasbourg reformer as being two-
faced and duplicitous. That said, these personal animosities can conceal an
important fact: On the question of Christian discipline, Bucer is, if anything,
simply developing Luther's own thinking.

In *The Liberty of the Christian,* published in 1520, Luther states that the
Christian is subject to none and servant of all. This is in many ways the
foundation of Luther's thought on both ethics and Christian discipline. It is
also fully in keeping with Bucer's own thinking. Indeed, three years later

---

[8] Martin Greschat, *Martin Bucer: A Reformer and His Times* (Louisville: Westminster
John Knox, 2004), 7.

[9] Brian Lugioyo, *Martin Bucer's Doctrine of Justification* (New York: Oxford University
Press, 2010), 85.

[10] Greschat, *Martin Bucer*, 18.

Bucer would say much the same thing in his first published work, which in English has been translated as *Instructions in Christian Love* but would be literally translated as "That No One Should Live for Himself, but for Others."

Likewise, the respective passages on the church in the Augsburg Confession and Tetrapolitan Confession, both published in 1530, the former representative of Luther's thought and written by Melanchthon and the latter written by Bucer and Wolfgang Capito, do not directly disagree on any point. The Augsburg Confession says simply that "The Church is the congregation of saints, in which the Gospel is rightly taught and the Sacraments are rightly administered."[11]

The Tetrapolitan is, to the surprise of no one who has ever read Bucer, both more wordy and more ambitious: "The Church of Christ, therefore, which is frequently called the kingdom of heaven, is the fellowship of those who have enlisted under Christ and committed themselves entirely to his faith; with whom, nevertheless, until the end of the world, those are mingled who feign faith in Christ, but do not truly have it."[12]

Technically speaking, there isn't anything here that the Lutherans would disagree with. After all, the reason the two separate confessions were written is not because the various reforming parties disagreed on the definition of the church. Both were happy, more or less, saying that the church consists of those who hear and respond to the Gospel, citing John 10:27–28 in support of their argument. The reason they wrote multiple confessions is because they disagreed on the issue of eucharistic presence.

That said, we do see Bucer attempting to develop Luther's thinking in ways that go beyond Luther's own initial work on the subject. Bucer does not add discipline as a mark of the church by saying something like "The church is the congregation of saints, in which the Gospel is rightly taught, the Sacraments are rightly administered, and Church Discipline is rightly practiced." *That* would be a real parting of the ways with Luther. Rather, in characteristic fashion, he has simply chunked together several different things that many treat as discrete, separate marks into a single definition of the church. He does much the same thing in his "Brief Summary of Christian Doctrine," when he says that Christ "urges (the church) to come to-

---

[11] Book of Concord, "Augsburg Confession," accessed May 23, 2016, http://bookofconcord.org/augsburgconfession.php#article7.

[12] Arthur C. Cochrane, ed., *Reformed Confessions of the Sixteenth Century* (Louisville: Westminster John Knox, 2003), 74.

gether in person whenever possible, to teach, guide, comfort and admonish one another with one mind, by means of the word of God and the holy sacraments, and by prayer and the discipline of the Lord."[13] The closest that Bucer comes to the distinct tripartite formula of word, sacrament, and discipline is later in the same document when he says that senior pastors have been "entrust[ed with] the ministries of teaching, the holy sacraments, and Christian discipline, that is to say, everything concerned with the cure of souls."[14] Even here, however, it is worth noting that Bucer does not seem to see this as three separate marks which, when occurring together, constitute a church; rather, he sees all of these things so often treated as distinct and separate as being parts of a single work: the cure of souls.

We might say then that the later distinction between the *esse* of the church and the *bene esse* does not necessarily exist in Bucer but that he tends to collapse them together. The marks of the church *are* the things necessary to the "cure of souls" so that those individuals within the church may grow in Christian love in obedience to God and for the good of their neighbor. Discipline, then, is not primarily seen as adherence to a rigid set of rules for Bucer. Rather, it is the submission of one's life and Christian liberty to the yoke of Christ so that this liberty can be used for the service of others in keeping with the sacrificial nature of Christian love. Though it goes beyond Luther, it is not a departure from the Wittenberg reformer. Consider Luther's own words in his Preface to the German Mass: "While, however, every man is bound on his conscience, in like manner as he uses such liberty himself, not to hinder nor forbid it to any one else, we must also take care that liberty be servant to love and to our neighbour. Where, then, it happens that men are offended or perplexed at such diversity of use, we are truly bound to put limits to liberty; and, so far as possible, to endeavour that the people are bettered by what we do and not offended."[15]

2. BUCER'S IRENICISM AND DISCIPLINE

With that foundation for understanding Bucer's general approach to discipline laid, we now turn to the question of how this emphasis on discipline

---

[13] Wright, *Commonplaces*, 83.

[14] Wright, *Commonplaces*, 83.

[15] Martin Luther, "Preface to the German Mass," accessed August 30, 2016, http://history.hanover.edu/texts/luthserv.html.

worked itself out in practice. To do that, we will first consider Bucer's general pattern of relating to other Christians. Then, we will look at Bucer's specific handling of those outside the state church who also affirm a third mark in their own way, the Anabaptists of Strasbourg. We'll pay particular attention to his handling of Pilgram Marpeck, which is uniquely valuable because of Marpeck's relatively mainstream theology.

To understand Bucer's relationship to other Christians, we must begin by noting that Bucer's situation in Strasbourg is *considerably* different from the situations of most other reformers. Not only is Bucer's position relative to the Strasbourg government something of an on-again-off-again problem, but Bucer also is forced to deal with a local church *far* more diverse than what you would find in most other places.

As a free imperial city, Strasbourg was largely self-governed and had its own legal code in place that dated back to the late 13th century.[16] They also had a wealthy merchant class as well as a number of thriving guilds in the city, all of which made the city financially independent. We have already mentioned the gardeners' guild, which was home to so many of the city's radicals. The combination of great commercial wealth and a legal code that concerned itself more with preserving the city's independence and material wealth caused the city to become something of a hub for dissidents in south Germany. Erasmus particularly admired the place—and he didn't admire many places. But in 1514 he spoke in glowing terms about the south German city: "At last I have seen a monarchy without tyranny, an aristocracy without factions, a democracy without tumult, wealth without luxury, prosperity without insolence. What greater happiness could be imagined than this harmony!"[17]

This reputation for tolerance, or to use Erasmus's term, harmony, is, in fact, part of what drew Bucer himself to the city. After a highly unstable, itinerant existence following his exit from the Dominicans, Bucer moved to Strasbourg, though he had also considered moves to Wittenberg or Zurich to study with Luther or Zwingli. That said, the relative stability offered by a city like Strasbourg, especially given the fact that Bucer's grandfather was a citizen of the city which would pave the way for Bucer to become a citizen as well, would have had a strong appeal to the reformer. This was particularly important in his case as he was newly married when he arrived in the

---

[16] Williams, *Radical Reformation*, 363.

[17] Wright, *Commonplaces*, 14.

city in 1523 to a former nun—a fact which made his position even more secure than that of a typical Luther-sympathizer. Yet it was precisely the openness of the city, which had once proven so attractive to Bucer, that would also be a regular cause of trouble and turmoil for the Strasbourg reformation.

After about one year in the city, Bucer would be given the pastorate at the aforementioned St. Aurelia's Church. Though theoretically under the dominion of the larger St. Thomas church, St. Aurelia's enjoyed a high level of freedom due to the strong influence of the gardeners' guild. This auton-omy afforded Bucer some level of freedom, but also made his situation quite complex. In the fall of 1524, only a few months after assuming the pastorate, Bucer oversaw the unearthing of the bones of St. Aurelia, which had been a relic for which the church was well-known. Up to that point Bucer's comments on icons and relics had been comparatively moderate. Of icons and statues he had said, "images are indifferent, statues and the use of them is a matter of indifference, but the abuse of them is not; namely if they are worshipped and adored."[18] But after a few months in this church heavily influenced by the radicals, Bucer began to shift on this question. Now, according to biographer Hastings Eells, Bucer said, "it was impossi-ble to have images without abusing them; consequently, they were forbid-den by the first and second commandments, were of no use in instructing the unlearned, and should be renounced even by those who did not abuse them, so that the weaker brethren might not be tempted."[19] This shift is representative of the ways that Bucer, particularly the younger Bucer, could be swayed by the combination of the influence of his friends and pastoral concern. Note that even here Bucer frames his objection to images around concern with shepherding "weaker brethren."

In time the gardeners' guild would become an even greater influence on the city. By the late 1520s, the radical presence in the city hit a critical mass, punctuated by the arrival of the recently radicalized Marpeck who had given up much of his family's spectacular wealth (he had loaned Emperor Ferdinand a sum equivalent to 20 years wages for the typical worker only a few years before) to join the Anabaptists.[20] Marpeck's arrival in 1528 sig-naled the beginning of a crisis moment in the Strasbourg reformation and in

---

[18] Hastings Eels, *Martin Bucer* (New Haven: Yale University Press, 1931), 37.

[19] Eels, *Martin Bucer*, 38.

[20] Boyd, *Pilgrim Marpeck*, 6.

Bucer's work as a reformer. 1529 saw the failure of the Marburg Colloquy, where the Zwinglian and Lutheran sides of the Reformation were unable to come together on the question of Eucharistic presence. This led to the submission of multiple confessions, including both the Tetrapolitan and the Augsburg, to Charles V in 1530 at a time when Charles already suspected that the young reform movement was schismatic. This alone would have been a major challenge for the reformation, but the difficulties were compounded by two additional factors that touched Bucer particularly: First, Johannes Oecolampadius and Ulrich Zwingli both died in quick succession in 1531, leaving the Swiss reformation leaderless. Second, church attendance in Strasbourg in the established church began to decline as more and more of the city's most committed church members began turning to the various Anabaptist sects now thriving in the tolerant Strasbourg. Something of Bucer's mood at this time can be gathered from what he wrote in December 1531 to his friend Ambrose Blaurer: "If it were not for you and what is left of those in Zurich who knows what might happen?"[21] Bucer's mood remained much the same a year later when he wrote, again to Blaurer, "Pray for our church. The heretics are ruining it incredibly. Through our misguided leniency they have gained such strength that this evil can be neither done away with nor properly remedied."[22]

There were four chief groups of radicals in the city. All four rejected infant baptism, but past that they tended to splinter. The Swiss Brethren, were marked by a strict biblicism, pacifism, and a refusal to take oaths. Michael Sattler, who the city had banished in 1526, was one of the more prominent members of this group. The followers of Melchior Hoffman formed the second group of radicals in the city. Hoffman was known for his eschatological teachings and believed that the radicals of Strasbourg were the beginning of the prophesied 144,000 witnesses of Revelation and that Strasbourg was where the apocalypse would begin. Third were the spiritualists led by Caspar Schwenkfeld, himself a close friend of Bucer's fellow reformer Wolfgang Capito. Schwenkfeld and his followers generally deemphasized the importance of Scripture in favor of the internal witness of the Holy Spirit. Capito himself was drawn to this movement as he had always "asserted that faith was grounded on the 'inner word' of God and that Old Believers, Lutherans, and Anabaptists all made the mistake of valuing the

[21] Boyd, *Pilgrim Marpeck*, 64.
[22] Greschat, *Martin Bucer*, 119.

external ceremonies too highly."[23] Finally there were the followers of Marpeck. This group had the *most* in common with the Swiss Brethren, however they did not reject all oath-taking as the Swiss Brethren did. This is a key point as it opened up the possibility of civil service for members of this group, which allowed them to be seen as more mainstream than the three other groups. Thus this group became the most prominent and successful of the four. They rejected the more fringe beliefs of the Hoffmanites and the spiritualists *and* by allowing some oaths to be taken they more easily integrated into the public life of Strasbourg. Their status was also bolstered by Marpeck's business acumen and considerable reputation. Prior to moving to Strasbourg, Marpeck had worked as a mining official who helped determine who had what rights to the mines in his native Tirol region. After coming to Strasbourg, he used this experience to help arrange a deal that provide much needed lumber to the city during 1530.[24] That said, the Marpeck followers still rejected infant baptism and separated themselves from the state church, insisting that the church could only consist of those who had publicly professed faith and pledged themselves to taking up the cross of Christ as understood within Marpeck's broader theological system. It is perhaps worth noting how much Marpeck's understanding of the church sounds like Bucer's at first glance.

In observing how he managed these controversies, we can see how Bucer's thinking worked itself out in practice as well the reasons he acted in the ways that he did. To begin, Bucer took a generally conciliar approach to these local issues, an approach that even he himself would later see as being too lenient as we already saw from his letter to Ambrose Blaurer. The reasons for this approach are multiple. In the first place, material necessity compelled him to take a more irenic route—a city like Strasbourg simply wouldn't allow a harsher reaction along the lines of Zwingli's famed response to the radicals, which was to give the re-baptizers a third baptism— death by drowning. Second, however, is the fact that Bucer, still in some ways a Dominican, genuinely believed in the possibility of persuasion via argumentation and believed that he had nothing to fear from giving the radicals a public hearing. Not only was Bucer a capable and somewhat intimidating scholar given his background with the Dominicans, he was also a masterful negotiator of whom one man, in something which could be read

---

[23] Boyd, *Pilgrim Marpeck*, 65.

[24] Boyd, *Pilgrim Marpeck*, 57.

as compliment or insult, said, "among all the theologians now living, [Bucer is] truly an excellent man for negotiating in theological affairs after the manner of the world."[25] He was, in other words, a consummate diplomat, adept at drawing disparate groups together. Some saw this work as peace-making *via* obfuscation to the point that both sides could "agree" because the statement they agreed to was so carefully parsed that each side could import its own meaning to the agreement. Others were more sympathetic to his efforts at reconciliation. In either case, Bucer did not fear face-to-face debate and was quite adept at winning over those who disagreed with him. Indeed, Bucer enjoyed greater success at bringing radicals back into the established church than any other reformer, most notably drawing the region of Hesse back from radicalism in the late 1530s and also converting the family of Idelette de Bure, the future wife of John Calvin, back from radicalism around the same time.[26]

The second reason for this conciliar approach is that Bucer's approach to the church is distinctive: The domain in which the institutional church acts is limited for Bucer because of his robust view of the Christian magistrate.[27] However, within its smaller domain (relative to that of late medieval Christianity's normal view of the institutional church) the church has a great deal it is expected to do in helping people to truly follow Christ by embracing Christian discipline. This has the effect of making the church both far more important in individual spiritual formation and far less pervasive within the public square since Bucer expects Christian magistrates, rather than Christian ministers, to do much of the large-scale cultural work needed to produce and protect a broader Christian society. Much of his irenical work, then, is trying to keep people unified enough that they can show Christian charity to one another, as is fitting with proper Christian discipline, and so that they can be sufficiently unified to live as neighbors in a Christian society.

It is worth noting that the key for Bucer is the earnest committing of one's life. He is content to live with some level of aberrant theology for a while, provided there is a commitment made by the individual to belong to the local church and to practice Christian discipline. If that is in place, he is

---

[25] Wright, *Commonplaces*, 48.

[26] Greschat, *Martin Bucer*, 148.

[27] Martin Bucer, *De Regno Christi*, in *Melanchthon and Bucer* (Philadelphia: Westminster Press, 1969).

happy to work alongside not only Lutherans, but also radicals and Catholics.[28]

In a letter written in 1532 to a leader in the Basel reformation, Simon Grynaeus, Bucer would strongly defend this understanding of the church. In the letter he wrote, "We are often too lenient towards those who agree with us and accept our teaching and too severe toward those who dissent and do not yet accept our teaching.… It is the greatest calamity to recognize as ours only those who accept all our doctrine, thereby neglecting many who truly belong to Christ."[29] Note the careful phrasing in the letter: "do not **yet** accept our teaching." The argument here is not for a kind of permanent theological pluralism in the church, but for patience and prudence in how we establish and enforce theological norms.

In her book *The Yoke of Christ*, Amy Nelson Burnett writes:

> The only essential doctrine was faith that 'Christ is the unique savior of mankind, true God, true man, from whom we await all things.' Bucer was ready to admit that this broad definition included Catholics: 'there are many who belong much more to Christ among those who are considered papists than among those who seem to be evangelical.' Likewise, neither Lutherans nor Anabaptists, both of whom would disagree with the Basel clergy over the interpretation of the Lord's Supper, were to be considered outside of the church because of their doctrinal disagreement.[30]

The centerpiece of Bucer's approach is patient, irenic discussion done with the goal of preserving Christendom by helping more nominal or confused Christians take up the yoke of Christian discipline. Understanding this point helps to explain Bucer's approach to Marpeck.

As we have already seen, things were coming to a head with the radicals in Strasbourg by late 1531.[31] Things accelerated still further when Wolfgang Capito's wife died that year and Capito soon developed an interest in the widow of a local radical leader named Sabina Bader. This prompt-

---

[28] Burnett, *The Yoke of Christ*, 63.

[29] Burnett, *The Yoke of Christ*, 64.

[30] Burnett, *The Yoke of Christ*, 64–65.

[31] Boyd, *Pilgrim Marpeck*, 64.

ed something of a local crisis that Bucer diffused through a mixture of argumentation and shrewd political maneuvering which, amongst other things, involved steering his friend Capito away from Bader and toward Wibrandis Rosenblatt, the widow of the recently deceased Basel reformer Johan Oecolampadius. Once the crisis had been averted, Capito's relationship to Schwenkfeld soured, which in turn led to the banishing of the radical leader from the city of Strasbourg. Hoffman's influence would fade as he proved to be too extreme in his views for even the radicals. The Swiss Brethren had not had as strong a presence in the city due in no small part to the earlier banishing of Sattler in 1526. This left only Marpeck and his followers. To address them, Bucer arranged for a behind-closed-doors meeting at town hall before the city counsel on Saturday December 9, 1531. On Wednesday the 13th the two leaders met again. On Monday December 18, the counsel decided to banish Marpeck unless he agreed to "retract his assertion that infant baptism was unchristian and to abstain from rebaptizing."[32] Marpeck refused and after a bit of written back-and-forth with Bucer, left the city in January of 1532. What was the nature of Bucer's objection to Marpeck? This is perhaps the point of greatest interest. Though Bucer never wavered in his support for infant baptism, his chief concern wasn't with baptism *in itself*. Rather, his critique was in the separatism of Marpeck and his followers. Bucer biographer Martin Greschat summarizes Bucer's response as follows: "Bucer was not left unmoved by the deep piety and exemplary moral conduct of this Anabaptist leader and his congregation. But he disapproved of their self-imposed separation all the more. How much more could be achieved, especially regarding church discipline, if all would together instead of against each other?"[33]

That formulation is striking: Bucer sees church discipline and unity as being closely related—the goal of discipline is love. When the body is splintered such that discipline cannot be practiced coherently within the church, that goal is compromised. We will let Bucer himself have the final word here as we observe his definition of heresy given in a letter to Margaret Blaurer, sister to his friend Ambrose, written in September of 1531:

> Heresy is not this or the other delusion or opinion, but rather a craving of the flesh by which one presumes, in con-

---

[32] Boyd, *Pilgrim Marpeck*, 67.

[33] Greschat, *Martin Bucer*, 120.

duct or doctrine, to undertake something apparently better than the divine custom in the common church, and therefore proceeds to separate oneself from the church and join a particular band or sect.... They claim to be holier than everybody else but flagrantly miss the goal of love, which alone lies—as God himself—at the essence of all piety. Therein lies the poison.[34]

3. BUCER'S ENDURING RELEVANCE

In his 2009 book *Deep Church*, Jim Belcher attempted to articulate a view of the church that could appease both of the rising groups within American evangelicalism—the young reformed movement and the emergent church movement. Belcher argued that one of the chief problems that divided the two groups was the question of who belonged to the church. Specifically, Belcher said, the question was which came first: Belief in Christian doctrine or belonging to the Christian church? Belcher argued, not unreasonably, that the Reformed consistently said that belief was primary while the emergents argued with equal passion that belonging must come first.

The difficulty this created is most clearly seen in how these two views cash out in the daily life of a congregation. Those churches which elevate belief embrace what Belcher called a "bounded set" mentality. They believe that the only way the church can be known is through carefully defined boundaries that are then regularly patrolled by qualified leaders. While Christians should never be unkind toward those outside the bounds of orthodoxy, they also should not treat those on the outside as brothers or sisters. The emergents, meanwhile, affirmed what Belcher called an "open set" approach to church life. For them, the first thing is the Christian community of believers gathered together for love and good deeds. The point is not to pass out doctrinal exams to all members of the church and threaten anyone who fails to pass with excommunication. Indeed, according to the emergents, such a spirit actually undermines the difficult work of Christian love and reconciliation within the body of Christ by creating a suspicion between brothers and an elevation of the intellectual and academic over more practical matters of Christian piety. If these debates call to mind the older debates between the scholastics and the humanists, you might anticipate Bucer's relevance to this question.

---

[34] Greschat, *Martin Bucer*, 120–21.

Belcher's solution to this debate was the rather ingenious idea of a "center set" church. To explain what this means, Belcher used the analogy of how shepherds care for their animals in the Australian Outback. The lands that the sheep can roam are so broad that fencing them in is impractical. Yet, Belcher said, the sheep still need to be fed and watered. The solution to this problem is simple: The shepherds build wells and trust that the sheep won't stray too far because, ultimately, they need to drink. They may wander a long way off from the well for a time, but eventually necessity will compel them to return. This, Belcher argued, is how the church ought to think about the question of belief and belonging: Setting up fences that clearly mark out the "orthodox" (or perhaps "biblical") position on every issue under the sun is unwise and impractical. Likewise, transforming the church into a doctrinal free-for-all where all beliefs are welcomed and affirmed is destructive to the life of the Christian community, which, after all, is called into being and preserved by the grace of God offered to it through the Gospel. Instead of these false alternatives, Belcher argued for a church that commits itself to the clear teaching of the Gospel and which confidently trusts that the sheep will not stray *too* far from that center because, eventually, they will need another drink.

This deeply practical understanding of the question, which anchors the identity of the church in the churches' proclamation of the Gospel for the life of the saints, is something that Bucer would sympathize with enormously. Like Belcher, Bucer was deeply suspicious of those who would prowl near the edges of orthodoxy and eagerly attack anyone who transgressed them. Throughout his life he labored to reconcile various Christian groups to one another, a work that he began in earnest with his attempts to mediate the supper strife of the mid-to-late 1520s and which continued through the late stages of his life as he labored for reunion with evangelical Catholics in Germany. Yet Bucer recognized that Christian community could only be preserved through the holding of a shared center. For Bucer, that center was not simply an affirmation of justification by faith, but was rather a more all-encompassing embrace of the Yoke of Christ, which would lead to the renewal of Christian society as individual believers embraced the call to die to self and serve the good of their neighbor.

It is here, then, that we see Bucer's sharpest departure from the later proponents of the third mark of the church. Whereas the radicals and later the Presbyterians of England would be marked by a sort of precisionist spirit that demanded full doctrinal purity before union could be assumed and joint work done, Bucer embraced a broadly irenic style of faith that sought common cause not only with radicals, but also with Roman Christians. Indeed, Bucer's overall approach shares a great deal with Belcher's idea of a "center-set church." Bucer's ecumenism, if we can use that term, was never unprincipled or lacking in theological roots. The goal was the promotion of Christian love within local churches and Christendom more broadly. Discipline served that goal. For Bucer the work of Christian reconciliation and Christian discipline are not only *not* at odds, they are one and the same.

BIBLIOGRAPHY

Avis, Paul D. L. *The Church in the Theology of the Reformers*. London: Marshall, Morgan, and Scott, 1981.

———. "The True Church in the Theology of the Reformation." *Scottish Journal of Theology* 30 (1977): 319–45.

Belcher, Jim. *Deep Church*. Downers Grove: InterVarsity Press, 2009.

Book of Concord. "Augsburg Confession." Accessed May 23, 2016. http://bookofconcord.org/augsburgconfession.php#article7.

Boyd, Stephen B. *Pilgrim Marpeck: His Life and Social Theology*. Durham: Duke University Press, 1992.

Burnett, Amy Nelson. *The Yoke of Christ: Martin Bucer and Christian Discipline*. Ann Arbor: Sixteenth Century Journal Publishers, 1994.

Cochrane, Arthur C., ed. *Reformed Confessions of the Sixteenth Century*. Louisville: Westminster John Knox, 2003.

Eells, Hastings. *Martin Bucer*. New Haven: Yale University Press, 1931.

Greschat, Martin. *Martin Bucer: A Reformer and His Times*. Louisville: Westminster John Knox, 2004.

Kirby, Torrance. *Richard Hooker's Doctrine of the Royal Supremacy*. Leiden: Brill, 1990.

Lugioyo, Brian. *Martin Bucer's Doctrine of Justification*. New York: Oxford University Press, 2010.

Luther, Martin. "Preface to the German Mass." Accessed August 30, 2016. http://history.hanover.edu/texts/luthserv.html.

Williams, George H. *The Radical Reformation*. Ann Arbor: Sixteenth Century Journal Publishers, 1992.

Wright, David, ed. *Commonplaces of Martin Bucer*. Appleford: Sutton Courtenay Press, 1972.

II:

WRITTEN MONUMENTS:
BEZA'S ICONES AS TESTAMENT TO AND PROGRAM FOR
REFORMIST HUMANISM

E.J. Hutchinson, Hillsdale College

1. INTRODUCTION

THE CHOICE to focus on Theodore Beza's *Icones* for a volume on "Confessionalism and Diversity in the Reformed Tradition" may seem *prima facie* to be an odd one. After all, the *Icones*,[1] first published in 1580, is not one of Beza's major works. Indeed, the illustrated Latin edition—the one I shall discuss in this essay—was not, to my knowledge, reprinted again until 1971,[2] unlike so many works of the major Protestant Reformers that saw numerous printings even during the authors' lifetimes. It is true that a French translation, by Simon Goulart and authorized by Beza,[3] was pub-

---

[1] The work's full title is: *Icones, id est verae imagines virorum doctrina simul et pietate illustrium, quorum praecipue ministerio partim bonarum literarum studia sunt restituta, partim vera Religio in variis orbis Christiani regionibus, nostra patrumque memoria fuit instaurata: additis eorundem vitae et operae descriptionibus, quibis adiectae sunt nonnullae picturae quas EMBLEMATA vocant.*

[2] Théodore de Bèze, *Icones* (Menston: Scolar Press, 1971).

[3] R.M. Cummings, "Note" to Bèze, *Icones* (Menston: Scolar Press, 1971), pages unnumbered.

lished the year after the Latin edition in 1581,[4] but it shows some marked differences from Beza's original.[5]

The work, then, is a minor one.[6] A further strike against it is the fact that it is not really a work of theology at all; so what could it contribute to the ongoing scholarly discussion of confessionalism and confessionaliza-tion? However, it is, paradoxically, precisely these "defects" that make it most serviceable for the topic: I shall endeavor to show that the *Icones* ought to widen our scope of what we mean by "diversity" (albeit it a diversity within a greater unity) in the Reformed tradition—a "tradition" that turns out to be not only theological, but cultural and humanistic as well—far be-yond what such a phrase normally signifies.[7] The fact, furthermore, that Beza could monumentalize the theological and humanistic culture of the Reformers with such extreme erudition[8] (more on this below) and with a catholicity that is at once confessional, geographical, and occupational or

---

[4] 1673 saw a hybrid and expanded edition by the printer Pierre Chouet. As Alain Dufour notes, "Chouet…s'avisa de retirer cet ensemble de gravures en un recueil pourvu d'un titre français: *Les portraits des hommes illustres*, mais ne contenant que les gravures, sans les textes (un exemplaire de ce recueil est conservé au Cabinet des estampes de la Bibliothèque publique et universitaire de Genève) et une édition latine: *Icones*, avec les textes." Introduction to Théodore de Bèze, *Les vrais portraits des hommes illustres* (Geneva: Slatkine Reprints, 1986), v. Cummings, "Note," gives 1683 for the date.

[5] For instance, it contains portraits not found in the Latin edition and all figures receive verse tributes, which is not true of the Latin edition.

[6] The *Icones* has not often been read as a work of literature–or read at all, for that matter. An exception is Catherine Randall (Coats), *(Em)bodying the Word: Textual Resurrections in the Martyrological Narratives of Foxe, Crespin, de Bèze, and d'Aubigné* (New York: P. Lang, 1992), 85–115, which does attempt a literary reading. It is hampered, however, by the fact that it investigates the text on the basis of Goulart's translation rather than the Latin original, and incorrectly states that the *Icones* was first pub-lished in 1581, the year of publication of the French translation (86). Much of the argument is reprised in briefer form in Catherine Randall (Coats), "Reactivating Textual Traces: Martyrs, Memory, and the Self in Theodore Beza's *Icones* (1581)," in *Later Calvinism: International Perspectives*, ed. W. Fred Graham (Kirksville, MO: Six-teenth Century Journal Publishers, 1994), 19–28.

[7] Randall, *(Em)bodying the Word*, 87, remarks on Beza's "apparent arbitrariness in his selection of material." The argument below will makes clear that, appearances not-withstanding, Beza's program is anything but arbitrary.

[8] On Beza's classical learning, see Kirk M. Summers, "Theodore Beza's Classical Library and Christian Humanism," *Archiv für Reformationsgeschichte/Archive for Refor-mation History* 82 (1991): 193–207.

vocational in a work that was not even one of his major productions but whose elegance, refinement, and learning he nevertheless expected his readers in both church and academy to understand and appreciate, demonstrates what common coin this culture used to be; our puzzlement at it is an index of how different we are from our fathers in the faith. In short, I shall try to commend to you Beza's *Icones* as a model of irenic polemicism, or polemical irenicism, in favor of a unitive Protestantism (including its academic culture) over against Roman tyranny, couched in and dependent upon the learned humanism of the sixteenth century. It is a program in which modern Protestants should be interested precisely because modern Protestants are so unlikely to be interested in it.

The *Icones*, then, as a work of unitive Protestantism is, as has just been indicated, deliberately anti-Roman. Thus at first glance we meet already with an enigma, for it seems very un-Protestant (and counterproductive to his purposes) for Beza to make a book of icons. But what he is actually doing is to take the Roman Catholic form of martyrology and iconography and turn it on its head, rendering it word- (and Word-)centered.[9] In order to indicate what this claim means, I should now say more about what kind of work the *Icones* is; I shall return to its anti-Roman tendencies later, which the interceding discussion will help to illuminate and place in proper perspective.

To be more concrete: in what follows, the *Icones* will be discussed under the three headings of (1) its contents; (2) its purpose, for which the dedicatory epistle to King James VI is singularly useful; and (3) some specific examples that illustrate its purpose. Throughout, and particularly in parts 1 and 3, I shall make special, though not exclusive, use of evidence from the sections of the *Icones* in Latin verse—because they are the most deliberately erudite parts of the work—to establish the argument.

2. WHAT IS THE *ICONES*?: CONTENTS

The *Icones* is a biohagiographical collection of portraits, both visual and verbal, of heroes of the Reformation, organized by region.[10] Many of the en-

---

[9] See Randall, *(Em)bodying the Word*, 86, 89–90, 95, though I disagree with the claim that he often undercuts the priority of word over image (cf. the claims on 96). Cf. Catherine Randall (Coats), "Reactivating Textual Traces," 21.

[10] The *Icones* is, in the words of Henry Martyn Baird, "[s]omewhat more than a mere collection of eulogies, yet decidedly less than a series of unprejudiced biographies." Nevertheless, he finds it on the whole trustworthy, with the possible exception of

tries have woodcut portraits, but at the time of the publication of the original Latin edition Beza had not been able to acquire portraits of many of the figures he treats.[11] (In the French version, on the other hand, more woodcuts are included.) Many of the entries also include tributes in verse—usually in Latin, though there are also three in Greek: one for Erasmus, one for Guillaume Bude, and one for Robert Estienne.[12] But, though Beza's subjects are his heroes of the Reformational movement, that does not mean that they are limited to those who would come to be called the (confessional) "Reformed." Erasmus and Bude have just been mentioned, but there are many others. Indeed, one of the most striking features of the *Icones* is its confessional *diversity*, one that is complemented by diversities of geography and occupation as well. As Alison Adams has claimed,

> In the years around 1580, Bèze had to some extent grown tired of the sectarian struggle. For a while he seemed to stand back from theological battles with, for instance, his Lutheran opponents, devoting himself to his study of the Psalms and the New Testament and their Christian significance. The *Icones* itself, which Bèze had been preparing for many years, does not limit its consideration to members of the Reformed church in the narrow sense, but includes all

---

the poems, which will form the bulk of my study the argument of which, it should be noted, does not depend on the historical accuracy of Beza's depictions: "[T]he *Icones*, notwithstanding the brevity of the sketches, constitute an important source of trustworthy information, to which we willingly admit our indebtedness on more than one occasion. For if the spirit of high appreciation pervades the work, the words of panegyric are, for the most part, reserved for the epigrams that are interspersed–a species of composition to which Beza was much addicted even down to his latest years." See Henry Martyn Baird, *Theodore Beza: The Counsellor of the French Reformation, 1519–1605* (New York: G.P. Putnam's Sons, 1899), 312, 314. Randall, *(Em)bodying the Martyrs*, 88, correctly notes the geographical organization of the *Icones*, but incorrectly states that the entries within the geographical subdivisions are "arranged alphabetically"; they are not.

[11] Cummings, "Note," remarks that this lack of completeness in the Latin edition "suggests an initial haste inspired by controversial motives." For Beza's historical context during the period surrounding the composition of the *Icones*, cf. Scott M. Manetsch, *Theodore Beza and the Quest for Peace in France, 1572–1598* (Leiden: Brill, 2000), 92–143.

[12] Erasmus also receives a poem in Latin: Theodore Beza, *Icones* (Geneva: Ioannes Laonius, 1580), sig. C.iii.r.

those who can be considered to have supported the return to true Christian values.[13]

Let us set this diversity out more precisely.

The *Icones* contains tributes to 93 named individuals, in addition to group tributes to Waldensian, Netherlandish, and Spanish martyrs,[14] of which 38 individual tributes include woodcuts.[15] As one might expect, many are figures of good Reformed pedigree (as the term "Reformed" later came to be understood): men such as John Calvin, Peter Martyr Vermigli, Martin Bucer, Wolfgang Musculus, Huldrych Zwingli, Heinrich Bullinger, and Johannes Oecolampadius, to name a few. In addition, however, is a sizable number of Lutherans—not simply mediating Lutherans such as Philip Melanchthon, or celebrities like Martin Luther, but also men such as Georg Anhalt, Johann Bugenhagen, and Caspar Cruciger. Beza praises, in addition, martyrs of the English church such as Thomas Cranmer, Hugh Latimer, and John Hooper, and the Pole John a Lasco. Not only that; there are a number of Roman Catholic entries as well. By this I do not mean pre-Reformation Western Christians in general, though there are those too (Wyclif, Hus, Jerome of Prague, and Girolamo Savonarola);[16] I refer to figures such as Johann Reuchlin, Michel de l'Hospital, King Francis I, and Marguerite of Navarre, in addition to Budé and Erasmus.[17]

At this point, it is worth reiterating that it is not confession that serves as the organizing principle of the work; the organizing principle is, rather, geography.[18] After the dedicatory epistle to King James VI of Scot-

---

[13] Alison Adams, *Webs of Allusion: French Protestant Emblem Books of the Sixteenth Century* (Geneva: Droz, 2003), 121.

[14] Within the group entries themselves, some individuals are named, but the title of the tributes is to the martyrs of those regions in general, irrespective of rank, age, and sex.

[15] Eleven are added in the French edition (Cummings, "Note").

[16] Obviously these figures are not "Roman Catholics" in any narrow sense of the term.

[17] The inclusion of these contemporaries of Beza as "Roman Catholics" ought not to obscure the ambiguity surrounding their personal convictions. On the contrary, it goes some way toward explaining that inclusion. It nonetheless remains true that Beza includes individuals who never formally separated from communion with the Bishop of Rome.

[18] For Beza as "spokesman for Protestants in the diaspora" and "reformer of the refugee church," see Manetsch, *Quest for Peace*, 1–8.

land (to which I shall return below) and the section on pre-Reformation martyrs referred to above, the work is divided into nine major sections based on region:[19] *Germania, Helvetia, Gallia, Anglia, Scotia, Gallia Belgica, Polonia, Italia,* and *Hispania* (roughly, Germany, Switzerland, France, England, Scotland, Belgium, Poland, Italy, and Spain).[20]

But no one is included in a particular region simply because he was born there, that is, simply because it was his native country. Instead, the criterion for the placement of a figure in a particular place seems to have been that it be a place from which his influence was felt—whether in church, school, or state.[21] Thus John Calvin, though from Picardy, is included in the section on *Helvetia,* as are the Germans Johannes Oecolampadius, Simon Grynaeus, and Konrad Pellikan, and the Italian Peter Martyr Vermigli.[22] It is evident, then, that Beza sees his comrades as part of an international movement for which mobility is a great good. Indeed, by mistreating a Reformer and forcing him into exile a country can forfeit her claim upon her native son, to her own great loss. Two poems can be taken to illustrate both of these points—geographical mobility and the forfeiture of progeny. These are the poems dedicated to Martin Bucer and Peter Martyr.

Theologians: Martin Bucer

Though many of the verse tributes in the *Icones* were re-issued from an earlier edition of Beza's *Poemata* (1569),[23] the poem to the Reformer of Strasbourg was new. Of Bucer, Beza writes:[24]

---

[19] Germany in fact receives two sections, *Praecipua Christianismi, nostra patrumque memoria, inter Germanos instaurati organos* and *Sex Germaniae eximii martyres.* When these two sections are combined, Germany receives more tributes than any other region (30 named individuals). *Gallia* is second (23 named individuals).

[20] Sometimes Beza uses the name of the region (e.g., *Helvetia, Italia*), sometimes that of the region's inhabitants (e.g., *inter Germanos, apud Polonos*).

[21] Another point to which I shall return.

[22] Some of these figures were itinerant; but for obvious reasons an individual can only be included in one section.

[23] Beza's *Poemata,* sometimes referred to as the *Juvenilia,* was first published in 1548 and went through several revisions. For the controversy surrounding the first edition, see Kirk M. Summers, *A View from the Palatine: The* Iuvenilia *of Théodore de Bèze* (Tempe, AZ: Arizona Center for Medieval and Renaissance Studies, 2001).

*Natales, Bucere, tuos **Germania** iactat,*
  Natalibus felix tuis.
*Quis vero et quantus fueris, **tua scripta** loquuntur,*
  Ad littus orbis ultimum.
*De vita si quis rogitet, **Germania** dicet,*
  Invita Bucerum expuli.
*Ast ego sic pulsum (pia dixerit **Anglia**) fovi,*
  Tandemque texi mortuum.
Verum mox eadem (factum o immane) sepulcro
  Flammis cremavit erutum.
Fallor ego, totus terraenae fecis an expers,
  Bucere sic caelum tenes?

Germany boasts of your birth, Bucer,
Happy because of your birth.
But who and how great you were, **your writings** say,
To the furthest shore of the world.
If anyone should ask about your life, **Germany** will say,
"I, unwilling, drove out Bucer."
"But I," pious **England** will say, "cared for him when he
was driven out,
And finally covered him over when he died."
But soon the same one (O monstrous deed!) burned
Him with flames when he had been dug out of his grave.
I am deceived, Bucer: do you thus hold heaven
Whole, or without earthly dregs?[25]

The last couplet is somewhat difficult; it presumably turns on a pun on Bucer's name, for a *Butze* is something that protrudes or projects.[26] The rest of it, however, is clear enough. Two markers of geography are mentioned. Though a native of Germany,[27] Bucer was eventually forced to make his

---

[24] Beza, *Icones*, sig. G.i.r. The meter is the First Pythiambic. All translations are my own.

[25] All translations are my own.

[26] I owe this observation to Stephen Naumann. The repetition of his name is significant, occurring in lines 1, 6, and 12 and thus acting as a thread holding the poem together. Cf. the poem on Hyperius, discussed below, where Beza does the same with his name in lines 1, 11, and 17.

[27] This is consistent with what was said above. Though a native of Germany, that is not the reason why he is included in the German section of the *Icones*, as the *titulus* to his entry makes clear: *Martinus Bucerus, Germanus, Selestadiensis, ecclesiae Argentinensis*

way to England, where he taught at Cambridge. But why are these places important? They are the locations from which the influence of his writings (*tua scripta*) was felt—it is a commonplace of the *Icones* that writings (as opposed to, say, images) constitute the true bridge to universality and immortality, allowing one a voice even from beyond the grave. The local is a staging-ground for the international, and the divide is crossed by literary productivity. We might additionally note in passing that, even when a Reformer has died, a country can still incur guilt on his behalf:

> thus does England, because of the posthumous burning of Bucer's body, along with that of Paul Fagius, at the hands of Mary I, or "Bloody Mary," on 6 February 1556.[28] It is no coincidence, given what has just been said about the transnational power of the word, that their writings were burned together with their remains in accordance with the law *De comburendo haeretico*.[29]

Theologians: Peter Martyr Vermigli

Similar is the poem to Peter Martyr in elegiac couplets (included, as noted above, in the section devoted to *Helvetia*), of whom Beza says:[30]

> *Tuscia te pepulit, **Germania** et **Anglia** fovit,*
> *Martyr, quem extinctum, nunc tegit **Helvetia**.*
> *Dicere quae si vera volent, te et nomine dicent,*

---

pastor, et demum in Academia Cantabrigiensi theologiae professor. Fagius receives the next entry, and his description is similar: *Paulus Fagius, Germanus, Tabernensis, ecclesiae Argentinensis pastor, ac tandem in Cantabrigiensi Academia theologiae professor*. Beza has already given the reader his principle in the heading of the section as a whole: *Praecipua Christianismi, nostra patrumque memoria, inter Germanos instaurati organos* ("Exceptional instruments of the renewal of Christianity, in the memory of us and our fathers, among the Germans").

[28] A similar point is made with respect to Zwingli's posthumous treatment in the poem dedicated to him. See Beza, *Icones*, sig. M.ii.r.

[29] See A. Edward Harvey, *Martin Bucer in England* (Marburg: Heinrich Bauer, 1906), 94–95. They were rehabilitated by Elizabeth I on 22 July 1560.

[30] Beza, *Icones*, sig. Piiir. The meter is the elegiac couplet. Unlike the poem to Bucer, this one was previously published, though without the final couplet. Its opening words (*Tuscia te pepulit*) perhaps echo the opening of the verses, also in elegiacs, that supposedly adorned Vergil's tomb (*Mantua me genuit*). Those verses, like Beza's, are about two things: geography and writing.

Hic fidus Christi (credite) **Μάρτυρ** *erat.*
*Utque istae taceant, satis hoc **tua scripta** loquuntur:*
*Plus satis hoc **Italis** exprobrat exilium.*

Tuscany begat you, **Germany** and **England** nourished you,
Martyr, whom, dead, **Switzerland** now covers.
If these places wish to speak the truth, they will also speak of you by name:
"This was a faithful (believe!) **Μάρτυρ** [witness] for Christ."
And even if they be silent, **your writings** sufficiently say it.
More sufficiently does this[31] reproach the **Italians** with your exile.

The primary motifs of this short poem are already familiar from the poem to Bucer: itinerancy, productivity, and the pun on his name (*Martyr*, of course, means "witness"). Though born in Italy, Peter Martyr made his way to Germany, England, and finally to Switzerland.[32] All of these places ought to testify to Martyr's status as "witness for Christ." But, in the end, no matter, for if they remain silent, his writings (again, *tua scripta*) will speak for him and continue to make him heard from beyond the grave.[33] His books, in fact, are a satisfactory rebuke to the Italians for having exiled him. Vermigli shares in the status of exile equally with Bucer, to the discredit of the homeland of each.

Within these geographical divisions, moreover, confessional identities are mixed. If we once again limit ourselves to those figures who receive poetic tributes, we see immediately that the section devoted to Germany (*Germania*) includes not only the Roman Catholic Erasmus,[34] but also the

---

[31] I.e. his status as *martyr* or "witness." *Hoc* is lengthened *metri gratia*.

[32] For a brief biography, see the *Oxford Encyclopedia of the Reformation*, ed. Hans J. Hillerbrand (Oxford: Oxford University Press, 1996), vol. 4, s.v. "Vermigli, Peter Martyr," 229–31 (hereafter *OER*).

[33] *Scripta* ("writings") feature prominently in the the poem to Grynaeus as well (Beza, *Icones*, sig. O.iii.r–v).

[34] Beza identifies Erasmus as *Batavus* ("Dutch"), and appears to include the inhabitants of *Batavia* (Holland or the Netherlands) among the *Germani*. I say "appears" because there is an alternative explanation, viz., that Erasmus lived for some time in Freiburg im Bresgau after Basel became officially Reformed. See Cornelis Augustijn, *Erasmus: His Life, Works, and Influence*, trans. J.C. Grayson (Toronto: Univer-

Lutherans Luther, Melanchthon, and Joachim Camerarius; not only these, but also the Reformed Martin Bucer and Wolfgang Musculus; and not only these, but also Andreas Gerhard Hyperius, who was neither quite Lutheran nor quite Reformed.[35] Again, the section on France (*Gallia*) includes the ambiguous Guillame Budé and Michel de l'Hospital, but also Calvin's (and Beza's) Greek teacher Melchior Wolmar and the printer Robert Estienne, not to mention Roman Catholics such as King Francis I and Marguerite of Navarre, as well as the unbeliever Francois Vatable.[36]

Theologians: Ioannes Oecolampadius

Not only are confessional identities mixed in each section, but—as may already be evident—professional identities are at first glance jumbled together as well. Beza, that is, is not interested only in theologians in any kind of narrow sense. This is not to say that he is not interested in theologians at all; he is. We can again avail ourselves of the poems for purposes of elucidation. First, a poem to the Basel Reformer Johannes Oecolampadius:[37]

> *Oecolampadius, serena nuper*
> *Lampas, aede sacra Dei coruscans,*
> *Qualis limpidiorve, puriorve*
> *Vix ullis micuit lucerna seclis,*
> *En mortis iacet obrutus tenebris.*
> *At vobis male sit, malae tenebrae,*
> *Lucis munere quae brevi fruentes,*
> *Eheu, nos miseros homunciones*

---

sity of Toronto Press, 1991; German original 1986), 158–60, 173–83. Though Beza mentions nothing of this move in his tribute, he often identifies figures geographically by their base of operations rather than by ethnicity (see above).

[35] Gerhard Rau notes similarities with both camps, but ultimately "because of his dogmatic method" groups Hyperius with "early Reformed orthodoxy." He nevertheless refers to him as "supraconfessional" and remarks that "in Hyperius there appeared a further developed Lutheran, a Reformed, and not least of all, an Erasmian ecclesiology." See *OER*, vol. 2, s.v. "Hyperius, Andreas," 299–300. It is worth remarking that Beza himself was still trying to reach agreement with the Lutherans as late as 1586 at Montbeliard. Cf. Jill Raitt, *The Colloquy of Montbéliard: Religion and Politics in the Sixteenth Century* (Oxford: Oxford University Press, 1993).

[36] These last three do not receive poems in the original Latin *Icones*; I include them only for the purpose of fuller illustration.

[37] Beza, *Icones*, sigs. M.ii.r–v. The meter is hendecasyllabic.

Nocte sic premitis tenebricosa.
Sed bene hoc cecidit, nigrae o tenebrae,
Quod dum ipsam petitis, malae, lucernam,
Laternam tamen obruistis unam:
Laterna ut lateat quidem hic sepulta,
Ipsa sed magis emicet lucerna.

Oecolampadius, recently a peaceful
Lamp, shining in the sacred abode of God,
Of such a kind that a clearer or purer
Light has scarcely shone forth in any age—
Behold, he lies covered in the darkness of death.
But may it go evilly for you, evil darkness,
Who thus oppress with darkness-shrouded night
Us wretched little men, who, for a brief time,
Were enjoying the gift of light.
But this has turned out well, O black darkness,
Because, although you, evil, attack the light itself,
You nevertheless cover the lantern alone,
Such that the lantern, indeed, hides buried here,
But the light itself shines out all the more.

As is his custom, Beza puns on the etymological meaning of his addressee: "Oecolampadius" means "house lamp," and Beza treats Oecolampadius as a light that continues to shine in God's house (or temple)[38] for God's people, even in the darkness and even after his death—presumably, once again, through his writings, for that is the only way in which he could continue to do so.

Theologians: Heinrich Bullinger

Likewise, Beza's poem to Heinrich Bullinger praises him for his *doctrina*, *pietas*, and *candor* (learning, godliness or practice of the true religion, and purity):[39]

Doctrina si interire, si Pietas mori,
Occidere si Candor potest,
Doctrina, Pietas, Candor, hoc tumulo iacent,

---

[38] *aedes* means both "house [of God or the gods," i.e. "temple," and "house [of man]," i.e., "dwelling."

[39] Beza, *Icones*, sigs. N.iiii.r–v.

Henrice, tecum condita.
Mori sed absit illa posse dixerim,
   Quae vivere iubent mortuos.
Immo interire forsan illa si queant,
   Subireque tumuli specum,
Tu tu illa doctis, tu piis, tu candidis,
   Et non mori certissimis,
Tenaci ab ipsa morte chartis asseras,
   Ipso approbante numine.
Foedus beatum! Mortuum illa te excitant,
   Et tu mori illa non sinis.
At hunc, amici, cur fleamus mortuum,
   Qui vivit aliis, et sibi?

If learning can perish, if piety can die,
If purity can be lost,
Learning, piety, purity lie in this tomb,
Heinrich, buried with you.
But far be it from me to say that those things can die
Which command the dead to live.
Nay, if by chance those things could perish,
And enter the cavern of the grave,
You, you by your learned, you by your pious, you by your
pure
writings, and most certain not to die,
Would liberate them from clinging death itself,
As divinity itself gives approval.
Happy covenant! Those things raise you up, though you
are dead,
And you do not allow them to die.
But why, friends, do we weep over him, dead,
Who lives for others, and for himself?

Beza first says that, if it were possible for learning, godliness, and purity to die, they have been buried with Bullinger. But he next reverses course: these qualities have not died, but live on in his writings (*chartis*),[40] which possess those same qualities of learning, godliness, and purity; and for that reason Bullinger himself can be said to continue to live. The pattern is so far consistent: the written word is the vehicle of immortality. Here it is combined

---

[40] Bullinger's writings primarily theological/doctrinal/pastoral, so I include him with the theologians

with the metaphor of manumission, signalled by the verb *asseras* ("you would liberate"), for Bullinger as author frees virtue from slavery to the bonds of death. Thus Beza heroizes Bullinger as a pious and erudite theologian in possession of a kind of poetic immortality.

Theologians: Josias Simmler

One final example with respect to theology, this one more specific. I refer to the poem for Josias Simmler, Bullinger's godson, who taught New Testament (from 1552) and theology (from 1560) at the Carolinum in Zurich.[41] Beza writes:[42]

> *Simlere, mi Simlere, quo superstite*
> *Tot mortui revixerant,*
> *Quos ira nobis numinis, tam pauculis*
> *Ademit annis plurimos.*
> *Simlere, quem treumuit renatus Arrius,*
> *Tremuit renatus Eutyches,*
> *Vastator ille Poloniae, hic Germaniae,*
> *Laesi flagella numinis.*
> *Heu subita et immatura te mors auferens*
> *Quam multa tecum sustulit!*
> *Lamenta amicis quanta, quot iustissimos*
> *Secum dolores attulit!*
> *Quos inter, ecce Beza quondam haud ultimus,*
> *His irrigat te lacrymis:*
> *Beza repetito vulnere isto saucius,*
> *Communis ad tumulum patris.*

Simmler, my Simmler, as long as you survived
So many of the dead had come back to life,
Very many of whom the divinity's anger took away
From us in so few years.
Simmler, at whom Arius reborn trembled,
At whom Eutyches reborn trembled—

---

[41] Scholarship on Simmler is rare. For a brief account, see the entry by Georg von Wyß in *Allgemeine Deutsche Biographie*, ed. Bayerische Akademie der Wissenschaften (München) Historische Kommission, Band 34 (Leipzig: Duncker and Humblot, 1892), 355–58.

[42] Beza, *Icones*, sig. P.iiii.v.

The former the devastator of Poland, the latter of Germany—
[you were] the scourge of the harmed divinity.
Alas, how much sudden and untimely death took away
When it carried you off!
How great the lamentations for friends, how many most just
Griefs it brought with itself!
Amidst these, behold Beza, by no means the last in former days,
Soaks you with these tears:
Beza, hurt again by that recollected wound,
At the tomb of a common father.

The poem begins with misdirection. The opening gesture toward resurrection is quickly deflated, for Beza is actually referring to particular heresies that had reared their heads again in his own day. The reference to "Arianism" in Poland indicates Simmler's stance against Socinianism; the reference to "Eutychianism" in Germany is directed toward certain Lutherans. Simmler as author is in the background here as in many of the other poems already discussed—though only implicitly, for Beza does not mention his writings. Indeed, the departure of the loved one in this poem seems much more final, as Beza makes no claim about Simmler continuing to live on through his books. And yet—paradoxically, perhaps—we can connect the references in the poem much more closely with particular works that was possible in the previous poems cited. Here one would include works such as his *Assertio orthodoxae doctrinae de duabus naturis Christi, servatoris nostri, opposita blasphemiis & sophismatibus Simonis Budnaei nuper ab ipso in Lituania evulgatis*, first published in 1575; his *De aeterno Dei filio domino et servatore nostro Iesu Christo & de spiritu sancto, adversus veteres & novos antitrinitarios, id est Arianos, Tritheitas, Samosatenianos & Pneumatomachos, libri quatuor* (1568); his *De vera Iesu Christi domini et servatoris nostri secundum humanam naturam in his terris praesentia, orthodoxa & brevis expositio* (1574); and his *Responsio ad maledicum Francisci Stancari Mantuani librum adversus Tigurinae ecclesiae ministros, de trinitate & mediatore domino nostro Iesu Christo* (1563).

Non-Theologians: Joachim Camerarius

In any case, it is now evident (and unsurprising) that theologians and theological writings play an important role in the imaginary hall of heroes Beza constructs in the *Icones*. But many other types of figures are included as well, particularly those who were renowned and admired for their liberal learning and exemplary pedagogy. As Baird comments, "To anyone that remembers the close connection which the Reformers always recognised as existing between the progress of letters and the advance of pure religion," the inclusion of such figures is not surprising.[43] Three poems will serve as examples. First, a short poem dedicated to the Lutheran Joachim Camerarius:

> *Extinctis olim, Musae, flevistis alumnis,*
> *Et vitam vestra restituistis ope.*
> *Nos contra vobis, Ioachimi in funere, Musae,*
> *Has miseri extinctis solvimus exequias.*
> *Namque omnes tecum, tecum, Ioachime, Camoenae*
> *Ut vixere simul, sic periere simul.*

In former times, O Muses, you wept over your dead foster-sons,
And you restored their lives by your aid.
We, on the other hand, at the funeral of Ioachim in wretchedness
Performed these funeral rites for you, Muses, dead.
For as all the Muses lived together with you, Joachim,
So they died together with you.

This thoroughly classicizing poem of lament, written fittingly in elegiac couplets,[44] is addressed to the Muses, invoked under both their Greek (*Musae*) and Italic (*Camoenae*) names. The first couplet alludes to the Muses'

---

[43] Baird, *Counsellor of the Reformation*, 313. He mentions in this connection figures such as Erasmus, Reuchlin, and Francis I (cf. above and Randall, *(Em)bodying the Word*, 99). Randall Coats, "Memorializing the Martyrs," 24, offers the following false dichotomy: "Beza's choices for inclusion in *Icones* are not always theologically motivated, but rather arise from subjective preference." First, one might coyly respond that his theological motivations are no less a matter of subjective preference than any other preference. Second—less cynically and therefore more importantly—one might resist too swift a use of "subjectivism" as a meaningful analytical category and, in the absence of an immediate logic of selection by objective criteria, continue investigating. *Pace* Randall Coats, such a logic of selection is in fact present, as will emerge in the remainder of this essay.

[44] See *Oxford Classical Dictionary*, 3rd ed., ed. Simon Hornblower and Anthony Spawforth (Oxford: Oxford University Press, 1999), s.v. "elegiac poetry, Greek," 516–18 (hereafter *OCD*).

resuscitation of singers beloved to them.[45] Then, the conceit: with the death of *this* poet, the Muses themselves have died. The link between Camerarius and the classical Muses—and, indeed, of Beza's transition from the Greek term to the Latin one—is appropriate, given that Camerarius devoted a great deal of time to translating classical Greek works into Latin, such as those of Homer, Sophocles, Theocritus, Herodotus, and Demosthenes. He also wrote commentaries on works such as Cicero's *Tusculan Disputations*[46] and Homer's *Iliad*.[47] In addition, he was a poet in his own right,[48] as well as a teacher of Greek. Though he had a significant role to play in the world of theology (he was involved in drafting the Augsburg Confession),[49] Beza says nothing about it here. Why? Perhaps because Beza was never able to come to terms theologically with the Lutherans. If that is the case, however, the fact serves to highlight another kind of catholicity all the more, for it does not prevent Beza from continuing to hold him in the highest esteem for the gifts he bestowed on humanistic learning—and therefore, implicitly, on the church.

Non-Theologians: Conrad Gessner

That we should not be too quick to read the theological omission polemically is made clear by our next example, a poem dedicated to the Reformed Conrad Gessner.[50]

> *Te caelo mutante solum, Gesnere, volucres*
> *Quaecunque pennis aera permeant,*
> *Replevere modis omnia tristibus,*
> *Migrantem amicum, extrema supra sidera,*
> *Omnes eum sonitu gravi insequutae.*

[45] I am, however, aware of no such instance in Greek myth. It is possible that he refers to a metaphorical resuscitation; the Muses' aid (*ope*) would in that case be memory, their peculiar province. (I owe this suggestion to Joseph Garnjobst.)

[46] The *Commentarii explicationum in M.T. Ciceronis Tusculanarum Quaestionum libros V*. https://archive.org/details/bub_gb_964YJ7bdqRYC.

[47] The *Commentarius explicationis primi libri Iliados Homeri*. https://archive.org/details/bub_gb_0svT_XAcCA8C

[48] The *Libellus continens Eclogas et alia quaedam poematia diversis temporibus et occasionibus* https://archive.org/details/bub_gb_j06-RLP8TGEC.

[49] See *OER*, vol. 1, s.v. "Camerarius, Joachim," 249.

[50] Beza, *Icones*, sigs. R.i.r–v.

Te caelo mutante solum, Gesnere, feroces
Gemuere in antris belluae,
Et stabulis pecudes relictis.
      Sibilis colubrite feri gemunt lugubribus,
Imisque quotquot sub cavernis
Occulta terrarum colunt:
Et flaccidum plantae virentes,
Et pallidum flores nitentes,
Et marcidum arbores comantes.
      Regna te per humida,
Et bellus qua ferit undique
Reboantia littora pontus,
Planctu sonoro deflet Amphitrite,
Et liquidis sub aquis pisces natantes mutitant.[51]
      Natura te omnis denique ut fidum suorum antistitem
Plorat sacrorum, muta
Futura deinceps, ni loquaris mortuus.
Haec inter tibi turbatus, Gesnere, parentat
Beza tuus, vati vates, et amicus amico,
His incompositis innumeris numeris.

When you exchanged earth for heaven, Gessner, whatever
Birds move on wings through the air
Filled all with gloomy strains;
They all followed him, their migrating friend,
Beyond the furthest stars with grave sound.
When you exchanged earth for heaven, Gessner, the fierce
Beasts lamented in their caves,
And the herds, having left their stables.
The savage snakes lamented you with hissing groans,
And however many creatures inhabit the secret
Parts of earth down in the deepest caves:
And you, feeble, the flourishing plants,
And you, pale, the shining flowers,
And you, withered, the leafy trees.
Through the realms of water and [the places]
Where the bellowing sea strikes
The re-echoing shores on every side,
Amphitrite weeps for you with loud complaint,

---

[51] The text is difficult. I read *mutitant* as an alternate spelling of *muttitant* (metrically impossible here) < *muttitare*, which is in turn a frequentative form of *mut(t)ire*, "to murmur."

And the fish swimming in the clear waters mutter in lament.
In short, all nature bewails you as the faithful priest
Of her rites, hereafter dumb,
unless you, though dead, should speak.
Amidst these, Gessner, your Beza, in turmoil, offers
Solemn sacrifice to you—a poet to a poet, and a friend to a friend—
With these disordered unmeasured measures.

Conrad Gessner, professor of Greek at Lausanne, of natural history and ethics at the Carolinum, and later a theology professor in the Prophezei, as well as the author of the important *Bibliotheca universalis* and other scholarly works of enormous significance,[52] was a great devotee of the study of nature and philosophy; in the accompanying prose section Beza calls for that reason him a Varro and a Pliny.[53] The lamentations of nature detailed in the poem are therefore manifestly appropriate to the addressee. Though Gessner was a Protestant, the poem says nothing at all about religion (the prose section mentions *pietas* once) even though, due to his religious confession, his scientific works were placed on the Roman Catholic list of prohibited books.[54] Beza instead views him as another humanist like himself: he offers the "sacrifice" of the poem as "a poet to a poet." A humanistic *captatio* is placed in the final line. The poem is metrically manifold and irregular, and so he refers to its meter with the phrase *innumeris numeris*. The phrase was originally used of Plautus; according to a remark of Varro preserved in Aulus Gellius' *Attic Nights*, Plautus himself coined it to describe the metrical aspect of his plays.[55] Beza does not make the link explicit, but Gessner, and anyone else with a similar education, would have understood it.

Non-Theologians: Michel De L'Hospital

Finally, a poem to Michel de l'Hospital:

[52] See *OER*, vol. 2, s.v. "Gessner, Conrad," 170–71.

[53] The reference is to Pliny the Elder.

[54] Indeed, all of Gessner's works were banned in the *Index librorum prohibitorum*, or "Pauline Index," promulgated by Pope Paul IV in 1559.

[55] Camerarius, treated above, remains one of the foremost technical scholars of Plautus of the entire modern period.

Talis Aristoteles oculos atque ora ferebas,
    Sculptoris docta nunc redivive manu.
Pars autem illa tui melior, melioribus olim
    Expressa in tabulis, nec peritura manet.
Sed quid opus sculptisve fuit scriptisve tabellis?
    En vivo in Xenio vivis Aristoteles.

You had eyes and face like Aristotle,
O you now renewed by the learned hand of the sculptor.
But that part of you was better, once expressed
In better writings, and it remains as one that will not per-
ish.
But what was the need for sculptures or written works?
Behold, Aristotle, you live in the living Host [i.e.,
l'Hospital].[56]

There are a number of conceits in play in this poem. First, there is the contrast between the image of l'Hospital and his writings. His physical appearance was like Aristotle's, but the better part of him was not his body at all; it was his writings. At the same time, the noun *tabulis* draws attention precisely to the materiality of those writings, and so Beza gives what has become a common trope for him in the *Icones* a further turn: while l'Hospital was alive, there was no need for writings at all, for Aristotle was reincarnated in l'Hospital himself.[57] Thus the second-person apostrophe shifts from l'Hospital at the beginning of the poem to Aristotle himself at the end, and his name is used to create a ring-composition that holds the poem together. Aristotle, both as himself and as l'Hospital, is the thread that runs through these six lines. This designation will perhaps strike the reader as somewhat odd. L'Hospital was primarily a man of action, a statesman—one who attempted to mediate between Roman Catholics and Protestants in order to restore peace to France—and not a scholar, though he did write Latin verse.

What is the relation, then? L'Hospital, Beza says in the prose section, put into practice the things only discussed by Aristotle while walking in the

---

[56] Beza puns on the meaning of l'Hospital by using a Latin transliteration of a Greek word of equivalent meaning, ξένιος.

[57] This is expressed arrestingly in the present tense, which paradoxically draws attention to the fact that l'Hospital is no longer alive.

Peripatos:[58] *forte tamen in eo dispari, quod (ut de pietate taceam) quae deambulans Aristoteles in umbra porticus disseruit, Hospitalius noster reipsa exercuit.* Beza's tribute, however, is not unambiguous: the accompanying woodcut shows L'Hospital with his back to a candle and thus criticizes his religious position:[59]

MICHAEL HOSPITALIVS.

---

[58] The reader should recall here that Aristotle was himself tutor to a man of action, Alexander the Great.

[59] Beza, *Icones*, sig. V.ii.v.

Beza criticizes such waffling in the dedicatory epistle to King James VI of Scotland.[60]

3. THE MAGISTERIAL TURN: THE PURPOSE OF THE ICONES IN BEZA'S LETTERS TO JAMES VI AND GEORGE BUCHANAN

We might use this remark about a man of action, deeply entrenched in public affairs directed toward the pacification of his country, but compromised in his service by his failure to commit fully, in Beza's opinion, to orthodoxy to serve as a transition to some remarks about the purpose of the *Icones*. Beza makes that purpose clear in two letters: the dedicatory letter to James just mentioned and another letter, not included in the front matter of the *Icones*, to his friend George Buchanan, who had served as James' childhood tutor.

The fact that the Latin *Icones* (as well as its French translation), written by a French-Swiss republican Genevan Protestant, is dedicated to the decidedly non-Presbyterian Scottish (and soon-to-be English) monarch is itself an index of the international and irenic scope of the movement of the Reformation in the sixteenth century.[61] I have already remarked on the "catholicity" of Beza's catalogue of heroes in the *Icones*; Beza remarks on it to the king as well:[62]

> ...*hunc sum ordinem sequutus, ut Gentium et Ecclesiarum, in quibus floruerunt, servata distinctione, ipsis et doctis eorum* παραστάταις, *utpote quorum ministerio nostra patrumque memoria Ecclesiae bonaeque literae sunt instauratae, primum hunc locum tribuerim: altero Regibus, Principibus, et civitatum Magistratibus, Ecclesiae nutritiis, militaribus denique fortissimis viris servato, qui pro tuenda vera religione sanguinem etiam profuderunt.*

---

[60] See Beza, *Icones*, sig. iii.r: *Quod autem iis quos nunc commemoro, nonnullos in ipso praesertim Galliae vestibulo adiunxi, quorum nonulli pietatem ipsam, non tamen certa (ut arbitror) improbitate, sed ignorantia oppugnarunt, alii religionem cum populo colere quam suae conscientiae rationem habere quantam oportuit maluerunt, nullus ut spero indignabitur, qui mei consilii causam ex ipsis eorum elogiis cognoverint.* I disagree with Randall, *(Em)bodying the Word*, 88, that the preface is "characterized by authorial ambivalence"; his purpose seems to me perfectly clear.

[61] Beza remarks on Knox later in letter and expresses his hope that the Scottish and Genevan churches will be bound closely together (Beza, *Icones*, sig. iiiv).

[62] Beza, *Icones*, sigs. *ii.r–*iii.v.

> ...I have aimed at the following sequence [in arranging the entries]: while preserving the distinction of nations and churches in which [my subjects] flourished, I have given the first place to those men and their learned helpers by whose service in our and our fathers' memory the churches and humane studies were renewed; the second place has been reserved for kings, princes, and city magistrates, nurses of the church, and finally to the very brave soldiers, who poured out even their own blood for the sake of protecting the true religion.

What Beza refers to as the "second place" seems to indicate a projected second volume that was never completed.[63] Be that as it may, we ought to note a number of things from this brief excerpt that confirm the foregoing observations: (1) his objects of praise are geographically diverse; (2) they come both from the secular and ecclesiastical spheres; (3) they are praised because they were instrumental in a project of renewal; (4) significantly, this project was not simply ecclesiastical, a fact that cannot be overstressed: the rapid growth of the Protestant outlook led to the renewal not just of the churches, but also of humane studies (*bonae literae*)—and one could add that the latter was of great use to the former, as can be clearly seen from the *Icones* itself; (5) magistrates, such as King James himself, have a role to play: they are to be nursing fathers (*nutriciis*) of the church;[64] (6) soldiers too have a role, in defending the practice of the true faith against hostile aggressors.

Beza assumes that James will be sympathetic to his position, and will do his part in advancing the Reformation movement—or, at the very least, he subtly exhorts him to be so and to do so by speaking as though it is already the case that he is and does:[65]

> *Quum enim te constet ab ipsa pueritia, divino quodam impulsu (adscitis etiam eruditissimis illarum doctoribus D. Georgio Buchanano, quem mihi liceat omnis liberalioris eruditionis ac praesertim poetices*

---

[63] See Dufour, introduction to *Les vrais portraits*, iv; many portraits of kings, princes, magistrates, and generals were added in the 1673 edition (ibid., v). It should, however, be noted that a few public figures are included already in the 1580 *Icones* (e.g., Francis I and Marguerite of Navarre).

[64] The reference is presumably to Isaiah 49.23.

[65] Beza, *Icones*, sigs. *iii.r–v.

parentem appellare, et D. Petro Iunio, eximia quoque doctrina prae-
dito) linguarum et bonarum artium studia tanta mentis contentione
tantoque successu amplexum, ut, favente Deo, veterum illorum, tum
rebus fortiter gestis tum etiam eruditione clarissimorum Regum me-
moriam nostro seculo renovaturus videare: atque adeo illos propemod-
um omnes in eo superaturus, quod te verae pietatis, quae illis pler-
isque defuit, studiosissimum re ipsa in primis ostendas: cui tandem
existimaverim gratiorem fore virorum et **doctrina** *et* **pietate**
praestantissimorum commendationem?

For since it is established that you, from your very boy-
hood, by some divine impulse, have embraced your studies
of languages and the humane disciplines (you also had the
most erudite teachers of those subjects, Dr. George Buchanan, whom I may call the father of all liberal education
and especially of poetry, and Dr. Peter Junius, also endowed with exceptional learning) with so great a striving of
mind and so great an outcome, that, with God favoring
[your enterprise], you seem about to renew for our age the
memory of those ancient kings most illustrious both for
deeds accomplished bravely and also for erudition, and
even to surpass nearly all of them, because you show your-
self to be in reality most zealous for the true religious faith,
which was lacking for most of them: to whom, finally,
could I judge that the commendation of men most excellent **both in learning and in religious faith** would be
more welcome?

Learning and piety receive almost equal treatment in Beza's description.
Indeed, James' study of languages and the humanities comes by a "divine
impulse." In his wise government, he will equal the best of ancient kings—
no, he will rather surpass them, because he professes the true (Reformed)
religion. He should therefore be very pleased to read about other such figures who excelled in learning and piety.

Beza goes on:[66]

Ad haec et illud accedit quod **quum Christi regnum** *quanto*
maximo animi ardore fieri potest **apud Scotos** *tuos* **promoveas,**
usque adeo ut ad extremas usque terras huius tuae singularis pietatis
fama permanarit, **sit autem huius Christi regni pars etiam**

---

[66] Ibid., sig. *iii.v.

*aliqua Genevensis haec Ecclesia, putavi mei esse officii me-
metipsum tuis populis aggregare, et gratam communis tanti beneficii
memoriam Regiae tuae Maiestati qua possem ratione testificari.*

To these things is also added the fact that, **since you are
promoting the reign of Christ among your own Scots**
with as great a zeal of mind as can possibly occur—and to
such an extent that the fame of this exceptional religious
faith of yours has flowed forth all the way to the ends of
the earth—**[and since], moreover, this Genevan church
is also a part of this reign of Christ**, I thought that it belonged to my duty to add myself to the flock of your peo-
ples and to testify to your royal majesty to the welcome
memory of so great a kindness in whatever way I could.

Taking this with the passages above, we may conclude that Beza conceives
of the "reign of Christ" (*Christi regnum*) rather broadly, encompassing not
merely the institutional church but the whole of society, both in Scotland
and elsewhere; the "church of Geneva" (*Genevensis Ecclesia*) is, after all, part
of the very same reign or kingdom of Christ, and Beza numbers himself
among the "flock" (*aggregare*) of James, a (foreign) monarch. Beza, then, sees
the Protestant domains of Europe and the British Isles to be closely connected and their fortunes to be closely intertwined. Thus James as a pious
prince is important not only for his own people, but for continental European Christians as well.

Beza closes the letter by expressing the hope that James may see his
reign flourish more and more; that Christ, as *Rex Regum*, King of Kings,
would make James' virtues to grow; and that James would not only meet,
but exceed, the expectation that has been aroused about him "in the whole
Christian world" (*in orbe toto Christiano*). The Scottish king, it seems, sums up
in his person the hopes of the Reformation movement, both theologically
and pedagogically, and Beza, through his lavish praise, hopes to stir him up
to act accordingly in the realms of letters and religion. Beza construed the
movement, and the *regnum Christi*, as having boundaries somewhat wider
than those we tend to conceptualize today, a day in which they are often
limited to the institutional church. For Beza, those expansive boundaries
encompassed church, school, and government—whether in Switzerland,
Germany, France, or Scotland—for he believed all to function within a *so-*

cietas Christiana that in certain respects respected national distinctions while at the same time transcending them.

Beza's purpose is made still clearer in a letter sent to George Buchanan on 16 March 1580, to which was attached a copy of the *Icones*. He begins by calling the work a "trifle": *Nugatus sum aliquid in re seria quod etiam Regi consecrare sum ausus* ("I have trifled somewhat in a serious matter, and I dared to dedicate it even to the king").[67] He therefore asks Buchanan to put in a good word with James, his former pupil. But his self-deprecation must not be allowed to obscure the fact that he had a serious purpose in his supposedly nugatory composition, which he at one point calls his "Attic Nights" (*noctuas Athenas*) in a reference to the *Noctes Atticae* of the second-century compiler Aulus Gellius:[68]

> *Quid autem hac mea qualicunque commentatiacula captem, ex ipsa praefatione cognosces, nempe ut quam de se expectationem in omnibus Ecclesiis concitarit, ubi Rex cognoverit, simul* **quod suum sit munus**, *variis istis optimis exemplis delectatus,* **magis ac magis intelligat**.

> You will recognize from the preface itself what I seek to obtain by means of this little composition of mine, of whatever sort it is—namely, **that the king**, when he has come to know the expectation he has aroused about himself in all the churches, at the same time **understand more and more**, once he has been delighted by these various examples of the best sort, **what his duty is**.

Notice the difference here. The flattery of the dedicatory epistle has been replaced by a forthright assertion of the king's *duty* (*munus*), a term that was missing in the letter to James. The *Icones* is in fact not just a trifle after all. Beza expects the king to be delighted—but to be delighted with a purpose. Beza's dedication of the work to the king serves notice that James has a wide reputation and that with that reputation comes a great responsibility. The delight that James will find in exemplars of piety and learning is to lead to an ever-deepening comprehension on his part of his obligations as a Christian prince not only to his own people, but to the *orbis Christianus* as a

---

[67] Note on term "trifle," light Latin poetry, etc.

[68] *Ep.* 31 in George Buchanan, *Opera omnia*, ed. Thomas Ruddiman, tom. 2 (Lyon: J.A. Langerak, 1725), 759.

whole. He has an architectonic role to play in the advancement of the Reformation of church and school. Beza's rhetorical strategy prevents him from being so forthright with the king himself, but he is able to speak more frankly to Buchanan, who, Beza hopes, will encourage James along similar lines.

4. JAMES VI, PIOUS DEFENDER AGAINST THE PAPAL MENACE: THE EXAMPLE OF ROMAN TYRANNY

Why this practical aim for King James? The answer is that Protestants in every region of Europe had a common enemy: the hierarchy of the Roman Catholic Church and the princes who supported it. Against this foe liberal learning and the true religion were powerful weapons, especially when aided by a legitimate Christian prince—and this in contrast to the popes, who had illegitimately usurped the throne in the view of the Reformers.

In this connection, it is not surprising that the theme of Roman "tyranny" appears several times over the course of the *Icones* directed toward King James. For example, Beza's tribute to the Waldensian martyrs refers to Roman tyranny; the term occurs in the section on Ioannes Bordellus, Matthaeus Vermellius, and Petrus Bordo, as well as in the tributes to Thomas Cranmer and John Knox; and the poem to Andreas Gerardus Hyperius refers to the "tyrant" (that is, to the Pope).

Furthermore, though they do not use the term "tyrant," the poems dedicated to Luther and Calvin can be taken as representative of Beza's general stance. First, the poem to Luther:[69]

> *Roma orbem domuit, Romam sibi Papa subegit,*
> *Viribus illa suis, fraudibus iste suis.*
> *Quanto isto maior Luterus maior, et illa,*
> *Istum illamque uno qui domuit calamo?*
> *I nunc, Alcidem memorato Graecia mendax,*
> *Luteri ad calamum ferrea clava nihil.*

Rome tamed the world, the pope subjugated Rome to himself,
The former by its own strength, the latter by his own tricks.

---

[69] Beza, *Icones*, sig. C.iiii.v.

> How much greater is Luther than the latter, greater also
> than the former,
> Who tamed both the latter and the former with one pen?
> Go now, let lying Greece remember Hercules,
> [whose] iron club is nothing in comparison with Luther's
> pen.

This short poem in elegiac couplets turns on the well-worn conceit that the pen is mightier than the sword. Beza takes us from the Roman Empire, which ruled through violence, to the papal empire, which ruled through deceit (and thus was presumably even less respectable than the pagan empire). And then he takes us to Luther, who overcame both with the pen— that is, with the power of the word (*de rigueur* in the *Icones*, as noted above). He caps the poem by making Luther superior even to the greatest Greek hero, Hercules, the patron saint of mankind. Even this comparison is itself anti-Roman, engaging as it does with a sixteenth-century polemic against Luther that depicted him negatively as Hercules, as seen in Hans Holbein the Younger's woodcut *Hercules Germanicus*.[70] Beza re-appropriates the comparison and turns it to positive use, and makes Luther superior to Hercules to boot.

The metrically promiscuous poem[71] to Calvin, on the other hand, approaches Rome from a different angle:[72]

> *Romae ruentis terror ille maximus,*
> *Quem mortuum legent boni, horrescunt mali,*
> *Ipsa a quo potuit virtutem discere virtus,*
> *Cur adeo exiguo ignotoque in cespite clausus*
> *Calvinus lateat, rogas?*
> *Calvinum assidue comitata modestia vivum,*

---

[70] See Sachiko Kusukawa, *The Transformation of Natural Philosophy* (Cambridge: Cambridge University Press, 1995), 46–48. Kusukawa notes, 48, that the woodcut is "in the spirit of Erasmus with whom the woodcut was associated at the time." Erasmus mentions Hercules in another connection in *Moriae Encomium* 40, in which he compares St. George to Hercules: *Iam vero Georgium etiam Herculem invenerunt, quemadmodum et Hippolytum alterum.* As Kusukawa further remarks, 48n98, Melanchthon was displeased with the comparison of Luther to Hercules in the woodcut.

[71] The poem consists of two iambic trimeters, two dactylic hexameters, and a glyconic in the poem's center; this is followed by another hexameter, a pentameter, and two more iambic trimeters.

[72] Beza, *Icones*, sig. R.iii.v. Beza also uses this poem in his Latin *Vita* of Calvin.

Hoc tumulo manibus condidit ipsa suis.
O te beatum cespitem tanto hospite!
O cui invidere cuncta possint marmora!

Calvin, that greatest terror of Rome rushing down to ruin,
over whom, dead, good men grieve, wicked men shudder,
from whom virtue herself was able to learn virtue—
do you ask why in burial he lies enclosed in ground
so slight and unknown?
Modesty, having continually accompanied Calvin as a man,
herself has buried him with her own hands in this tomb.
O you ground blessed by so great a guest!
O [you] whom all marble monuments could envy!

Though Beza draws attention to Calvin's writings in the accompanying prose section, he focuses instead on Calvin's virtue (and, by implication, Rome's vice) in the verse tribute—virtue herself could learn virtue from Calvin! The unassuming nature of his tomb—indeed, his tomb was un-marked—contrasts with the Roman extravagance denoted by *marmora*. Beza surely has conspicuous Roman shrines to the saints and popes in view; one need only think, for example, of Michelangelo's tomb for Pope Julius II, particularly his originally design that was never realized. To such monuments the resting-place of this Protestant saint stands in sharp contrast. Without an ostentatious grave monument, Calvin can only be memorialized by words—here, by Beza's words.[73] Just as Luther's pen was, so Calvin's virtue is sufficient to assure the destruction of Rome, already in the process of falling headlong (*ruentis*). Both contribute to her destruction, moreover, without the weapons of worldly warfare (power, deceit, wealth) held in common by pagan and ecclesiastical Rome, which in Beza's view continued to hold the Roman church in bondage.

---

[73] As he is again in Beza's *Ioannis Calvini Vita*, referred to in the previous note. Commenting on the eulogy for Calvin in the *Icones*, Randall, *(Em)bodying the Word*, 111, remarks, "His portrait of Calvin is a bodily image in woodcut only; the majori-ty of his development concerns Calvin as a verbal entity, a producer through his bodily existence, of crucial texts. For de Bèze, Calvin's significance is in the correct alignment of his word in relation to Scripture, to the Word, as manifested by his textual productions."

5. EX ARCE TARPEIA

One motif in particular is used several times to refer to Roman illegitimacy, and that is the classicizing motif of the Tarpeian Rock, the cliff on the Capitoline Hill in Rome whence traitors were thrown down to their deaths.[74] The site was named after an early episode in Roman history recounted in Livy 1.11.5–9, in which Tarpeia, daughter of Spurius Tarpeius, betrays the Romans and allows the Sabines into Rome, and is then killed—by the Sabines!—for her treachery.

This Tarpeian motif appears already in the second entry in the *Icones*, dedicated to Jan Hus, though the first, to Wycliffe, has set the stage through references to the "Roman harlot" (*Romanae meretrici*) and to Rome as "Antichrist" (*Antichristo*). I include here the brief entry on Hus in its entirety:[75]

> *O vigilis anseris hoc (enim patria Bohemorum lingua cognomentum illud sonat) minime obstreperum, sed suavissimum, ac plane tempestivum clangorem! quo coelitus potius quam ex terra sonante, veternosi tot seculis Christiani sunt excitati, non ut, anserum Capitolinorum exemplo, **Tarpeia rupes** adversus invasores servaretur, sed contra ut immanis praedo ex illa eadem arce, partim astu, partim vi occupata, in Christianum orbem diu grassatus, deturbaretur. Ut autem illum idem iste perfide correptum ustularit, quid aliud tamen effecit, quam quod tum sibi ipsi, tum aliis suis mancipiis indelebilem perfidiae notam inussit,[76] tu vero, Husse, quasi ex cavea in coelum emissus ingrata terra relicta evolasti? Quin etiam (dictu mirabile) tot illos qui et iam tum sunt auditi, et nunc adhuc audiuntur olores tibi succinentes, cur non merito velut ex foecundissimis tuis phoenicis potius, quam anseris, cineribus (quod etiam diceris iam iam moriturus praedixisse) enatos dixerimus?*

> O what a sound of the sentinel-goose (for in the native tongue of the Bohemians that is what his surname means), not at all clamorous, but most pleasant, yea, and a clanging manifestly sounding at the right time! When [Hus] was sounding forth from heaven more so than from earth,

---

[74] See *OCD* s.v. "Tarpeian Rock," 1474.

[75] Beza, *Icones*, sig. A.iii.r.

[76] This phrase echoes the immediately preceding entry for Wycliffe (*...hoc vel uno scelere Antichristo sibi ipsi quidem perpetuam crudelitatis notam inurente...*). Beza, *Icones*, sig. A.ii.r.

Christians—sleepy for so many centuries—were roused, not in order that the **Tarpeian Rock** might be preserved against invaders according to the example of the Capitoline geese, but, in contrast, in order that the monstrous robber, long having raged against the Christian world, might be thrust down from the same citadel, besieged partly by craft, partly by violence. When, moreover, that same [robber] burned him after he was treacherously arrested, what else—contrary to intention—did it accomplish than to brand an indelible mark of treachery both upon him himself and upon his slaves?—while you, Hus, flew away, sent forth from the cage into the sky, having left behind the ungrateful earth? Nay, more (wondrous to say!), why should we not rightly say that so many swans, who already at that time were heard and even now are heard singing together with you, were born from your most fertile ashes as of a phoenix rather than of a goose ([an outcome] which you are even said to have predicted already at that time when about to die)?

As we have seen several times already, Beza puns on the meaning of the name "Hus," but in this instance in a more complex way: "Hus" means "goose" in the "native tongue of the Bohemians," but that provokes Beza to draw a simile between him and the Latin *anseres*, the geese that saved Rome from utter destruction at the hands of the Gauls in 390 BC.[77] Beza, then, has now referred to two treacherous attempts against Rome from early in Rome's history, that of the Sabines and that of the Gauls. It is now, however, not Rome that is saved; it is the "Christian world" that is saved from Rome itself, which has laid siege to the world through "craft" and "violence."[78] Through the use of *Christianus orbis*, moreover, paralleled in the dedicatory epistle, the reader is to recall the preface to James and to see both James (the statesman) and Hus (the priest and reformer) as fighters against a common enemy. Finally, it is worth noting that the entry's bird imagery abounds beyond the goose, whether Roman or Bohemian: from this goose were born swans who rose from his ashes like the phoenix, the most potent classical symbol of resurrection and immortality.

---

[77] See Livy 5.47.

[78] Cf. the poem to Luther above; but here, in contradistinction to the poem, the church of Rome has the characteristics of *both* the pagan empire *and* the medieval church as they are set out those verses.

In sum, this entry, with its reference to an event in early Roman history and its allusion to a common Roman symbol, is designed to have an impact on a certain kind of reader—that is, a Protestant and humanistically educated reader. The shared culture upon which Beza presumes provides the vocabulary and syntax, as it were, for a playful critique of the church of Rome that is at once subtle and devastating, calculated to produce the frisson-like effect of wry recognition in the knowing reader—an effect greater in the cultured reader in proportion to the allusive artifice with which the critique is presented.

The next place we find a reference to the Tarpeian Rock is in the prose section of the Luther entry. There, after referring to Luther as the "scourge of the Roman Antichrist" (*Antichristi Romani flagellum*) in the section heading and calling him a "herald roused...by God the Best and Greatest" (*praeco a Deo Opt. Max.*), using the traditional Roman title of Jupiter,[79] Beza writes that Luther was[80]

> ...*ad repurgandam Dei templum evocatus, eo ipso Antichristo occasionem ei praebente, quem arrepto verbi Dei flagello erat ex occupata Christi domo profligaturus: quem non Caesares, non Reges, non fulmina ex arce **Tarpeia** vibrata, non ullae innumerabilium Sophistarum phalanges, vel tantillum terruerunt....*

> ...called forth for purging the temple of God, when the Antichrist himself was offering opportunity to him, whom he [Luther], when he had seized in hand the scourge of the Word of God, was going to drive out of the besieged house of Christ—whom [again, Luther] not Caesars, not kings, not thunderbolts hurled **from the Tarpeian citadel**, not any of the innumerable troops of sophists, terrified even the slightest bit....

There are a number of classical references in this passage: not only the Caesars (who, combined with *reges*, are meant to evoke secular rulers who have set themselves against the Protestants), but also Jupiter, who is called to mind through the thunderbolts (*fulmina*)—his regular iconographic accom-

---

[79] This designation is common in texts of this period–it is a regular feature in, e.g., Peter Martyr Vermigli's *Preces sacrae ex Psalmis Davidis desumptae* (Zürich: Christopher Froschauer, 1564).

[80] Beza, *Icones*, sig. C.iiii.r.

paniment—cast down from the Capitoline Hill. This image of thunderbolts should be read as a reference to the papacy, such that Beza first steals the title of the pagan god ("Best and Greatest") for the Christian God, and then identifies the pope with this same pagan god; the papacy presumably can be glossed as pagan because it is antichristian. His use of *Tarpeia*, rather than some other epithet for the Capitoline citadel, to describe the height from which the pope thunders reminds the reader of Rome's treachery, as is true of the poem to Luther as well. Both prose and verse section, in fact, contain a similar fusion of classical Rome, the church of Rome, and duplicitous Greece (the Greek term *sophistarum* in the prose section, *mendax* in the poem) to stand for that which is opposed to Christian Reformation. Again, this *mélange* is intended for the humanistically educated reader, because only he can grasp the full force of Beza's allusivity, an allusivity that pulls the rug out from under Rome's supposedly noble and supposedly ancient heritage. The pope liked to fancy himself the *pontifex maximus*, heir of Roman might and prestige. Beza wishes to make him swallow the Roman spirit, altars and all.

Finally, the image of the Tarpeian Rock appears in two poems, both times in poems that are new to the *Icones*. The reader first encounters it in the poem dedicated to Wolfgang Musculus.[81]

> *Magnum dicere musculum pusillum*
> *Quum sit auribus insolens latinis,*
> *Magnum hunc dicere Musculum quod ausim,*
> *Quamvis pulvere conditum pusillo,*
> *Si causam rogitas, viator: audi.*
> *Haud quaquam fuit iste mus pusillus,*
> *(ipsum si libeat vocare murem)*
> *Illarum ex numero famelicarum*
> *Quae felis rapidos verentur ungues:*
> *Sed qui ipsos potius catos rapaces,*
> *Quantumvis solitos potentiorum*
> *Ipsis cum dominis domos vorare,*
> *Vivus perculit, et suo paventes*
> *Adhuc nomine territat sepultus.*
> *Immo quem tremuit quoque illa **rupis***
> ***Tarpeiae arcibus** incubans leaena,*
> *Orbis magnanimos vorans monarchas.*

---

[81] Beza, *Icones*, sig. H.ii.v–H.iii.r.

Magnum et dicere Musculum pigebit,
Quanvis pulvere conditum pusillo?

Although it is not customary to Latin ears
To call a very meager little mouse great,
As to the fact that I dare to call this Musculus great,
Although buried in very meager dust,
If you ask the reason, traveller: hear.
By no means was that very meager mouse
(if it be right to call him a mouse)
From the number of those famished does
Who fear the quick claws of the queens,
But rather one who, while alive, smites the greedy toms,
however much accustomed to devouring houses
with their masters, and still terrifies them, fearful,
With his name when he's been buried.
Nay, rather: one at whom that lioness, too,
Trembled, when she lay down on **the citadel of the Tar-**
peian Rock,
Devouring the great-hearted monarchs of the world.
And will it annoy you to call Musculus great,
Although buried in very meager dust?

Yet again, Beza puns on the meaning of the name of his subject (*musculus* means "little mouse"). For our present purposes, however, it is the invocation of the Tarpeian Rock that is of interest. In this instance, the Roman citadel (*arcibus*), in another striking locution, is identified precisely by means of the rock used to execute traitors.[82] "Rome," called now a "lioness," is thus once again synonymous with treachery. But though this terrifying animal has consumed powerful and lofty kings, she is herself terrified by a tiny mouse. So great is the power of the spokesman for Protestant truth that he causes fear even from beyond the grave.

Beza returns to the motif once more in a set of verses in dactylic hexameter addressed to Andreas Gerardus Hyperius:[83]

Non Hyperis dedit hoc, Hyperi, tibi patria quondam.
Quod superis potius ducis cognomen ab oris:
Nec tibi sors olim tribuit temeraria nomen,

---

[82] Cf. *ex arce Tarpeia* above in Beza's tribute to Luther.

[83] Beza, *Icones*, sigs. I.ir–v.

Andreae: at ipsa suo ornavit te nomine virtus.
Hoc sancti mores, teneris hoc omnis ab annis
Vita probat, superum curae caeloque sacrata.
Ecquis enim melius, quisnam te fortius uno
Tarpeia aggressus depellere rupe tyrannum?
Certius an quisquam erranti per devia turbae
Commonstravit iter superas quod ducit in artes?
Macte igitur vertute, Hyperi, quem nec fera totum
Mors domuit, totum nec servant claustra sepulcri,
Quin superi meliore fovent iam parte receptum,
Altera dum tumulo quae nunc pars clausa quiescit,
Exanimisque licet iam coeli ad lumen anhelat,
Evigilet foelix: et quod tu diceris, illud
Evadas, Hyperi, tum re, tum nomine totus.

Your sometime Hyperian country did not grant this to you,
Hyperius:
That nickname you draw rather from the heavenly climes;
Nor did rash chance once bestow your name on you,
Andreas: but virtue itself adorned you with her own name.
This his holy character, this his whole life from his tender
Years proves, consecrated to care for things above and for
heaven.
For who better, who more bravely than you alone
Fell upon the tyrant to drive him off of the Tarpeian
Rock?
Or did anyone more certainly show to the masses wander-
ing in pathless
Wastes the route that leads to the heavenly arts?
O Hyperius, honored for virtue, whom neither savage
death
Subdued whole, whom the barrier of the tomb does not
preserve whole—
Nay, rather, those above care for you already, received in
the better part,
Until the other part, which now rests in the barrier of the
grave,
Awakes, happy: and that which you are called, as that may
you
Rise, Hyperius, both in fact and in name, whole.

Beza, after still more puns on a dedicatee's name—"Hyperius" refers
both to his native city Ypern in West Flanders and to the Greek word ὑπέρ,

"over, above";[84] "Andreas" is related to the Greek ἀνδρεῖος, "manly, coura-
geous"—yet again links Rome and despotic treachery: the pope is a tyrant,
and Hyperius has thrust him to his execution from the cliff classically employed for such traitors. Beza envisions Hyperius accomplishing this feat
despite Hyperius' theological location somewhere between the Lutherans and
the Reformed, as noted above. In either case, his Protestant credentials are
unquestioned, and his confessional ambiguity makes for no hindrance to his
efficacy in what Beza sees as the common cause of both groups against the
Roman menace. Indeed, in the accompanying prose section Beza praises
him explicitly as a theologian who was a gift not only to his hometown and
the academy at Marburg, but to the entire Christian church.[85]

The foregoing remarks on Roman tyranny and treachery can be elucidated by *Emblema* 25, which, together with *Emblema* 24, offers a general
comment on the issue. Catherine Randall Coats has argued that the *Emblemata*,[86] appended to the end of the work, provide a sort of interpretive
key to orient readers in their approach to the foregoing *Icones*; regardless of
whether that holds good for the collection as a whole, it surely does with
respect to this particular issue. The image is itself programmatic.[87] On the
right is Castel Sant' Angelo, connected by a bridge or tunnel, it seems, to a
heavily stylized St. Peter's with unfinished dome.[88] Originally constructed as
the mausoleum of the Roman Emperor Hadrian, in Beza's day it was the
fortified bastion of the Roman bishop. Its erstwhile function as a tomb,
however, is not lost on Beza—indeed, that fact is of essential symbolic significance. Thus in the accompanying verses he writes:

---

[84] Cf. the Greek name for the sun-god, Hyperion.

[85] Beza, *Icones*, sig. I.i.r. All of Hyperius' books, too, were placed on the "Pauline Index" in 1559.

[86] The *Emblemata* are a series of 44 often difficult images with accompanying explanations in verse appended to the end of the *Icones*. Beza says to James in the dedicatory epistle: *Subiunxi praetera EMBLEMATA quadraginta et quatuor, quae, quod graves et
pias sententias complectantur, eruditis lectoribus non ingrata fore mihi persuasi. Sunt autem,
opinor, sic appellata, quod imagines eiusmodi sententiosae operae tesselato parietibus aut vasis
inseri consueverint* (Beza, *Icones*, sig. *iiir). For more on the *Emblemata*, see Adams,
Webs of Allusion, 119–53.

[87] Beza, *Icones*, sig. Nn.iiiv.

[88] Adams, *Webs of Allusion*, 136.

Caesareos cineres quae moles clauserat olim,
  Arx est Romano nunc sacra Pontifici.
Quam bene qui mortis nunc est mortalibus auctor,
  Morti sacratas obtinet iste domos.

The heap that once had enclosed the ashes of the Caesars
  Is now the sacred citadel for the Roman Pontiff.
How well does he who is now the author of death for the
death-bound
  Hold a house consecrated to death.

Beza makes his connections explicit here. The *arx* that had previously been (and in point of fact was) the Capitoline Hill has now been reimagined as Hadrian's tomb. But note that the mausoleum is connected by a passageway to St. Peter's. Such a passageway did exist historically for defensive purposes. But the image is located in a metaphorical register as well. We should remember that St. Peter's and Castel Sant'Angelo are on the same side of the Tiber, though the image is ambiguous on this score; from the woodcut, one might conclude that they are not. Why? Perhaps to reinforce the symbolic point that the pagan Empire, for which the Capitoline, on the other side of the river, had traditionally been a cipher but which is in this picture epitomized by Hadrian's Mausoleum,[89] is from Beza's perspective

---

[89] The reason for this change is explained in lines 3–4 of the poem.

one with St. Peter's: therefore a bridge connects pagan Rome to the symbol of Christian Rome by a bridge across the water.

The link between pagan and Christian Rome is further reinforced by what appears to be happening on the unfinished dome of St. Peter's: two men are throwing themselves to their deaths. In the *Icones* proper, the church of Rome had been equated with the Capitoline, which was in turn equated with the Tarpeian Rock, departure point for traitors. The layers of metaphor are now concretized in St. Peter's dome (connected to a potent symbol of pagan and imperial Rome, one that naturally invokes the spectre of death) as men plummet to their demise. This explanation goes some way toward elucidating an image whose events Adams calls "mysterious."[90] Where she writes that "it looks *almost* as if two of [the people on the tower] were throwing themselves off,"[91] it is now possible to conclude that they are, and also to say why.

Can we tie all this together? Let us use *Emblema* 24 to try:[92]

---

[90] Adams, *Webs of Allusion*, 136n31. I first found the suggestion of suicide in Adams, and, seen in light of the foregoing discussion, one can now speak of it with less tentativeness than she does.

[91] Adams, *Webs of Allusion*, 136n31 (emph. mine).

[92] Beza, *Icones*, sig. Nn.iii.r.

What we see is a prince surrounded by two cardinals, as the winds blow on the sea to trouble it. The verse-caption reads:[93]

> *Tranquilli immotique prius velut aequoris undas*
> *Unica ventorum vis agitata ciet,*
> *Sic mundum meretrix Romana. Hanc tollite, Reges,*
> *Pacatus subito (credite) mundus erit.*

Just as the force of the winds alone will rouse the waves
Of a previously tranquil and motionless sea,
So the Roman prostitute has done to the world. Take her away, kings:
Suddenly (believe!) the world will be calm.

The rousing of a storm at sea has obvious classical precedents, of which the storm in *Aeneid* 1 is the most influential. One perhaps catches a hint of it here (the church would then be linked to Aeolus, the pagan god of winds). More to the point, however, is the moniker used for Rome: *meretrix Romana*, an epithet already used in the tribute to Wycliffe in the work's very first entry. Given all that we have so far observed, it is hard to resist recalling the story of Romulus and Remus—for the she-wolf (*lupa*) that suckled the abandoned twins was only called a wolf, according to one tradition, because she was a prostitute (for which *lupa* was slang).[94] The Roman kings, of course, were eventually driven out for their perceived tyranny. The church of Rome has once again been identified with a pagan symbol—but one whose meaning would only have been accessible to and effective for a reader who had been classically educated in those selfsame Roman traditions. And who has the duty of driving her out? Kings—Christian and Protestant kings, kings like James VI, to whom the *Icones* is dedicated.

5. CONCLUSION

When the reader of the *Icones* looks at this work synthetically, then, he is presented with a sophisticated vision of a united pan-Protestantism that is integrated throughout the social order, in church, school, and magistracy. For Beza, piety must be Protestant, but it must also be intelligent (hence his inclusion of non-Protestant figures intellectually useful to the Protestant

---

[93] On this image, cf. Adams, *Webs of Allusion*, 135–36.

[94] Cf. the account in Livy 1.4.

cause). Finally, it must be established through the power of the pious magistrate. All three legs of this stool must work in common cause against a common enemy—or, to put it more positively, must present a united and defensible witness to the truth over against Rome. To Beza, a classically-informed, erudite, and orthodox Protestant humanism, aided by a pious prince, provided the best resources for advancing the cause of intelligent piety and the freedom of the gospel. It is a vision at once comprehensive and, if we would heed its wisdom, compelling.

BIBLIOGRAPHY

Adams, Alison. *Webs of Allusion: French Protestant Emblem Books of the Sixteenth Century*. Geneva: Droz, 2003.

Augustijn, Cornelis. *Erasmus: His Life, Works, and Influence*, translated by J.C. Grayson. Toronto: University of Toronto Press, 1991; German original 1986.

Baird, Henry Martyn. *Theodore Beza: The Counsellor of the French Reformation, 1519–1605*. New York: G.P. Putnam's Sons, 1899.

Bèze, Théodore de. *Icones, id est verae imagines virorum doctrina simul et pietate illustrium, quorum praecipue ministerio partim bonarum literarum studia sunt restituta, partim vera Religio in variis orbis Christiani regionibus, nostra patrumque memoria fuit instaurata: additis eorundem vitae et operae descriptionibus, quibis adiectae sunt nonnullae picturae quas EMBLEMATA vocant*. Menston: Scolar Press, 1971.

Buchanan, George. *Opera omnia*, edited by Thomas Ruddiman, tom. 2. Lyon: J.A. Langerak, 1725.

Cummings, R.M. "Note" to Bèze, *Icones*. Menston: Scolar Press, 1971.

Coats, Catherine Randall. *(Em)bodying the Word: Textual Resurrections in the Martyrological Narratives of Foxe, Crespin, de Bèze, and d'Aubigné*. New York: P. Lang, 1992.

———. "Reactivating Textual Traces: Martyrs, Memory, and the Self in Theodore Beza's *Icones* (1581)." In *Later Calvinism: International Perspectives*, edited by W. Fred Graham, 19–28. Kirksville, MO: Sixteenth Century Journal Publishers, 1994.

Dufour, Alain. Introduction to Théodore de Bèze, *Les vrais portraits des hommes illustres*. Geneva: Slatkine Reprints, 1986.

Graham, W. Fred, ed. *Later Calvinism: International Perspectives*. Kirksville, MO: Sixteenth Century Journal Publishers, 1994.

Harvey, A. Edward. *Martin Bucer in England*. Marburg: Heinrich Bauer, 1906.

Hillerbrand, Hans, J. *Oxford Encyclopedia of the Reformation*. Oxford: Oxford University Press, 1996.

Hornblower, Simon, and Anthony Spawforth, eds. *Oxford Classical Dictionary*. 3rd ed. Oxford: Oxford University Press, 1999.

Kusukawa, Sachiko. *The Transformation of Natural Philosophy*. Cambridge: Cambridge University Press, 1995.

Manetsch, Scott M. *Theodore Beza and the Quest for Peace in France, 1572–1598*. Leiden: Brill, 2000.

Raitt, Jill. *The Colloquy of Montbéliard: Religion and Politics in the Sixteenth Century*. Oxford: Oxford University Press, 1993.

Summers, Kirk M. "Theodore Beza's Classical Library and Christian Humanism." *Archiv für Reformationsgeschichte/Archive for Reformation History* 82 (1991): 193–207.

———. *A View from the Palatine: The* Iuvenilia *of Théodore de Bèze*. Tempe, AZ: Arizona Center for Medieval and Renaissance Studies, 2001.

Vermigli, Peter Martyr. *Preces sacrae ex Psalmis Davidis desumptae*. Zürich: Christopher Froschauer, 1564.

Von Wyß, Georg. "Josias Simmler." In *Allgemeine Deutsche Biographie*, edited by Bayerische Akademie der Wissenschaften (München) Historische Kommission, Band 34. Leipzig: Duncker and Humblot, 1892.

III:

A REFORMED IRENIC CHRISTOLOGY: RICHARD HOOKER'S ACCOUNT OF CHRIST'S "PERSONALL PRESENCE EVERY WHERE" IN 16ᵀᴴ-CENTURY CONTEXT

W. Bradford Littlejohn, The Davenant Trust

1. THE QUESTION OF HOOKER'S CHRISTOLOGY

A. Introduction

EVEN NOW, after more than a quarter century of revisionist scholarship, Richard Hooker remains something of a marginalized misfit in conversations or conferences about Reformed orthodoxy, the awkward kid in the corner whom no one is quite sure who invited him to the party. The reasons for this persistent bias are rooted in deep-seated prejudices of theological identity within the church, as well as outdated disciplinary divides within the academy. It can't be because Hooker is English and Reformed historical theology is Continental, although scholarship has been choked at times by the perennial fog in the Channel—after all, no one hesitates to discuss Perkins and Ames in the context of Reformed orthodoxy. Presumably it is because the latter were "Puritan," and only card-carrying Puritans cared about what was going on in the broader world of Reformed theology. Except that it has become increasingly clear that there is no non-question-begging criterion that would link figures like Perkins and Ames together on one side of a gulf that lies between them and "Anglicans" like Hooker and Davenant.

One area of Hooker's theology where suspicions about his Reformed credentials have stubbornly persisted is his Christology, one of the few theological loci to which Hooker dedicates a protracted systematic discussion in the course of his rather practically- and polemically-oriented *Laws of Ecclesiastical Polity*. Of course, this is one area where the standard suspicions—that Hooker is somehow building a bridge to medieval Catholic theology, anchored chiefly on Aquinas's *Summa Theologiae*—will hardly do. For it does seem that Hooker leaned heavily on the *Summa* for his exposition of the doctrine of the person of Christ, but so did the Reformed generally.[1] No, here the charges must be more creative—that Hooker's Christology is tinged with Lutheranism or "Alexandrianism," and thus sub-Reformed in ways that will in due course put him in bed with Anglo-Catholicism.

If Hooker's Christology does lean Lutheran, then it would be chiefly at the point of the doctrine of ubiquity, the main point at which the otherwise united Reformed and Lutheran Christologies parted ways. This was the Lutheran doctrine that, in order to explain the real presence of Christ at the Eucharist, insisted on a real communication of certain proper attributes of the divine nature to the human nature of Christ, so that it was made capable of bodily omnipresence, along with sundry other uncreated gifts. The Reformed protested that such a formulation was philosophically incoherent and theologically disastrous—a physical body could not, in the nature of the case, have the property of omnipresence, and if Christ's humanity was somehow gifted with such a property, it would cease to be truly human, thus overthrowing the Chalcedonian definition and the basis of our redemption. As it turns out, Hooker was clearly aware of this important debate, devoting nearly one-third of his entire discussion of the person of Christ to the question, "Of the personall presence of Christ every where, and in what sense it may be granted he is everywhere present according to the flesh" (chapter 55 of Book V of the *Laws*).

B. Initial Survey of Hooker on Ubiquity

At first glance, Hooker's discussion is not very encouraging to those who would see in him secret Lutheran sympathies. Even before he begins his

---

[1] W. David Neelands highlights Hooker's dependence on Aquinas in his Christology in "Christology and the Sacraments," in *A Companion to Richard Hooker* (Leiden, Netherlands: Brill, 2008), 372.

treatment of ubiquity proper, he seems implacably Reformed on the key points of difference. Chapter 53, unpromisingly entitled, "That by the union of the one with the other nature in Christ there groweth neither gain nor loss of essential properties to either," begins by asserting that the hypostatic union involves

> no abolishment of natural properties appertaining to either substance, no transition or transmigration thereof out of one substance into another, finally no such mutual infusion as really causeth the same natural operations or properties to be made common unto both substances; but whatsoever is natural to Deity the same remaineth in Christ uncommunicated unto his manhood, and whatsoever natural to manhood his Deity thereof is uncapable. (V.53.1)[2]

This is a firm rejection of the Lutheran understanding of the *communicatio idiomatum* (the "communication of attributes,") as we shall see at more length later. In case there were any doubt what this meant in concrete terms, he lists several such "true properties of deity," including "to be every where present, and enclosed nowhere" (V.53.1). Even though admitting in chapter 54 that the human nature has been elevated by its union with deity, he again insists that in no way was it infused with "the natural forces and properties of his Deity" (V.54.5). Later, again focusing on the question of ubiquity, he asks, "But shall we say that in heaven his glorious body by virtue of the same cause hath now power to present itself in all places and to be every where at once present?" After surveying the many ways in which Christ's body has been glorified, he concludes, "Notwithstanding a body still it continueth, a body consubstantial with our bodies, a body of the same both nature and measure which it had on earth" (V.54.9).

In chapter 55, he continues this theme, coming right out of the starting gate with the infamous Reformed principle *finitum non capax infiniti* ("the finite is not capable of the infinite"), which the Lutherans considered blas-

---

[2] All quotations from Hooker are taken from the Keble edition to make use of its (relatively) modernized spelling: Richard Hooker, *The Works of that Learned and Judicious Divine Mr. Richard Hooker with an Account of His Life and Death by Isaac Walton*, 3 vols., arranged by John Keble, 7th edition revised by the Very Rev. R.W. Church and the Rev. F. Paget (Oxford: Clarendon Press, 1888). Citations, however, are given using simply the book, chapter, and section.

phemous: "All things are in such sort divided into finite and infinite, that no one substance, nature, or quality, can possibly be capable of both" (V.55.2).[3] Expounding this distinction further, he argues that "nothing created can possibly be unlimited, or can receive any such accident, quality, or property as may really make it infinite (for then it should cease to be a creature)" (V.55.2). He then goes on "somewhat more plainly to show a true immediate reason wherefore the manhood of Christ can neither be every where present, nor cause the person of Christ so to be," specifying that it is not mere creatureliness in general but "his being *man*, a creature *of this particular kind*, whereunto the God of nature hath set those bounds of restraint and limitation" (V.55.5). In case there were still any ambiguity, he goes on, "The substance of the body of Christ hath no presence, but only local," and "If his majestical body have now any such new property by force whereof it may every where really even *in substance* present itself, or may at once be in many places, then hath the majesty of his estate extinguished the verity of his nature" (V.55.6). Finally, he says, "To conclude, we hold it in regard of the forealleged proofs a most infallible truth that Christ as man is not every where present" (V.55.7). Case closed, right? It would be hard to ask for greater clarity.

Well, not quite. In the next sentence, Hooker acknowledges that there are some who disagree—"There are [those] which think it as infallibly true that Christ is every where present as man"—and then, somewhat surprisingly, says, "Which peradventure in some sense may well enough be granted" (V.55.7). He goes on to summarize three senses in which it may be granted, using similar language—"Again as the manhood of Christ may after a sort be every where said to be present" (V.55.8) and "And even the body of Christ itself although the definite limitation thereof be most sensible doth nothwithstanding admit in some sort a kind of infinite and unlimited presence likewise" (V.55.9).

---

[3] For a good survey, see Steven Wedgeworth and Peter Escalante, "A Compound Person and Complex Questions (Part 1): Addendum to 'Do We Have a Christology Crisis," and "A Compound Person and Complex Questions (Part 2)," both at *The Calvinist International*, March 18, 2012, https://calvinistinternational.com/2012/03/18/a-compound-person-part-1/, and https://calvinistinternational.com/2012/03/18/a-compound-person-part-2/.

2. LUTHERANIZING INTERPRETATIONS

The questions that must be asked by interpreters wishing to make sense of Hooker's Christology, then, are (1) whether these concessive statements do indeed stand in tension with the peremptory affirmations and denials that filled the preceding pages, and (2) if so, why Hooker would have been so equivocal on such an important question. Unfortunately, the few scholars who have given close attention to this passage have often skipped straight to the second question without first taking the time to answer the first. Indeed, of the relatively scant scholarly attention that has been paid to Hooker's Christology (for instance, just 3 ½ pages in the otherwise excellent recent 600-page collection *A Companion to Richard Hooker*),[4] a remarkable proportion has been dedicated to this question of ubiquity and the *communicatio idiomatum*. The majority of scholars, to be sure, have noted in passing that Hooker seems to take the Reformed side,[5] but a significant and persistent minority report has argued the opposite.

A. Ronald Bayne (1902)

Ronald Bayne's frequently cited 1902 introduction to Book V is more equivocal than dogmatic on the subject, suggesting that Hooker is a man torn between a Lutheran *id* and a Reformed *super-ego*: "With Luther's conviction 'that the divine nature and its substance ... was able to possess and to be conscious of, all that is purely human as its own' Hooker is by temperament in full sympathy; but this sympathy with Luther is implicit, not explicit, in these chapters. Formally and consciously Hooker is not Lutheran."[6] Bayne goes on to grant that Hooker explicitly accepts Calvin's doctrine of the *communicatio idiomatum*, of the *finitum non capax infiniti*, and the rejection of ubiquity, before returning again to say that "it will be felt that Hooker in his 55th and 56th chapters is willing to go as far as he can in the

---

[4] Neelands, "Christology and the Sacraments," 369–73.

[5] Thus Neelands and also Barry Rasmussen, "Presence and Absence: Richard Hooker's Sacramental Hermeneutic," in *Richard Hooker and the English Reformation*, ed. W.J. Torrance Kirby (Dordrecht, Netherlands: Kluwer Academic Publishers, 2003), 159–60.

[6] Ronald Bayne, "Introduction," *Of the laws of the ecclesiastical polity, the fifth book* (London: Macmillan, 1902), cviii–cix, quoting Isaak August Dorner, *History of the Development of the Doctrine of the Person of Christ* (Edinburgh: T. & T. Clark, 1889), II.ii.102.

Lutheran direction." His conclusions against the ubiquitarian position, Bayne feels, "are not pressed with rigorous logic: on the contrary they are largely qualified and discounted."[7] In a lengthy footnote spanning these two pages, Bayne's evasiveness continues. "Formally and consciously," he again admits, "Hooker belonged to the Sacramentarians," and his views are "in close accord at many points" with those of Vermigli's classic *Dialogue on the Two Natures of Christ* and indeed Beza's works as well. "But," he concludes, "these treatises lack the Lutheran heat which is in Hooker, and Beza's facility seems thin when compared with the large humanity of the Elizabethan divine."[8] One cannot but feel that Bayne's resort to the metaphorical language of "thinness" and "heat" is an attempt to compensate for a lack of coherent argumentation.

B. Gunnar Hillderdal (1962)

Bayne's halting gesturings toward a Freudian Hooker with repressed Lutheran longings were embellished to grand effect by the Swedish scholar Gunnar Hillerdal in his very influential 1962 *Reason and Revelation in Richard Hooker.* After four chapters of arguing for Hooker's Thomistic attempt to harmonize nature and grace against the unfortunate bifurcations of Calvinism, Hillerdal turns his attention to the matter of Christology, which he thinks is at the heart of Hooker's re-thinking of reason and revelation, nature and grace. Crucial, thinks Hillerdal, is Hooker's affirmation that "The very cause of his [the Word's] taking upon him our nature was to change it, to better the quality, and to advance the condition thereof, although in no sort to abolish the substance he took, nor to infuse into it the natural forces and properties of his deity" (V.54.5). "The last words" of this quote, Hillerdal says,

> are necessary, if the churchly tradition and the decisions made in the ancient church are to be respected. However, there can be no doubt that Hooker's real interest is to emphasize that something wonderful has happened to man's nature. Hooker has to stay within certain limits, and yet he takes some steps which make it questionable whether or

---

[7] Bayne, "Introduction," cix–cx.

[8] Bayne, "Introduction," cix–cx, fn7.

not he has really crossed the border-line that he feels himself obliged not to step over.[9]

Hillerdal continues this basic mode of exposition, dividing Hooker's statements into those which he *has to say* and those which he *wants to say*, and often playing off different clauses of the same sentence against one another:

> To be sure, he says that as no alteration takes place in the nature of God at the moment of incarnation, "so neither are the *properties of man's nature* in the person of Christ by force and virtue of the same conjunction so much altered, as not to stay within those limits which our substance is bordered withal." However, Hooker proceeds with these words: nor is "the *state* and quality of our substance so unaltered, but that there are in it many glorious effects proceedings from so near copulation with Deity." Hooker tries to solve this apparent contradiction by the additional statement that "albeit the natural properties of Deity be not communicable to man's nature, the supernatural gifts, graces, and effects thereof are."[10]

It is startling that Hillerdal evinces so little concern with whether Hooker's statement merely *tries* to resolve the apparent contradiction or in fact *succeeds*, or even whether there *is* actually any contradiction in the first place. This predilection for philosophical fuzziness continues in the following sentences:

> From one point of view the denial of the change of man's nature is just a battle with words. Traditional Christian doctrinal theology forbids Hooker to admit that the substance of man has been altered. However, the whole line of argumentation, in spite of this hesitation, tends toward stressing the idea that a remarkable change has taken place.[11]

---

[9] Gunnar Hillerdal, *Reason and Revelation in Richard Hooker* (Lund, Sweden: CWK Gleerup, 1962), 122–23.

[10] Hillerdal, *Reason and Revelation in Richard Hooker*, 123.

[11] Hillerdal, *Reason and Revelation in Richard Hooker*, 123.

Hooker theologizes, according to Hillerdal, less in obedience to reason than to primal urges: "Hooker at all times strives to go in a very special direction. He wants to make some statements on the ubiquity of the Lord's glorified body. In order to be able to do so, he makes a new start, now discussing the question of God's presence in the world."[12]

> Hillerdal then surveys the territory of Book V, chapter 55 that we have sketched above, acknowledging that it appears at first glance hostile to his thesis and to what we know is Hooker's secret desire. However, he considers most of this material to be mere ground-clearing and flank-protecting so that Hooker can finally draw the conclusion he desires. The humiliation of Deity that took place in the incarnation resulted, from one point of view, in the marvelous exaltation of man's nature!... We must not hesitate any longer to say that "even the body of Christ itself, although the definite limitation thereof must be sensible, doth notwithstanding admit in some sort a kind of infinite and unlimited presence."[13]

But why, asks Hillerdal, is "Hooker so eager to show that Christ can be bodily present everywhere?" Hillerdal is only too eager to tell us: "Hooker thinks that the bodily conjunction of Deity gives to the body of Christ 'a presence of force and efficacy throughout all generations of men.'" Thus "if that body can be present everywhere, then the sins of all generations can be atoned for wherever Christ's body is present." In short, "a remarkable possiblity opens up. The 'deification' of human nature that took place in Jesus Christ can be renewed over and over again within the church!"[14]

In short, for Hooker the back-door adoption of a Lutheran doctrine of ubiquity is in fact a mere ploy for establishing an altogether un-Protestant doctrine of salvation by sacramental *theosis* and of the church as the continuation of the Incarnation. Of course, it might be objected that in the very next chapter, discussing "the union or mutual participation which is between Christ and the Church of Christ in this present world," Hooker peremptorily declares that the hypostatic union "doth therefore impart such life [to Christ] as to no other creature besides him is communicated....

---

[12] Hillerdal, *Reason and Revelation in Richard Hooker*, 123.

[13] Hillerdal, *Reason and Revelation in Richard Hooker*, 125.

[14] Hillerdal, *Reason and Revelation in Richard Hooker*, 125–26.

Wherefore God is not so in any, nor any so in God as Christ... All other things ... because their substance and his wholly differeth, their coherence and communion either with him or amongst themselves is in no sort like unto that before mentioned" (V.56.5). However, Hillerdal is clearly less interested in Hooker's actual words than in what, he assures us, are his earnest unspoken desires.

C. Drew Martin (2016)

Hillerdal might seem to present something of an easy target; however, he merits consideration because the substance of his argument has re-appeared in somewhat more sophisticated form in a recent essay by Andrew J. Martin, which deserves careful engagement. Dr. Martin, as a disciple of Peter Lake, can give more plausibility to Hooker's inner struggle, seeing it as an attempt to shield himself from the ire of the "Calvinist consensus" that dominated Elizabethan England. Hooker had to *appear* Reformed, if he wanted to make any headway whatsoever with his views, but since he was inwardly unhappy with the Reformed *status quo* of late Elizabethan England, he had to point the way to a new "Anglican" religion by subtle insinuations which often ran contrary to his explicit statements.[15] Martin, like Hillerdal and others, wishes to argue that this is particularly the case with Hooker's understanding of the church and sacraments, in which Hooker hopes to break down the barrier between the visible and invisible churches, reassert an *ex opere operato* conception of sacramental grace, and ultimately break the stranglehold of the Reformed doctrine of predestination by showing that salvific grace is automatically available to all who participate in the glorified flesh of Christ that is physically offered in the Eucharist. And like Hillerdal, Martin sees Hooker's Christology—and the doctrine of ubiquity that he thinks can be discerned in it once we read between the lines—as the key to this whole reconception of the Christian faith.

Martin argues that Hooker's statements on the matter of ubiquity "straddled the fence dividing John Calvin from the Gnesio-Lutherans on

---

[15] For this basic interpretation of Peter Lake's, see *Anglicans and Puritans: Presbyterianism and English Conformist Thought - Whitgift to Hooker* (London: Unwin Hyman, 1988), ch. 4, and "Business as Usual: The immediate reception of Hooker's Ecclesiastical Polity," *The Journal of Ecclesiastical History* 52, no. 3 (2001): 456–86.

the subject of the post-ascension location of Christ's human nature."[16] Indeed, although recognizing that Hooker appeals to precisely the same passage from Augustine that Calvin did in his dispute with Westphal to demonstrate Christ's local bodily presence in heaven, Martin asserts that he did so "for a distinctly different purpose."[17] It is not entirely clear what this different purpose is, since Hooker himself says that he invokes Augustine to prove that if Christ's body were "every where present," it "doth thereby cease to have the substance of a true body," which would seem to be precisely Calvin's point. But Martin thinks that the language of ubiquity even only "after a sort" puts an enormous gap between Hooker and Calvin. He goes on to quote the *Consensus Tigurinus*, the Heidelberg Catechism, the Belgic Confession, the Scots Confession, and the 39 articles, all affirming a local presence of Jesus Christ in heaven rather than on earth, to show that "Hooker's willingness to speak of the ubiquity of Christ's human nature, albeit only 'after a sorte' and by virtue of his conjunction with the divine nature, appears to have run against the grain of the Reformed symbols on the continent and in England."[18] Unfortunately, he makes no more effort than Hillerdal to inquire just what Hooker said and meant when he spoke of presence "after a sort," and whether any of the authors or defenders of these confessional symbols spoke similarly.

Martin goes on to argue that Hooker's use of the doctrine of the *communicatio idiomatum* set him apart from Calvin and Beza—not formally, he admits, but in terms of "emphasis" and "preference." Hooker had a "preference for speaking of the differences according to the person rather than the two natures." This, says Martin "is significant" because it "increased his freedom to depict the communication of attributes as well as the physical

---

[16] Drew Martin, "Richard Hooker and Reformed Sacramental Theology," in W. Bradford Littlejohn and Scott N. Kindred-Barnes, eds., *Richard Hooker and Reformed Orthodoxy* (Göttingen: Vandenhoeck and Ruprecht, 2017), 299.

[17] Martin, "Richard Hooker and Reformed Sacramental Theology," 300. The quote, from Ep. 57 to Dardanus, runs: "Make thou no doubt or question of it, but that the man Christ Jesus is now in that very place from whence he shall come in the same form and substance of flesh which he carried thither, and from which he hath not taken nature, but given thereunto immortality. According to this form he spreadeth not out himself into all places. For it behoveth us to take great heed, lest while we go about to maintain the glorious Deity of him which is man, we leave him not the true bodily substance of a man" (*Laws* V.55.6).

[18] Martin, "Richard Hooker and Reformed Sacramental Theology," 301.

presence of the ascended word incarnate."[19]   On the question of ubiquity specifically, Martin also emphasizes preference and emphasis:

> whereas the symbols of the Reformed tradition typically emphasized the local presence of Christ's human nature in heaven, Hooker did not deny this presence but nevertheless grounded his discourse of Christ's "power" and "dominion over the whole universal world," including the church, on the foundation of Christ's ubiquity.[20]

In a footnote, Martin grants that Hooker did not formally adopt the Lutheran position or explicitly deny the Reformed position, but states that "his statements were ambiguous," and intentionally and strategically so.[21] However, since he himself does not offer any detailed analysis of the logic of Hooker's statements, it is difficult to judge just how ambiguous they are or are not.

D. Evaluating the Methodology of these Interpretations

Each of these studies suffers from significant methodological flaws that warrant highlighting before we move on to further consideration of Hooker's doctrine. Although Quentin Skinner a half century ago rightly attacked attempts to hammer a writer's thought into a single consistent argument,[22] scholars seem now inclined to err in the opposite direction. True, no human being is perfectly consistent, and we must beware of trying to impose consistency where it is lacking. At the same time, though, most of these early modern intellectual giants were far cleverer and more learned than their modern interpreters, and so we probably owe them the assumption of intellectual consistency unless and until it is manifestly clear that contradictions are present. To first assume inconsistency, and then to claim the psychoanalytical expertise to determine which side of the inconsistent claims represent the author's *real* intention and which are mere masks, or holdovers from earlier views now discarded, is extraordinarily bold on the part of the

---

[19] Martin, "Richard Hooker and Reformed Sacramental Theology," 301.

[20] Martin, "Richard Hooker and Reformed Sacramental Theology," 302.

[21] Martin, "Richard Hooker and Reformed Sacramental Theology," 302n25.

[22] Quentin Skinner, "Meaning and Understanding in the History of Ideas," *History and Theory* 8, no. 1 (1969): 16–18.

modern historian. To be sure, such rhetorical decoding is often an important part of the intellectual historian's task, but it is only appropriate if first motivated by other textual or extratextual evidence that the writer would desire to speak out of both sides of his mouth on a given question. In the present case, I am aware of no evidence that would suggest distinctively Lutheran leanings or influences on Hooker, or even that Lutheran Christological distinctives were being seriously entertained in England during his time; certainly, none of the three scholars we have considered here offer such evidence. In the absence of it, we cannot help suspecting that the claim that Hooker "wants to go in a very special direction" means only that the historian "wants to go in that very special direction" himself, or at any rate wants Hooker to.

Similar remarks must be made of "emphasis" arguments, such as Bayne resorts to in general, and Martin on the matter of the *communicatio idiomatum*. Once again, if we already have compelling reason to believe that an author is determined to move in a different direction than his contemporaries, then the detection of pronounced differences in emphasis may lend additional corroborating evidence of a departure from the consensus. However, in the absence of such compelling evidence, it becomes weaker even than a mere argument from silence, for pause to consider the logic of the claim: it is not that Hooker actually *affirms* Lutheran distinctives, nor is it even that he *fails to affirm* Reformed distinctives; it is rather that he fails to affirm Reformed distinctives with what the contemporary historian considers to be the clarity and vigor that the contemporary historian would have expected. Only an historian with a comprehensive grasp of the relevant primary source material could possibly be authorized in drawing much of a conclusion from this evidence.

Martin and Bayne at least, unlike Hillerdal, can lay some claim to familiarity with the relevant source material, but in Martin's exposition in particular, we detect another methodological flaw that has bedevilled Hooker scholarship. For although Martin does cite seven 16th-century texts for purposes of comparison with Hooker, there is an important discontinuity in terms of date and genre. First, he cites Calvin's 1550s writings against Westphal as a point of comparison, and indeed no move is more common among writings on Hooker and Reformed theology than to try and play him off against the Genevan Reformer. But as any student of Muller knows, or indeed any Reformed dogmatician before 1900, Calvin's unquestionable greatness never lay in his exhaustive precision. On many questions subsequently deemed of considerable dogmatic importance, Calvin speaks only loosely and generally, preferring rhetorical punch to philosophical precision. Almost invariably, the later dogmatic tradition (and indeed more scholastic contemporaries of Calvin like Vermigli) went on to treat the same issues with considerably greater nuance. Certainly, Calvin's statements on the presence of Christ's flesh do not add the nuanced qualifications that Hooker's do. But the same banal conclusion would emerge from a comparison of Calvin and Ursinus, Calvin and Zanchi, Calvin and Keckermann, etc. Second, Martin then appeals to the Reformed confessions of 1549–71. Not only do the same objections about date apply here, but so do considerations of genre. Confessions, which at least at this period were supposed to cover the entire scope of theology within the course of a few pages, were of necessity relatively minimalist in their claims, omitting most of the scholastic distinctions that would of course appear in dogmatic and polemical works. Indeed, it was Zanchi's indulgence in such scholastic detail in his *De Religione Christianae Fides* that doomed it as the pan-Reformed confession in was meant to be.[23] Although Hooker's discussion of Christology and sacraments is relatively brief as dogmatic treatises go, it is some 17 times longer than that which appears even in the *Consensus Tigurinus*, and at least 44 times longer than that of the Thirty-Nine Articles![24]

So if our purpose is, as I think it should be, to determine what Hooker, given his historical context, could plausibly have intended by his statements on the ubiquity of Christ's body, then I would submit that only the following methodology will do: first, determine what the standard and accepted terminology and reasoning on this subject were among contemporaries and near-contemporaries of Hooker, preferably by examining discussions of similar or greater levels of detail; second, ask to what extent Hooker's statements map onto these parallels; and only if they do not, can we then go on and ask third, why they might not. This, then, is the methodology I shall pursue.

---

[23] Luca Baschera and Christian Moser, "Introduction," to *De Religione Christianae Fides/On the Confession of the Christian Religion* (Leiden, Netherlands: Brill, 2007), 14–19.

[24] Book V, chapter 55 of the *Laws* alone is around 2,700 words, as compared to 157 words in the English translation of Articles 21 and 25 of the *Consensus Tigurinus*, and just 44 words in the whole Art. 4 of the Thirty-Nine articles, "Of the Resurrection of Christ."

3. HISTORICAL CONTEXT OF THE UBIQUITY DISPUTES
A. The Standard Narrative

Before undertaking such study, however, it may first be desirable to set some of the historical context. Indeed, I will suggest that a distorted grasp of the historical narrative of 16th-century Christological controversies is partly the culprit for failures to understand either Hooker, or Reformed orthodoxy more generally at this point.

The standard narrative runs something like this: In the beginning, there was the Lutheran Reformation. The character of the Lutheran church was set indelibly from the first by the theological distinctives of Martin Luther, and his intemperate polemical temperament, which had little toleration for anything that departed from these distinctives. Very shortly after this beginning, there was Zwingli, who founded the Reformed branch of the Reformation. While the character of the Reformed churches were, to be sure, determined to a considerable extent by Calvin and other second-generation figures, here too Zwingli's own distinctives put an indelible stamp on this second tradition. Accordingly, when Zwingli and Luther found themselves at loggerheads at Marburg in 1529 over the matter of the Eucharist, the two traditions were doomed for lasting estrangement (if indeed they had not already been doomed at birth). Melanchthon's Augsburg Confession of 1530 solemnized the breach, adopting language about the Lord's Supper that no Reformed theologian could accept: "the body and blood of Christ are truly present, and are distributed to those that eat in the Lord's Supper." Undergirding this theology of "consubstantiation" was of course the idea that Christ's resurrected body could be physically present in multiple places at once, over against the Reformed emphasis on the ascension, and that "Christ, regarded as man, must be sought nowhere else than in heaven."[25] To be sure, a period of murky ambiguity, partly a result of political considerations, aided and abetted by Bucer's (and also Melanchthon's) overweening desire for everyone to get along, blurred the boundaries a bit in the 1530s and 1540s. Melancthon's 1540 *Variata* version of the Augsburg Confession, which bent over backwards to give an olive branch to the Reformed and perhaps Calvin in particular, was the apogee of this irenic muddiness, rewording the key article 10 to state "with bread and wine

---

[25] Jaroslav Pelikan and Valerie R. Hotchkiss, eds., *Creeds and Confessions of Faith in the Christian Tradition* (New Haven: Yale University Press, 2003), 2:811.

are truly exhibited the body and blood of Christ to those that eat in the Lord's Supper." This was enough for Calvin to sign, though no doubt with reservations, and could only put a band-aid over the Reformed-Lutheran breach. Once Calvin joined in 1549 with Heinrich Bullinger to sign the more Zwinglian *Consensus Tigurinus* to present a united front against the Lutherans, the breach was certain to re-open, as it did in 1552 with the arch-Lutheran Joachim Westphal's ferocious assault on Calvin. In the polemical writings of the 1550s, Calvin burned all his bridges with the Lutherans at the worst possible time. When the 1555 Peace of Augsburg codified the status of the Augsburg Confession as a legitimate standard of faith within the Holy Roman Empire, the Reformed were left out in the cold—hence the awkwardness of Elector Frederick III's position in the Palatinate when he edged toward Calvinism in the early 1560s. Although he weakly protested that he could subscribe to the 1540 Variata Augsburg Confession, the Heidelberg Catechism he commissioned Ursinus to write in 1563 suggested otherwise, with its statement in Question 80 that "Christ with His true body is now in heaven at the right hand of the Father." During the 1560s and 1570s, the Lutheran churches were engaged in trying to expunge crypto-Calvinists who sought to hide behind the Variata, efforts culminating in the unambiguous 1577 Formula of Concord, with its codification of the original 1530 Augsburg Confession and the complementary doctrine of the ubiquity of Christ's body, and its formal anathematization of the Calvinists. The Reformed accepted this formal break, with both sides digging in for prolonged polemical trench warfare in the 1580s or beyond.

Unfortunately, despite its widespread acceptance, there are profound problems with this narrative. We cannot go into all of them here, but it is particularly important to reconsider Melanchthon's role in the narrative, which is likely to place the entire story in a different light.

B. Melanchthonian v. Ubiquitarian Lutheranism

First, although it is true that from early on Luther affirmed that Christ could be physically present in the Supper because the properties of his divine nature had been communicated to his flesh, he does not appear to have ever developed this Christological point with much precision prior to his disputations against Schwenkfeld in 1539–40.[26] Melanchthon from the very beginning avoided Luther's language of an "oral partaking" of Christ's body, and never adopted Luther's formulation of the *communicatio idiomatum*, though he did claim that Christ could "be where he wishes when he wishes in whatever mode he wishes according to his will."[27] He was particularly keen to insist that Christ never resided locally in the bread and wine such that they might be venerated. The 1540 revision of article X of the Augsburg Confession thus appeared to Melanchthon as a natural clarification, and the authoritative modern Lutheran discussion of the background to the Formula of Concord declares emphatically, "None regarded his revisions as a betrayal of his original purpose or of Luther's teaching."[28] Indeed, there is some reason to believe that Calvin and Bullinger drafted the Consensus Tigurinus as an overture to Melancthonian Lutheranism, not a declaration of war.[29] By the late 1550s, indeed, Melanchthon was even more emphatically rejecting any hint of local presence based on the ubiquity of Christ's human nature and even adopting Zwingli's affirmation that the body of Christ was present only in heaven.[30] Far from Westphal's polemics against Calvin reflecting a general Lutheran hostility toward the Reformed, in fact they may have helped provoke Melanchthon's shifts towards more Reformed language. Indeed, say Kolb and Arand, "Melanchthon responded

---

[26] Joar Haga, *Was there a Lutheran Metaphysics? The Interpreation of Communicatio Idiomatum in Early Modern Lutheranism* (Göttingen: Vandenhoeck and Ruprecht, 2012), 54–73.

[27] Charles P. Arand, Robert Kolb, and James A. Nestingen, *The Lutheran Confessions: History and Theology of the Book of Concord* (Minneapolis, MN: Fortress Press, 2012), 229.

[28] Arand, Kolb, and Nestingen, *Lutheran Confessions*, 174–75. Indeed, Gunnoe notes that the Variata "had been the most widely used version after 1540 and in fact had legal status in the empire as the basis of the Peace of Augsburg" ("The Reformation of the Palatinate and the Origins of the Heidelberg Catechism, 1500–1562," in Bierma et. al., eds., *Introduction to the Heidelberg Catechisim*, 43). To be sure, Diarmaid MacCulloch suggests otherwise in his *Reformation: Europe's House Divided, 1490–1700* (London: Allen Lane, 2003), 228; however, he has retracted this claim since (private email correspondence, 11/4/16).

[29] So Emidio Campi has argued recently ("Re-Evaluating the Consensus Tigurinus," unpublished conference paper, Sixteenth Century Society Conference, October 26, 2013).

[30] See also Haga, *Was there a Lutheran Metaphysics?*, 91–113.

[to Westphal] with venom in private letters, labeling Westphal's view 'bread worship'."[31]

The intra-Lutheran strife rapidly escalated between 1557 and 1560 with disputes between Johann Timann and Albert Hardenberg at Bremen and between Tilemann Hesshus and Wilhelm Klebitz at Heidelberg. Timann and Hesshus had both adopted Westphal's virulently anti-Reformed eucharistic theology and demanded that the Bremen and Heidelberg churches purge the so-called Zwinglians among them. The disputes were not lacking in drama; Hesshus, Arand and Kolb tell us, "deposed [his deacon] Klebitz after tussling with him over the chalice in front of the altar of the Holy Spirit church in Heidelberg because he believed it impious for someone who denied Christ's real presence in the Sacrament to distribute it."[32] Melanchthon intervened against Timann and in favor of Hardenberg at Bremen—not too surprising given that Hardenberg was a friend and former student—but more surprisingly, also sided against Hesshus, considered one of his favorite former students.

In response to these developments, the territory of Wurttemberg first formalized the ubiquitarian doctrine in the Wurttemberg Confession of 1559, drafted by their lead theologian, Johannes Brenz. Brenz shortly thereafter published a full-throated defense of the doctrine in his *De Personali Unione Duarum Naturarum in Christo*. Unfortunately, Melanchthon died in 1560 in the midst of these growing controversies. Accordingly, the task of answering Brenz was left to those we know as "Reformed." From Zurich Peter Martyr Vermigli published a masterful critique of Brenz in his *Dialogue on the Two Natures of Christ* (1561), while in Heidelberg, Elector Frederick III dismissed Hesshus and asked another of Melanchthon's star students, Zacharias Ursinus to draft a catechism that could serve as a fuller confession of faith than the Variata Augsburg Confession, to which Frederick had subscribed.[33] The Wurttembergers and other Gnesio-Lutherans, now increasingly led by Brenz's protegé Jakob Andreae, led the charge against the

---

[31] Arand, Kolb, and Nestingen, *Lutheran Confessions*, 233.

[32] Arand, Kolb, and Nestingen, *Lutheran Confessions*, 237.

[33] For more on the background of the Catechism, see Gunnoe, "Reformation of the Palatinate," and also, on Ursinus's Melanchthonian background, Bierma, "The Purpose and Authorship of the Heidelberg Catechism," in *Introduction*, 67–74, and "The Sources and Theological Orientation of the Heidelberg Catechism," in *Introduction*, 75–102.

Palatinate and began insisting for the first time on the original Invariata as the only valid form of the Augsburg Confession. Meanwhile, in Wittenberg, Melanchthon's students who now led the Faculty of Theology at the University, began developing the doctrine that Melanchthon had articulated in his closing years in order to reject any hint of ubiquitarianism or local presence. The key figure in this movement, Christoph Pezel, authored the Wittenberg Catechism in 1571, which, as Arand and Kolb summarize, "taught that Christ's human nature is immovably fixed in heaven."[34] Pezel and his colleagues further defended it with a treatise, *The True Church's Firm Foundation: On the Person and Incarnation of Our Lord Jesus Christ*, which firmly rejected Brenz's doctrine of a communication of attributes from the divine nature to the human nature and defended the Reformed understanding of a communication of attributes only to the person of Christ.[35] Although figures like Pezel have long been described as "crypto-Calvinists," Arand and Kolb deny a Calvinistic influence and insist that they should be called "crypto-Philippists."[36] As war waged between these Lutheran factions, Pezel at Wittenberg and Andreae at Wurttemberg, a new theological luminary, Martin Chemnitz of Swabia, stepped forward to offer something of a mediating position, known as "multi-voli-presence," which hearkened back to Melanchthon's 1530s teaching. Christ could be physically present in the Eucharistic elements, but not because his human nature had received the divine attribute of omnipresence as a new natural property, as Brenz and Andreae insisted, but simply because Christ, as God, had the power to make himself present whenever and wherever he wished, including, by some unfathomable mystery, in multiple places at once. This was good enough for the Wurttembergers, and Andreae joined forces with Chemnitz to compose the 1577 Formula of Concord, which sought to put an end to the intra-Lutheran strife by unambiguously rejecting "sacramentarian" doctrines, even if it maintained a studied ambiguity about the precise meaning of its own crucial doctrine of ubiquity.[37]

---

[34] Arand, Kolb, and Nestingen, *Lutheran Confessions*, 243.

[35] Arand, Kolb, and Nestingen, *Lutheran Confessions*, 245.

[36] Arand, Kolb, and Nestingen, *Lutheran Confessions*, 241.

[37] See Heinrich Schmid, *The Doctrinal Theology of the Evangelical Lutheran Church* (Minneapolis: Augsburg Pub. House, 1961), 298–99.

C. Persistence of Debate after the Formula of Concord

Despite the intended finality of the Formula, things were still not quite settled in the 1580s and beyond. Many Lutheran territories refused to accept it, sometimes on account of its doctrine, sometimes simply in protest of its exclusive language. Jill Raitt recounts that "When the king of Denmark received beautifully bound copies of the Book of Concord from his sister, he carried them to the fire and burned them. He then made it a capital offense to import, sell, or even own the Book of Concord."[38] Even in Lutheran Germany, fully one-third of the territories held out against the adoption of the Formula despite Andreae's intense lobbying in the 1580s.[39] Over the ensuing decades, several of these more Philippist polities formally aligned themselves with the Reformed and their more irenic confessions.[40]

The Reformed themselves, for their part, did their utmost to unite with the non-ubiquitarian factions in the aftermath of the Formula. In response to the Formula's claim to be the only true and authorized exposition of the Augsburg Confession, had been esteemed by many of the Reformed as the only pan-Protestant confession, Girolamo Zanchi was commissioned to draft an alternative confession of similar length to the Formula that could become a rallying-point for the anti-ubiquitarians. Zanchi being Zanchi, his confession ran to much greater length than was feasible for such a document, and was replaced with the *Harmonia Confessionum*, a book of confessions bringing together portions of the Tetrapolitan, Basel, Helvetic, Belgic, Augsburg, Saxon, and Wurttemberg Confessions (four Reformed and three Lutheran) as a single common confession.[41] The document failed to gain traction, but a promising opportunity for mutual understanding was presented by the 1586 Colloquy of Montbeliard. Montbeliard, a small German territory that bordered France, was trying to figure out how to handle the presence of Huguenot refugees who could not accept the Formula or its eucharistic liturgy, and determined to call a colloquy of Lutheran and Reformed representatives. From Geneva Theodore Beza was summoned,

---

[38] Jill Raitt, *The Colloquy of Montbeliard: Religion and Politics in the Sixteenth Century* (New York: Oxford University Press, 1993), 58.

[39] See Arand, Kolb, and Nestingen, *Lutheran Confessions*, 277–80.

[40] See Philip Benedict, *Christ's Churches Purely Reformed* (New Haven: Yale University Press, 2002), 217–27.

[41] Baschera and Moser, "Introduction," to *De Religione Christianae Fides*, 14–19.

while to represent the Lutherans, unfortunately Jakob Andreae was summoned, rather than the more irenic Chemnitz. Beza and the Reformed were
initially a bit distrustful of Andreae, and asked that a transcript of the debate
be made by a neutral representative and then be reviewed by both parties
before being published.[42] Their request was denied, and their mistrust was
well-warranted. Andreae had his own secretary record the debate, and subsequently edited the manuscript to embellish and flesh out his own statements, pare down those of Beza, and add marginal notes critiquing and
mocking Beza, plus a sharply critical preface for good measure.[43] When Beza tried to set the record straight in a published response, Andreae responded with a treatise "the language of which," says Jill Raitt "was so extreme that it discredits its own arguments," betraying, she says, a "hatred
for the Calvinists" whom he referred to as "devils."[44] Hooker began writing
his *Laws* this same year, though Book V was not published until 1597.
Around the same time, Zanchi wrote a lengthy and comparatively irenic
treatise, *De Incarnatione Filii Dei* (published posthumously in 1593).[45]

4. THE NATURE OF THE DOGMATIC DISPUTE

A. General Observations

With this background in place, we are now in a better position to consider
in detail the "Reformed" and "Lutheran" positions, and Hooker's relationship to them. It must be acknowledged that despite the greater Lutheran
fervor on the matter, the Reformed position was expressed with much
greater precision, the Lutherans being content with paradoxical formulations and an appeal to mystery. For instance, on the specific issue of the
bodily ubiquity of Christ, Andreae insisted at Montbeliard that if we are

---

[42] Raitt, *The Colloquy of Montbeliard*, 160–61.

[43] Raitt, *The Colloquy of Montbeliard*, 119.

[44] Raitt, *The Colloquy of Montbeliard*, 164–65.

[45] While Zanchi scholar Patrick O'Banion believes that the *De Incarnatione* is mostly
derived from lecture material from his lectures on Philippians at Neustadt in the
early 1580s (private email correspondence), Stefan Lindholm, whose thorough
study of the *De Incarnatione* has just recently been published as *Jerome Zanchi (1516–
90) and the Analysis of Reformed Scholastic Christology*, Reformed Historical Theology 37
(Göttingen: Vandenhoeck and Ruprecht, 2016), believes that Zanchi worked on the
text extensively in the middle to later 1580s (private email correspondence), perhaps in light of events at Montbeliard.

"speaking of Christ's body … as a body only" then it is true that he is not present on earth; "when Scripture speaks of Christ's absence, it means the absence of the body of Christ purely as corporeal."[46] After summarizing his position, Raitt expresses as much bafflement as Beza did when confronted with the idea of speaking of a body otherwise than as a body. Raitt goes on, quoting Andreae, "this is a truly miraculous mode of presence, that the body of Christ, existing and remaining in heaven according to the mode of a true body (*secundum quid*), without any local motion, by another mode is present (*simpliciter*) in all places." Andreae, she says, "denied that such a presence is physical, local, or relative, but rather said that it is mystical and, as such, to be believed rather than understood."[47] Beza, on the other hand, presented Andreae with three different kinds of presence: "(1) definitive: without circumscription, proper to spirits; (2) repletive: without definition, proper to divinity and therefore nontransferrable; and (3) local: circumscribed, proper to bodies and therefore nontransferrable."[48] Beza went on to argue that to truly attribute repletive presence to Christ's body by virtue of the hypostatic union, as the Lutherans did, would have the effect of denying any special presence in the Eucharist, as they intended, "since he [Christ] would have been there [in the bread and the wine] just as much from the very moment of the hypostatic union."[49]

B. The Genus Idiomaticum

Given Hooker's willingness to assert vaguely that Christ's humanity is everywhere present "after a sort" and "in some sense," he might indeed seem at first glance to be in sympathy with the Lutherans. Thankfully, however, Hooker does not leave us in the dark as to in *what* sense and after *what* sort, but expounds his senses with some precision, closely paralleling standard Reformed formulations of his time on all three of the key disputed points, which Lutheran dogmatics, following Chemnitz's authoritative 1570 *De Du-*

---

[46] Raitt, *The Colloquy of Montbeliard*, 85.

[47] Raitt, *The Colloquy of Montbeliard*, 86.

[48] Raitt, *The Colloquy of Montbeliard*, 90. The threefold division derives from the late scholastic Gabriel Biel, and was invoked by Luther in his early critiques of the sacramentarians. See Haga, *Was there a Lutheran Metaphysics?*, 55–60.

[49] Beza, *Ad Acta Colloquii Montisbelgardensis Tubingae edita, Responsio* (Geneva: 1588), 35, translated in Raitt, *The Colloquy of Montbeliard*, 90.

abus Naturis in Christo, designated the *genus idiomaticum*, the *genus apotelesmati-cum*, and the *genus maiestaticum*.[50] The first was that whereby the properties of each nature were shared with and properly attributed to the one person of the God-man. The second was that whereby both natures participated to-gether, each according to its properties, in the common action and work of the God-man. The third was that whereby the properties belonging to and proper to the divine nature of the Word were communicated to, which is to say, shared with the human nature, so that it was endowed with powers such as omniscience and omnipresence.

On the first genus, the *genus idiomaticum*, both parties were largely agreed, affirming that by virtue of the union of the two natures in the one person of the *Logos*, and the fact that both natures subsisted in and the per-son and were never themselves the subjects of action, we can truly predicate everything that Christ does of the person. Accordingly, we can certainly say, to use examples offered by Zanchi, among others, "God suffered, or "the Lord of Glory was crucified."[51] Indeed, we may go the other way just as appropriately; there is no question, insists Zanchi, "whether a man (indicat-ing Christ) or the Son of Man is everywhere and omnipotent and so on." These are examples of what was called, following scholastic usage, *concrete predication*. What we cannot do is say that "the Deity of Christ suffered," nor, to get to the point of chief debate, can we say that "the humanity is everywhere"; in these cases, we would be using *abstract predication*, and one cannot rightly predicate of a nature, considered in the abstract, something that does not belong to it.[52] The Lutherans would seem to concur at least with this formulation of the *genus idiomaticum*, which Heinrich Schmid sum-marizes in his magisterial collation of Lutheran dogmatics thus: "it is only to

---

[50] Note that the order is not always consistent; sometimes, as in Schmid, the *maies-taticum* is treated second, the *apotelesmaticum* third. See discussion of the rationales for different ordering on *Doctrinal Theology*, 290.

[51] Girolamo Zanchi, *H. Zanchii De Incarnatione Filii Dei Libri Duo [...]* (Heidelberg: J. Harnisch, 1593), 577. I am profoundly grateful to Ben Merkle, Angela Miller, Sam-uel Taylor, and Michelle Bollen of the Wenden House program at New Saint An-drews College, and to Jonathan Roberts and Charles Carman of the Davenant Latin Institute for their great assistance in translating key sections of Zanchi's text.

[52] On the distinction of concrete and abstract predication, and the related distinc-tion of predication *secundum quid* and *simpliciter*, see Haga, *Was there a Lutheran Meta-physics?*, 71–87; cf. Lindholm, *Jerome Zanchi (1516–90) and the Analysis of Reformed Scholastic Christology*, 118–20; Raitt, *The Colloquy of Montbeliard*, 83–85.

the person that, without further distinctions, the idiomata of the one or of the other nature can be ascribed; but this can in no wise happen between the natures themselves, in such a sense as though each of them did not retain the idiomata essential to itself."[53] Of course, the Lutherans will go on to say, by virtue of further distinctions, that one can make such ascriptions via the *genus maiestaticum*, but as far as the *idiomaticum* is concerned, they agree that this is always a matter of personal, or concrete predication— "God," "man," "Christ," "Son of God," "Son of Man," etc., made possible by the hypostatic union.

So was there any tension on this first point? Well yes, in fact. First, the Lutherans frequently insisted that although the Reformed *claimed* to be able to affirm a true, real predication of both natures through the one person of Christ, that they couldn't really, because they were closet Nestorians, sundering the two natures and thus reducing the *communicatio idiomatum* to a figure of speech—we could *talk* as if the Son of God suffered, but he didn't really. Few accusations are more frequently found on Lutheran lips in these debates both in the sixteenth century and beyond, and many historical theologians have uncritically parroted the charge. But in fact the Reformed consistently denied it, and insisted that personal or concrete predication is real, and it is only predication of natures, or abstract predication, that is merely nominal. Consider Zanchi, from *De Incarnatione*:

> when it is said that the man Christ is eternal and omnipresent, the proposition is true and real, with regard to the subject or person, but when it refers to the human nature itself, it is actually altogether false, and in word only is it fitting to it, in the same way that this honor is communicated to his human nature—that is, that he should be called God.[54]

Nonetheless, from the Reformed insistence that we observe proper distinctions when speaking according to the natures, there arose the suspicion among their opponents that they really preferred to speak of Christ

---

[53] Schmid, *Doctrinal Theology*, 283.

[54] *De Incarnatione*, 468. *Sic cum dicitur, homo Christus, eternus et ubiq. est, propositio vera est, et realis, spectato subiecto sue persona; sed de natura ipsa humana, falsissima est realiter, et verbotenus tantummodo ei congruit, quo nimirum modo eidem etiam humanae naturae, hic honos communicatur, ut Deus vocetur.* Cf. Heppe, *Reformed Dogmatics* (London: Allen & Unwin, 1950), 441–43.

according to the two natures rather than according to the one person, and hence implicitly divided up his agency into two subjects, giving the humanity a distinct identity and power of operation, and hence were implicitly Nestorian. One can see this claim repeated in Martin's attempt to distance Hooker from the Reformed. He draws attention to "Hooker's preference for speaking of Christ's attributes and operations after the incarnation according to his person rather than assigning them to one or the other of his natures,"[55] seeing this as something that pulls him away from his Reformed colleagues toward the Lutheran pole. In some ways, however, the opposite was the case. Whether one reads Vermigli's *Dialogue on the Two Natures of Christ*, Zanchi's *Confession of the Christian Religion* or *De Incarnatione*, Beza's disputations at Montbeliard, or the collected testimonies in Heppe's *Reformed Dogmatics*, one finds an unequivocal insistence on the anti-Nestorian, indeed Alexandrian point, that, in Heppe's words,

> The humanity taken up into the personality of the Logos is, then, not a personal man but human nature without personal subsistence…. This is why in the incarnation of the Logos it was not a new third thing that arose by the union of the divine and human natures. It was the human finite mode of being that was added to the eternal and infinite mode of being of the Logos, by the human nature being taken up into His personal subsistence.[56]

Moreover, says Zanchi,

> we believe and confess the force of this union of the two natures in the person of Christ to be so great, that first, whatsoever Christ is or doth according to the divine nature, that same whole Christ, the Son of man, may be said to be or to do. And againe, whatsoever Christ doth or suffereth according to his human nature, that same whole Christ, the Son of God, God himself, is said in the holy scriptures to be, to do and to suffer.[57]

---

[55] Martin, "Richard Hooker and Reformed Sacramental Theology," 301.

[56] Heppe, *Reformed Dogmatics*, 416.

[57] Zanchi, *Confession of the Christian Religion* (Cambridge, 1599), 217 (spelling modernized).

Indeed, so insistent were the Reformed on the propriety of predicating according to the person that they were quite concerned that it was the *Lutherans* who had unwittingly fallen into Nestorianism. Beza raised this concern several times against Andreae at Montbeliard, particularly when Andreae said, "The man assumed by the Son of God in the unity of person fills all. Therefore that assumed man is present everywhere."[58] The language of *assumed man* rather than *assumed humanity* would, if seriously meant, be a denial of the basic anti-Nestorian contention that Christ's humanity existed only as *enhypostatic* within the Logos. Heppe repeats the charge in his *Dogmatics*: "*Lutheran* Christology rests upon the essentially *Nestorian* assumption, that the incarnation of the Logos was the union of the divine nature with the human nature to be conceived in a previous subsistence, and that in it the result is the deification of the human nature by the pouring into it of the divine attributes."[59]

While the language of *assumptus homo* may have been a slip on Andreae's part, the charge does in fact go to the heart of the matter. For the Reformed felt that the Lutherans equivocated on the issue of concrete vs. abstract predication: to speak of the nature considered merely in itself, *qua* nature, was abstract and in this sense it would be invalid to say "humanity is everywhere," but they nonetheless contended that one could speak of the *nature as hypostatized*, the nature *as united in the one Person*, and this was a form of "concrete" predication.[60] Accordingly, they insisted that the concrete of each nature, in Quenstedt's words, "truly receives and partakes of the peculiar nature, power, and efficacy of the other, through and because of the communion that has occurred,"[61] so that there are two concretes that participate in each other, rather than one concrete person as the subject of predication.

In any case, a look at Hooker's language suggests a clear affinity with the Reformed on this point. First, he expressly denies the language of "mu-

---

[58] Andreae, *Ad Acta Colloquii Montisbelgardensis Tubingae edita* (Tubingen: 1587), 313, translated in Raitt, *The Colloquy of Montbeliard*, 116.

[59] Heppe, *Reformed Dogmatics*, 418–19.

[60] See Heppe, *Reformed Dogmatics*, 442; Raitt, *The Colloquy of Montbeliard*, 113, 122.

[61] *Theologia Didactico-Polemica*, III.102, quoted in Schmid, *Doctrinal Theology*, 289. Note, however, that Zanchi considered that Chemnitz, at least, got it right in his treatment of abstract and concrete predication in his ch. 13 of his *De Duabus Naturis* (see Lindholm, *Jerome Zanchi (1516–90) and the Analysis of Reformed Scholastic Christology*, 118; *De Incarnatione* 318).

tual participation" between the natures which the Lutherans used, and then defines the *communicatio idiomatum* thus:

> A kind of mutual commutation there is whereby those concrete names, *God* and *Man,* when we speak of Christ, do take interchangeably one another's room, so that for truth of speech it skilleth [i.e., matters] not whether we say that the Son of God hath created the world, and the Son of Man by his death hath saved it, or else that the Son of Man did create, and the Son of God die to save the world. Howbeit, as oft as we attribute to God what the manhood of Christ claimeth, or to man what his Deity hath right unto, we understand by the name of God and the name of Man neither the one nor the other nature, but the whole person of Christ, in whom both natures are. (V.53.4)

More importantly, though, once we understand the Reformed emphasis on the one person, we are in a position to understand Hooker's first apparent concession to the Lutherans. Here it is in full:

> Yet because the substance is inseparably joined to that personal Word which by his very divine essence is present with all things, the nature which cannot have in itself universal presence hath it *after a sort* by being *nowhere severed* from that which every where is present. For inasmuch as that infinite Word is not divisible into parts, it could not in part but must needs be wholly incarnate, and consequently, wheresoever the Word is, it hath with it manhood, else should the Word be in part or somewhere God only and not Man, which is impossible. For the *Person of Christ is whole,* perfect God and perfect Man wheresoever, although the parts of his Manhood being finite and his Deity infinite, we cannot say that the *whole of Christ* is simply every where, as we may say that his Deity is, and that his Person is by force of Deity. For *somewhat of the Person* of Christ is not every where in that sort, namely his manhood, the *only conjunction* whereof with Deity is extended as far as Deity, the actual *position* restrained and tied to a certain place; yet presence *by way of conjunction* is in some sort presence. (V.55.7)

The claim here is that the complete unity of the person means that, wherever the person is, the human nature is still inseparably joined with it, such that the *whole Christ* (*totus Christus*) is present. However, it must at the same time be said that the manhood *as such* is not present, and thus the *whole of Christ* (*totum Christi*) is not present. This *totus/totum* distinction was in fact a commonplace of Reformed Christology over against the Lutherans; Beza appealed to it at Montbeliard,[62] and Heppe cites it in various 17th-century divines.[63] On the basis of this kind of distinction, one can find Hooker's predecessors Vermigli, Ursinus, and Zanchi all appealing to the same idea of the presence of the humanity by way of conjunction; in fact, this was a direct response to one of Luther's favorite arguments against Zwingli, his appeal to the inseparability of the Logos.[64] For the sake of time, we will quote just Vermigli on this point.

> You do not interpret *unseparated* and *inseparable* the right way. You think that there is a tearing apart of the person if the divinity is held to be where the humanity is not present. This is completely untrue, because it suffices for the divinity, although immense and infinite, to support and sustain by its hypostasis the humanity wherever it is. Granted then that the body of Christ is in heaven and no longer dwells on earth, still the Son of God is nonetheless in the Church and then everywhere; he is never so freed from his human nature that he does not have it engrafted in him and joined in the unity of his person in the place where his human nature is.[65]

---

[62] Raitt, *The Colloquy of Montbeliard*, 121.

[63] Heppe, *Reformed Dogmatics*, 443, 447.

[64] On Luther's inseparability argument, see Lindholm, *Jerome Zanchi (1516–90) and the Analysis of Reformed Scholastic Christology*, 159–62.

[65] Vermigli, *Dialogue on the Two Natures in Christ*, ed. John Patrick Donnelly, The Peter Martyr Vermigli Library, vol. 2 (Kirksville, MO: Sixteenth Century Journal Publications, 1995), 24. Compare also Ursinus: *Theses De Officio et Persona Unici Mediatoris*, in *Zachariae Ursini [...] Volumen Tractationum Theologicarum* (Neustadt, 1584), 662: "Christ nevertheless is everywhere whole and entire. [*ubique totus et integer*]. For wherever the *logos* is, there the *logos* is a man, that is, united to his body, and existing at the same time one and at the same time whole both within and outside that body. Thus while he is infinite as he exists beyond the body, he does not on that account separate from the body nor is he estranged from it, although that body is not dragged with him into every place" (quoted in Andrew T. McGinnis, *The Son of God Beyond the Flesh: A Historical and Theological Study of the Extra-Calvinisticum*, T & T

In fact, in case there were still any room for ambiguity on this point, Schmid himself affirms that this presence by conjunction was never at issue between the Lutheran and Reformed, but that both parties agreed that "the *logos* never and nowhere is without or beyond His flesh, or this without or beyond Him, but, where you place the *logos*, there you also place the flesh, lest there be introduced a Nestorian disruption of the person subsisting of both natures."[66]

C. The Genus Apotelesmaticum

Thankfully, the next *genus*, the *apotelesmaticum*, will take considerably less time. On this point, there is little difference between the Reformed and Lutheran. Schmid summarizes the *genus* as "that by which, in official acts, each nature performs what is peculiar to itself, with the participation of the other,"[67] and Heppe as "the unitary action of the person of Christ in the work of redemption, in which both natures participate." This shared participation is so absolute that, in Zanchi's words, "Yea, Christ the mediator according to his humanity never did or doth anything, wherein his divinity did not or doth not work together, and he never performed any thing according to his divinity, whereunto his humanity was not assisting or consenting."[68] Hooker's language is very similar: "And that Deity of Christ which before our Lord's incarnation wrought all things without man, doth now work nothing wherein the nature which it hath assumed is either absent from it or idle" (V.55.8). This is particularly important for Hooker in his treatment of

---

Clark Studies in Systematic Theology [London: T & T Clark, 2014], 109). And Zanchi, *Confession of the Christian Religion*, Observations 11.XII.6 [p. 547]: "Add this moreover for better explication's sake, that the Word, although wheresoever it be (and it is in all places), there also the same is not only God, but also man, and that because it hath in all places the human nature united therunto by hypostasis, yet, wheresoever it is itself, it doth not make itself an hypostasis or personal to the human nature, but only there, where the same nature existeth; namely so, as that nature is sustained, borne and wrought or moved by it" (spelling modernized).

[66] Schmid, *Doctrinal Theology*, 297. It should be noted that while this quote might appear at first glance to be a polemic against the Reformed doctrine of the *extra Calvinisticum*, Schmid affirms it in earnest as a point on which the Reformed and Lutherans were united, apparently having in mind such affirmations as those of Vermigli just quoted.

[67] Schmid, *Doctrinal Theology*, 283.

[68] Zanchi, *Confession of the Christian Religion*, 217 (spelling modernized).

Christ's session at the right hand of God (which comes up again in the political theology of Book VIII of the *Lawes*): "This government therefore he exerciseth both as God and as Man, as God by essential presence with all things, as Man by co-operation with that which essentially is present" (V.55.8).

Of course, it was just this session or "most near and powerful dominion" to which the Lutherans appealed as that according to which Christ must be omnipresent.[69] Accordingly, Hooker's second "concession" comes in the context of this *apotelesmatic* cooperation: "Again, as the manhood of Christ may after a sort be every where said to be present, because that Person is every where present, from whose divine substance manhood nowhere is severed: so the same universality of presence may likewise seem in another respect appliable thereunto, namely by *co-operation* with Deity, and that *in all things*" (V.55.8). In other words, the resurrected and ascended Christ is ruling and governing all things everywhere, and the human nature is assisting in that work, and thus is present by way of its effects everywhere. This is easy to understand with reference to Christ's soul—"by knowledge and assent the soul of Christ is present with all things which the Deity of Christ worketh" (V.55.8). But what might it mean of his body?

Here we encounter Hooker's third "concession": "And even the body of Christ itself, although the definite limitation thereof be most sensible, doth notwithstanding admit in some sort a kind of infinite and unlimited presence likewise" (V.55.9). This, Hooker notes, is true in two ways: first by way of conjunction, as argued more generally earlier—"For his body being a part of that nature which whole nature is presently joined unto Deity wheresoever Deity is, it followeth that his bodily substance hath every where a presence of true conjunction with Deity," and second according to the *apotelesmatic* genus: "And forasmuch as it is by virtue of that conjunction made the body of the Son of God, by whom also it was made a sacrifice for the sins of the whole world, this giveth it *a presence of force and efficacy* throughout all generations of men" (V.55.9).

Given that the Reformed at no point disputed such a presence by way of shared activity, these should not really be considered concessions at all. Indeed, Hooker's at first surprising language about the life-giving power of Christ's flesh is paralleled and elucidated by a lengthy discussion of this

---

[69] Schmid, *Doctrinal Theology*, 297, quoting Quenstedt, *Theologia Didactico-Polemica*, III.185.

issue (and the Lutherans' frequent invocation of John 6 in this connection) in Zanchi's *De Incarnatione*.[70]

D. The Genus Maiestaticum

What then of the third genus, the *genus maiestaticum*, which was the real focus of controversy? We find the matter stated clearly in Schmid:

> the Reformed "differ from us when the question is stated concerning the impartation abstractly considered, or of a nature to a nature; because they deny that, by the hypostatic union, the properties of the divine nature have been truly and really imparted to the human nature of Christ, and that, too, for common possession, use, and designation, so that the human nature of our Saviour is truly Omnipresent, Omnipotent, and Omniscient."[71]

The Lutherans indeed acknowledged that Christ did not exercise these full powers during the time of his humiliation, hiding them under his servant form most of the time, but with his resurrection and ascension, they were fully exercised. It is sometimes suggested that since the Reformed opposed this notion of the transformation of Christ's human nature, they must have rejected any kind of transfer of glory from the divine to the human nature. So we saw above that Hillerdal expressed confusion as to how Hooker could say, "nor [are] that the *state* and quality of our substance so unaltered, but that there are in it many glorious effects proceedings from so near copulation with Deity" (V.54.5).

But in fact the Reformed had no difficulty making such affirmations. Zanchi, in a set of careful distinctions in his *De Incarnatione*, argues that there is a major and important difference between saying that the natural properties of the divine were transferred to the human and saying that the *effects* were so transferred.[72] Hooker, in the passage Hillerdal quotes, goes on to make the same distinction: "For albeit the natural properties of Deity be

---

[70] Zanchi, *De Incarnatione*, 536–38.

[71] Schmid, *Doctrinal Theology*, 296, quoting Cotta's edition of Gerhard's *Loci Communes*, IV, Diss. I, 50.

[72] Zanchi, *De Incarnatione*, 469–72.

not communicable to man's nature, the supernatural gifts graces and effects thereof are" (V.54.5).

Indeed, where the Lutherans spoke of the *genus maiestaticum*, the Reformed spoke rather of the *habitual graces*, which went over and above the *grace of union* that was involved in the *genus idiomaticum*.[73] Not only was the human nature made to belong to the person who was God, but it also received unique excellencies, such as the gift of impeccability, beyond what normally belonged to human nature, indeed, in Heppe's words, "the highest gifts of the spirit which a creature can receive at all; still, they are essentially finite, created gifts."[74] This difference was key—the principle *finitum non capax infiniti* still remained. Moreover, because they were finite, they were capable of increase, and indeed, the Reformed liked to appeal to Lk. 2:52— "And Jesus increased in wisdom and in stature and in favor with God and man"—to argue against the Lutherans that Jesus was made omniscient from the outset. The hypostatic union was once-for-all, not progressive, but the habitual graces were bestowed on Christ throughout his life, and especially at his resurrection and ascension, resulting in a progressive glorification of his flesh.

Hooker has a good deal to say about this doctrine in Chapter 54 of Book V of the *Laws*. Curiously, he does not use the more standard Reformed (and indeed Thomistic) language of "habitual graces," but rather, "the grace of unction." This same language, however, also appears in Zanchi's *De Incarnatione*,[75] in response to the Lutheran use of Psalm 45:7 to argue that the "anointing with the oil of gladness" referred to the *genus maiestaticum* (Hooker also refers to this passage). Hooker poses the question regarding the "grace of unction" as follows: "did the parts of our nature, the soul and body of Christ, receive by the influence of Deity wherewith they were matched no ability of operation, no virtue or quality above nature?" He answers in the affirmative, "the Deity of Christ ... hath imparted unto it all things, he hath replenished it with all such perfections as the same is any

---

[73] For the Thomistic background of this Reformed category, see *ST* III Q. 7. The Lutherans, it should be noted, did not deny the existence of the category, but considered the *genus maiestaticum* to go above and beyond it. (See especially Q. 7 a. 11, where Aquinas argues against the habitual graces being infinite, invoking something very like the *finitum non capax infiniti* principle.)

[74] Heppe, *Reformed Dogmatics*, 434.

[75] Zanchi, *De Incarnatione*, 522–24.

way apt to receive" (V.54.6). This last phrase, however, is the key one, as we see when Hooker goes on to explain why it is that the grace of unction *cannot* be used to explain how Christ might be personally present everywhere.

And concerning the grace of unction, wherein are contained the gifts and virtues which Christ as man hath above men, they make him really and habitually a man more excellent than we are, they take not from him the nature and substance that we have, they cause not his soul nor body to be of another kind than ours is. Supernatural endowments are an advancement, they are no extinguishment of that nature whereto they are given (V.55.6).

In other words, however far Christ's human nature has been elevated by its union with deity, it must still remain within the bounds of a recognizably human nature; otherwise the whole point of the Incarnation is overthrown, for Christ is not truly man.

Hooker's qualifications here find parallels in many Reformed treatments. Beza had contended at Montbeliard that "We also confess that the highest gifts of Deity which can fall upon the creature and of which human nature is capable,"[76] distinguishing between gifts that were "above nature, or 'hyperphysical,'" as opposed to those "contrary to nature, or 'antiphysical'." Similar language had been used by Melanchthon's disciple Christoph Pezel, who argued that the habitual gifts were only παραφυσικὰ or ὑπερφυσικὰ, and must not "be confused with the properties or attributes of the divine nature."[77]

The Lutherans, for their part, denied that the doctrine of ubiquity fundamentally compromised the integrity of the human nature and its local limitation; rather, the *genus maiestaticum* made possible a new mode of presence that surpassed our understanding. Thus, says Raitt, Andreae denied against Beza, "that such a presence is physical, local, or relative, but rather said that it is mystical and, as such, to be believed rather than under-

---

[76] Heppe, *Reformed Dogmatics*, 446, quoting Beza, *Responsio*, 265.

[77] Pezel, *Argumenta et obiectiones: de praecipuis capitibus doctrinae Christianae, cum responsionibus* (Neustadt, 1581), I:207–8, quoted in Heppe, *Reformed Dogmatics*, 446. See also the extensive quotes on Heppe, *Reformed Dogmatics*, 494–96, and Vermigli, *Dialogue*, 83: "We too confess that the body of Christ transcends everything human, but it does not thereby cease being the body of a man. It still retains its limbs, shape, limits, and limiation. It transcends everything human which pertains to the weakness, infirmity, and necessities of this life."

stood."[78] Or as later Lutheran dogmatician David Hollaz summarized the doctrine: "The doctrine concerning the reality of the flesh of Christ is not overthrown by the ascription of omnipresence to it, for it is not omnipresent by a physical and extensive, but by a hyperphysical, divine, and illocal presence, which belongs to it not formally and *per se*, but by way of participation, and by virtue of the personal union."[79]

Hooker, however, was adamant that while it might be difficult for us in our current state to imagine what all the glorified state of humanity might involve, surely, if we can know anything at all about human nature, we can know that there are certain basic properties of bodies that we can be confident are not taken away in this state—foremost among them being localized finite extension in space. Accordingly Hooker insists (and in this his opposition to the Lutheran formulations is unambiguous): "The substance of the body of Christ hath no presence, neither can have, but only local.... There is no proof in the world strong enough to enforce that Christ had a true body but by the true and natural properties of his body. Amongst which properties, definite or local presence is chief" (V.55.6).

6. CONCLUSIONS

Given the conclusiveness with which we would seem to have demonstrated Hooker's allegiance to Reformed orthodoxy at this point, the question must naturally arise why scholars should be so eager to conclude otherwise. There are any number of reasons connected to the curious historiographical biases in relation to Hooker because of centuries of anti-Reformed Anglican self-understanding, but I want to conclude by reflecting briefly on a somewhat different issue, that of polemicism and irenicism. It is certainly true that Hooker's writing throughout this section, while really quite unambiguous in its argument, is surprisingly amicable in tone. Nowhere are his

---

[78] Raitt, *The Colloquy of Montbeliard*, 86.

[79] *Examen Theologicum Acroamaticum*, 718, quoted in Schmid, *Doctrinal Theology*, 298. Cf. Brenz, *De personali unione duarum naturarum in Christo* (Tubingen: Ulrich Morhard, 1561), fol. 12r (translated in Vermigli, *Dialogue*, 92): "The term *everywhere* has to be understood rightly. In normal usage it includes locality, that is, diffused in itself and extended everywhere. But in this [latter] way of speaking the humanity of Christ is everywhere. The word *everywhere* does not mean any locality. For the Godhead itself is not diffused or spread locally. How could we say that the humanity united to the Godhead is spread and extended locally?"

Lutheran opponents named and shamed, nor do we find the kind of aggressive language that we often expect from 16th-century polemics, dwelling upon the absurdities and impieties of the opposing view. And then of course there is the fact that he ends his discussion with three concessions, which, while clearly not going as far as the Lutherans wanted to, do seem genuinely intended to extend an olive branch, as we see in these words which conclude his discussion of Christology proper: "Which things indifferently every way considered, that gracious promise of our Lord and Saviour Jesus Christ concerning presence with his to the very end of the world, I see no cause but that we may well and safely interpret he doth perform both as God by essential presence of Deity, and as Man in that order, sense, and meaning, which hath been shewed" (V.55.9). This is as if to say, "Look, everything of theological importance that you want to say, we think we can say too—we can just say it without falling into philosophical absurdity, since we qualify it in these ways," and indeed we find this same manner of exposition in Hooker's treatment of Christ's eucharistic presence a bit further on.

To scholars who think that theological polemics of this period must always be harsh and uncompromising, Hooker's irenic tone leads them to furrow their brow in suspicion. Surely he must be up to something, surely he must have a secret unfulfilled longing to be a Lutheran (so that, Hillerdal would have it, he can be an Anglo-Catholic!). But what if Hooker's relative irenicism on this point was in fact fairly standard for Reformed theologians of this period?

The evidence surveyed here suggests that is the case. Consider the fact that the Reformed saw themselves as also upholding the Augsburg Confession, and indeed doing so in accord with the meaning intended by its own author, Philipp Melanchthon. Their approach to confessions was deliberately inclusive; the *Harmonia Confessionum* which Beza and others worked to put together in the aftermath of the Formula of Concord was a hybrid of four Reformed and three Lutheran confessions, seeking to demonstrate their basic harmony. Their Gnesio-Lutheran opponents, however, took a very narrow view of confessions. In the discussions surrounding the colloquy, Montbeliard's Lutheran ministers protested that they could not set the dangerous precedent of conceding that there might be any valid confessions beyond the Augsburg Confession of 1530 and the Wurt-

temberg Confession of 1559.[80] And indeed, the most noxious feature of the
Formula of Concord to many of its contemporaries was not its actual positive theological expressions, which owed more to the moderation of Chemnitz than they did to Andreae's more problematic formulations, but the extensive condemnations appended to the chapters on the Lord's Supper and
the Person of Christ, which sought to deliberately exclude Calvinists and
Melanchthonian Lutherans.[81] The result was fragmentation and division of
the Reformed churches at a time when unity was of the utmost importance.
Arand and Kolb write,

> Their [the Reformed's] concerns about the political conse-
> quences of the Formula, particularly in regard to the ability
> of Calvinist churches to win protection under the provi-
> sions of the Religious Peace of Augsburg, were shared by
> the English government of Queen Elizabeth, who wanted
> to preserve the broadest possible consensus among the
> opponents of the papacy in princely courts throughout
> Europe. They believed that the Lutherans were playing in-
> to the hands of the papal foes with what they considered
> too narrow and restrictive definitions of doctrine as well as
> outright false teaching in the Formula.[82]

And so it was that much of the Reformed writing on the subject refused to fight fire with fire, seeking persuasion and conciliation, rather than
capitulation. Such is the tone not merely of Hooker, but of Vermigli's *Dialogue*, and of much of Zanchi's *De Incarnatione* as well. Indeed, Zanchi goes
out of his way to narrow down as precisely as possible the points of disagreement, and even enumerates fourteen different points which the Lutheran theologians themselves grant which, he thinks, logically entail agreement
with the Reformed position, so that they are not so much impious as just
confused or unclear.[83] In a remarkable passage later on, he seeks to make
sense of Chemnitz's seemingly-contradictory statements, and concludes
"that Chemnitz likewise senses and teaches what we [teach] about this ques-

---

[80] Raitt, *The Colloquy of Montbeliard*, 167.

[81] Arand, Kolb, and Nestingen, *Lutheran Confessions*, 279.

[82] Arand, Kolb, and Nestingen, *Lutheran Confessions*, 278.

[83] Zanchi, *De Incarnatione*, 478–83.

tion."[84] Zanchi, like Hooker, writes often as if he were simply trying to help his adversaries out of philosophical difficulty into which they have gotten themselves by too much zeal without knowledge. We see the same thing with Beza at Montbeliard, who frequently complained that Andreae's main difficulty was his inability to employ consistent logical and philosophical terminology.[85] At the Colloquy and in its aftermath, Beza sought to enumerate as many areas of agreement as possible, and Andreae kept rejecting them. Raitt says, "From time to time in the *Responsio*, Beza appealed for peace based on points of agreement. Andreae would have none of it. In fact, in the *Brief Recueil*, the French edition of Andreae's *Epitome*, his response to Beza's *Responsio*, Andreae argued that heretics like Beza should be prosecuted by the civil police."[86] Raitt herself suggests that the relative irenicism of the Reformed owed much perhaps to their relatively disempowered political position; since the Lutherans had most of the powerful princes of Germany on their side, they felt like they could demand capitulation while the Reformed merely asked for toleration. This explanation, however, seems inadequate when we look beyond the immediate German context. In Denmark, for instance, a much more lenient policy prevailed, and in England, where Elizabeth and later James enjoyed a nearly island-wide monopoly on the nature of the religious establishment, they used their power to carve out space for doctrinal flexibility on many points, rather than demanding complete uniformity.

The real nature of the difference might have more to do with the different approaches to the use of philosophy in theology. When the Reformed protested that their adversaries were simply being philosophically incoherent, many of the Lutherans responded by glorying in the accusation. Luther had contended that the incarnation had introduced a "new language," before which all merely human philosophy must give way:

> 20. Nonetheless it is certain that with regard to Christ [*in Christo*] all words receive a new signification, though the thing signified is the same [*in eadem re significata*]. 21. For "creature" in the old usage of language [*veteris linguae usu*] and in other subjects signifies a thing separated from divin-

[84] Zanchi, *De Incarnatione*, 582.

[85] See for instance Raitt, *The Colloquy of Montbeliard*, 113.

[86] Raitt, *The Colloquy of Montbeliard*, 122.

ity by infinite degrees [*infinitis modis*]. 22. In the new use of language it signifies a thing inseparably joined with divinity in the same person in an ineffable way [ineffabilibus modis]. 23. Thus it must be that the words man, humanity, suffered, etc., and everything that is said of Christ, are new words.[87]

Thus the ubiquitarians, confronted with the Reformed's impatient insistences that they were saying things that just didn't make sense, the former could dismiss such accusations with a wave of the hand, saying that of course it didn't make sense—why should it?[88] Accordingly, as Stefan Lindholm shows in his careful study of Zanchi and Chemnitz, Chemnitz simply does not seem to have felt bound to the canons of scholastic rigor that Zanchi demanded of both his adversaries and himself.[89] And Heinrich Schmid admits that the Formula is frankly rather opaque on the crucial questions, but since the main point is simply to insist on the real presence in the Eucharist, that is alright.[90] Indeed, many Lutherans argued that the rigor of the Reformed substituted Aristotle for Christ, and that their statements of what God could and could not do, like the *finitum non capax*, were simply blasphemous.[91] For both Luther himself and many later defenders of his doctrine, a radical Ockhamist understanding of God's *potentia absoluta* underlay their insistence that the normal rules of metaphysics were suspended

---

[87] Martin Luther, "Disputation On the Divinity and Humanity of Christ February 27, 1540", translated by Christopher B. Brown. Available online: http://www.iclnet.org/pub/resources/text/wittenberg/luther/luther-divinity.txt. Cited in Lindholm, *Jerome Zanchi (1516–90) and the Analysis of Reformed Scholastic Christology*, 119–20. Cf. Haga, *Was there a Lutheran Metaphysics?*, 82–89.

[88] This dynamic is well illustrated at several points in Vermigli's *Dialogue*, which quotes or paraphrases extensively from Brenz's *De Personali Unione* see especially pp. 48–50.

[89] Lindholm, *Jerome Zanchi (1516–90) and the Analysis of Reformed Scholastic Christology*, 122. See also Raitt, *The Colloquy of Montbéliard*, 88: "Andreae was scornful of Beza's demand that the debate proceed by way of syllogisms, and the few that Andreae used are, to say the least, simplistic. In each case, his first premise was the heart of the debate and so could not be used as a first premise, which must be above debate. Beza recognized this problem in his *Responsio*. It is difficult to know whether Andreae was simply unskilled in logic or despaired of its application."

[90] Schmid, *Doctrinal Theology*, 298–99.

[91] Arand, Kolb, and Nestingen, *Lutheran Confessions*, 240.

when it came to Christ's body.[92] Here as on many other points, the Reformed were by and large faithful to the Thomistic rather than the voluntarist tradition (despite the frequent claims to the contrary in the tertiary and sometimes even the secondary literature).[93]

It defies our modern stereotypes that the side which insisted on greater philosophical rigor and dogmatic precision should have been the more irenic, but perhaps it ought not surprise us on further reflection. In areas of fervent disagreement over important matters, one generally has to resort to one of two basic explanations: one must conclude that one's opponent is guilty either of a failure in reasoning or a moral failure, and it makes an important difference which explanation one takes. While many academics might much rather be accused of moral failure than of rational failure, most rational people would consider it worse to be accused of wickedness than of stupidity. The value, then, of demanding philosophical rigor in theology is that it takes the dispute out of the arena of basic fidelity to the gospel. All parties, it can be charitably assumed, love God and want to serve him, and the persistence of disagreements can then be safely attributed to the persistence of careless reasoning. If, however, one insists (as many do today far more insistently than Luther) that you just need to shut up, believe the Bible, and embrace the mystery, no matter how little sense it makes, then failure to do so can only be a failure of faith. Hence one will have little choice but to conclude that one's adversaries are demonically-inspired heretics.

Many Reformed folks today have been burned by a doctrinal exclusivism that seemed addicted to hair-splitting distinctions, and have gravitated in response to theologies that dispense with logic and metaphysics and thrive on feeling, mystery, and an air of piety. Let us hope that this foray

---

[92] Arand, Kolb, and Nestingen, *Lutheran Confessions*, 228: "His Ockhamist training had prepared him to recognize that God's power is not bound by definitions that limit God's ways of accomplishing his will within his creation: God can do with his creation what he wants. Luther believed that the creator can place his power and his incarnate presence where and in whatever form he wishes."

[93] Indeed, in the field of Hooker scholarship, one still far too often encounters the claim that Hooker's Thomism somehow sets him over and against the Reformed tradition. A.J. Joyce makes such suggestions repeatedly in *Richard Hooker and Anglican Moral Theology* (Oxford: OUP, 2012); see also Alexander S. Rosenthal, *Crown Under Law: Richard Hooker, John Locke, and the ascent of modern constitutionalism* (Lanham, MD: Lexington Books, 2008), 61–72.

into arcane 16th-century polemics will remind us that hair-splitting, rightly understood, can in fact be used as a tool of charity, toleration, and persuasion.

BIBLIOGRAPHY

Andreae, Jacobus. *Ad Acta Colloquii Montisbelgardensis Tubingae edita.* Tubingen, 1587.

Arand, Charles P., Robert Kolb, and James A. Nestingen. *The Lutheran Confessions: History and Theology of the Book of Concord.* Minneapolis, MN: Fortress Press, 2012.

Baschera, Luca, and Christian Moser. "Introduction" to *De Religione Christianae Fides/On the Confession of the Christian Religion.* Leiden: Brill, 2007.

Bayne, Ronald. "Introduction." *Of the laws of the ecclesiastical polity, the fifth book.* London: Macmillan, 1902.

Benedict, Philip. *Christ's Churches Purely Reformed.* New Haven: Yale University Press, 2002.

Beza, Theodore. *Ad Acta Colloquii Montisbelgardensis Tubingae edita, Responsio.* Geneva: 1588.

Bierma, L.D. "The Purpose and Authorship of the Heidelberg Catechism." In *Introduction to the Heidelberg Catechism: Sources, History, and Theology*, ed. L.D. Bierma et al., 49–74. Grand Rapids: Baker Books, 2005.

———. "The Sources and Theological Orientation of the Heidelberg Catechism." In *Introduction to the Heidelberg Catechism*, 75–102.

Brenz, Johannes. *De personali unione duarum naturarum in Christo.* Tubingen: Ulrich Morhard, 1561.

Campi, Emidio. "Re-Evaluating the Consensus Tigurinus." Unpublished conference paper, Sixteenth Century Society Conference, October 26, 2013.

Dorner, Isaak August. *History of the Development of the Doctrine of the Person of Christ.* Edinburgh: T. & T. Clark, 1889.

Gunnoe, Charles, D. "The Reformation of the Palatinate and the Origins of the Heidelberg Catechism, 1500–1562." In *Introduction to the Heidelberg Catechisim*, ed. L.D. Bierma et. al., 15–47.

Haga, Joar. *Was there a Lutheran Metaphysics? The Interpreation of Communicatio Idiomatum in Early Modern Lutheranism*. Göttingen: Vandenhoeck and Ruprecht, 2012.

Heppe, Heinrich. *Reformed Dogmatics*. London: Allen & Unwin, 1950.

Hillerdal, Gunnar. *Reason and Revelation in Richard Hooker*. Lund: CWK Gleerup, 1962.

Hooker, Richard. *The Works of that Learned and Judicious Divine Mr. Richard Hooker with an Account of His Life and Death by Isaac Walton*, arranged by John Keble, 7th edition revised by the Very Rev. R.W. Church and the Rev. F. Paget. 3 vols. Oxford: Clarendon Press, 1888.

Joyce, A.J. *Richard Hooker and Anglican Moral Theology*. Oxford: OUP, 2012.

Kirby, Torance, ed. A *Companion to Richard Hooker*. Leiden: Brill, 2008.

———. *Richard Hooker and the English Reformation*. Dordrecht: Kluwer Academic Publishers, 2003.

Lake, Peter. *Anglicans and Puritans: Presbyterianism and English Conformist Thought - Whitgift to Hooker*. London: Unwin Hyman, 1988.

———. "Business as Usual: The immediate reception of Hooker's Ecclesiastical Polity." *The Journal of Ecclesiastical History* 52, no. 3 (2001): 456–86.

Littlejohn, W. Bradford, and Scott N. Kindred-Barnes, eds. *Richard Hooker and Reformed Orthodoxy*. Göttingen: Vandenhoeck and Ruprecht, 2017.

Lindholm, Stefan. *Jerome Zanchi (1516–90) and the Analysis of Reformed Scholastic Christology*. Vol. 37 of *Reformed Historical Theology*. Göttingen: Vandenhoeck and Ruprecht, 2016.

Luther, Martin. "Disputation On the Divinity and Humanity of Christ February 27, 1540", translated by Christopher B. Brown. Available online: http://www.iclnet.org/pub/resources/text/wittenberg/luther/luther-divinity.txt.

MacCulloch, Diarmaid. *Reformation: Europe's House Divided, 1490–1700.* London: Allen Lane, 2003.

Martin, Drew. "Richard Hooker and Reformed Sacramental Theology." In *Richard Hooker and Reformed Orthodoxy,* ed. W. Bradford Littlejohn and Scott N. Kindred-Barnes, 295–318. Göttingen: Vandenhoeck and Ruprecht, 2017.

McGinnis, Andrew T. *The Son of God Beyond the Flesh: A Historical and Theological Study of the Extra-Calvinisticum.* T & T Clark Studies in Systematic Theology. London: T & T Clark, 2014.

Neelands, David. "Christology and the Sacraments." In *A Companion to Richard Hooker,* ed. Torrance Kirby, 369–402. Leiden: Brill, 2008.

Pelikan, Jaroslav and Valerie R. Hotchkiss, eds. *Creeds and Confessions of Faith in the Christian Tradition.* New Haven: Yale University Press, 2003.

Pezel, Christoph. *Argumenta et obiectiones: de praecipuis capitibus doctrinae Christianae, cum responsionibus.* Neustadt, 1581.

Raitt, Jill. *The Colloquy of Montbeliard: Religion and Politics in the Sixteenth Century.* New York: Oxford University Press, 1993.

Rasmussen, Barry. "Presence and Absence: Richard Hooker's Sacramental Hermeneutic." In *Richard Hooker and the English Reformation,* ed. W.J. Torrance Kirby. Dordrecht: Kluwer Academic Publishers, 2003.

Rosenthal, Alexander S. *Crown Under Law: Richard Hooker, John Locke, and the Ascent of Modern Constitutionalism.* Lanham, MD: Lexington Books, 2008.

Schmid, Heinrich. *The Doctrinal Theology of the Evangelical Lutheran Church.* Minneapolis: Augsburg Pub. House, 1961.

Skinner, Quentin. "Meaning and Understanding in the History of Ideas." *History and Theory* 8, no. 1 (1969): 3–53.

Ursinus, Zacharias. *Theses De Officio et Persona Unici Mediatoris.* In *Zachariae Ursini [...] Volumen Tractationum Theologicarum.* Neustadt, 1584.

Vermigli, Peter Martyr. *Dialogue on the Two Natures in Christ,* edited by John Patrick Donnelly. Vol. 2 of *The Peter Martyr Vermigli Library.* Kirksville, MO: Sixteenth Century Journal Publications, 1995.

Zanchi, Girolamo. *H. Zanchii De Incarnatione Filii Dei Libri Duo [...].* Heidelberg: J. Harnisch, 1593.

———. *Confession of the Christian Religion.* Cambridge, 1599.

IV:

GEORGE CARLETON'S REFORMED DOCTRINE OF EPISCOPAL AUTHORITY AT THE SYNOD OF DORT

Andre Gazal, Trinity Evangelical Divinity School

1. INTRODUCTION

RICHARD Montagu, in his severe criticism of the Synod of Dort, forth-rightly justified his refusal to subscribe to the famed Canons against Armin-ianism which this assembly of Reformed churches produced, as well as other aspects of its work: "For my part, I nor have, nor ever will subscribe that Synode absolutely, and in all points (for in some, it condemneth upon the Bye even the discipline of the Church of *England*), but so farre forth onely, as their Determinations shall bee found and made conformable unto the doctrine of OUR *Church*."[1]

In addition to his strong disagreement with the Synod's position regarding the nature and function of salvific grace as stated in its Canons, another reason Montagu gives for his refusal to accede to most of the Synod's pronouncements is its condemnation of the "discipline of the Church of England," or specifically, its government by bishops. Throughout this work, *Appello Caesarem*, Montagu charges the British delegation to the Synod with not accurately representing the doctrinal position of the Church of England in its general approval of the Canons as well as acquiescence to-

---

[1] Richard Montagu, *Appello Caesarem* (London: H. L. for Matthew Lownes), 181. See also Anthony Milton, *The British Delegation to the Synod of Dort* (Woodbridge, Suffolk, UK: Boydell, 2005), 387.

wards the Continental delegates' opposition to episcopacy. Montagu was not alone in this assessment of the Synod of Dort and the manner in which the British delegation represented the Church of England as other prominent ecclesiastics such as Lancelot Andrewes and William Laud also echoed it.

Yet, in his appraisal of the Synod in general, and the work of the British delegation specifically, Montagu speaks in something of a cautious tone, especially in mentioning one of its most prominent members, George Carleton (1559–1628), who at the time was bishop of Llandaff: "I derogate nothing from that *Synode*, nor any particular man in that *Synod*. For those Divines that were there of our Church, the Principall of them sometime was my worthy friend and acquaintance; since is my Reverend and much reverenced *Diocesan*."[2] Composing these remarks in 1625, six years following the adjournment of the Synod, Montagu attempts to display an apparent air of deference to Carleton, as he was by this time bishop of Chichester, where Montagu was serving, and therefore his Diocesan. However, this seeming obsequiousness thinly veils what is in reality a stinging reproof of the bishop and his colleagues. For shortly following this politic gesture towards Carleton is a refusal to accept unreservedly the Canons, which he, as a delegate to the Synod approved. "I have nothing to do with their Conclusions, farther than they doe consent and agree to the Conclusions and Determinations of that *Synod* of *London*, which established the Doctrine of our Church, to which I am bound, and have subscribed.[3] The implication of this statement is apparent: Bishop Carleton and his other colleagues representing the Church of England at the Synod of Dort, generally acceded to doctrines related to grace and church government that in some respects contravene those confirmed by ecclesial authorities of the said national church. Montagu's critique of the Canons of Dort generally, and particularly his suggestion that Carleton and his other colleagues compromised on the disciplinary matter of episcopacy, prompted a response by the bishop. This reply came in the form of *An Examination Wherein the Author of the Late Appeale Holdeth the Doctrines of the Pelagians and Arminians to be the Doctrines of the Church of England* to which was appended a vindication against Montagu's charge of the British delegation's tolerance of the Synod's alleged censure of episcopacy, *A Joint Attestation Avowing that the Discipline of the Church of Eng-*

---

[2] Montagu, *Appello Caesarem*, 69; see Milton, *British Delegation*, 384.

[3] Montagu, *Appello Caesarem*, 71; see Milton, *British Delegation*, 384.

ANDRE GAZAL

land Was Not Impeached by the Synod of Dort.[4] As clearly conveyed by the title, Carleton argues in this work that the Canons of Dort fully accord with the Church of England's stated doctrines concerning grace, and that to associate the said Church's teachings with those of Arminianism is to characterize it as sympathetic to the ancient heresy of Pelagianism. In the *Joynt Attestation* Carleton maintains that he and his colleagues contended very strongly for episcopacy towards which (or so the bishop reports) the other delegates were actually sympathetic.

Throughout Carleton's extensive discussions regarding the Synod of Dort and the Canons which it produced as well as his recorded orations given at the Synod, a steadily recurring theme is the dual necessity of defining doctrine and refuting heresy in order to ensure the unity of the Reformed churches. When examined in the light of his other principal works, it becomes apparent that the bishop regarded these tasks of affirming doctrine and condemning heresy within the larger context of his conceptions of *sola Scriptura* and catholicity. Believing that Scripture as generally interpreted by the church fathers and applied by the early church is the final authority in determining articles of faith and the broader matters of ecclesiastical governance,[5] Carleton discerned from the same a divinely prescribed order of church government whose purpose was to protect doctrine by defining it while simultaneously condemning heresy in order to protect the Church's unity. This order of ecclesiastical discipline was one in which centered around episcopacy. As the form of ecclesiastical governance *iure divino*, epis-

---

[4] George Carleton, *An Examination of Those Things Wherein the Author of the Late Appeale Holdeth the Doctrines of the Pelagians and Arminians to be the Doctrines of the Church of England, Whereunto Also There is Annexed a Joynt Attestation Avowing that the Discipline of the Church of England Was Not Impugned By the Synod of Dort* (London: Michael Sparkes, 1626).

[5] Although generally held by the magisterial reformers of the sixteenth century, the first major apologist of the Elizabethan Church, John Jewel (1522–71), specifically understood and applied this principle in terms of the Scriptures, early church fathers, first four ecumenical councils, and custom of the early church. Scripture was the ultimate authority but its interpretation and application needed to be verified by these necessary secondary authorities. This approach reflects one view of the relationship between Scripture and tradition identified by the late Heiko Oberman as "Tradition A." See John Jewel, *Apology of the Church of England*, trans. Ann Bacon, ed. John Booty (New York: Church Publishing, 2002), 17; Heiko Oberman, "*Quo Vadis, Petre?* Tradition from Irenaeus to *Humani Generis*," in Heiko Oberman, *Dawn of the Reformation: Essays in Late Medieval and Early Reformation Thought* (Grand Rapids: Eerdmans, 1992), 269–96.

copacy safeguarded doctrine, thereby preserving the order and peace of the Church. Because the episcopacy is divinely ordained to protect truth, it is the primary means of maintaining catholicity since it rests upon the truth whose maintenance is entrusted to the bishops. While such a view of episcopacy was not unique to Carleton, as it was espoused by other English churchmen as Richard Bancroft (1544–1610) and Matthew Sutcliffe (1550–1629),[6] several factors warrant a close examination of the bishop's particular exposition and defense of the doctrine. First, Carleton was leader of the British delegation to the Synod of Dort. The continental delegates accorded Carleton respect not only because of his role as head of this delegation, but also on account of his office as a bishop, to the utter annoyance of other participants like Franciscus Gomarus, the primary spokesman of the anti-Remonstrants.[7] Indeed, official synodical documents refer to Carleton as "Bishop" rather than simply "Doctor."[8] Furthermore, Carleton walked at the head of the procession of divines at the end of the synod.[9] Also as the principal member of a foreign delegation, he would be the first to speak whenever opinions were expressed in synodical sessions.[10] Very significantly, Carleton was the only member of the British delegation who served on the Synodical committee which drafted the Canons.[11]

Although the Synod of Dort concerned itself mostly with the soteriological issues raised initially by James Arminius (1560–1609) and by the Remonstrants, it did give consideration to the subject of ecclesiastical discipline, or polity. Whereas most of the delegates subscribed to classical, or Presbyterian polity, Carleton was the principal spokesman of *iure divino* episcopacy as a Reformed doctrine best capable of preserving Protestant ortho-

---

[6] Richard Bancroft, *A Suruey of the Pretended Discipline* (London, 1593); Matthew Sutcliffe, *A Treatise of Ecclesiastical Discipline* (London, 1591); see Patrick Collinson, *Richard Bancroft and Elizabethan Anti-Puritanism* (Cambridge: Cambrdige University Press, 2013), 83–102.

[7] For instance, various prints of the Synod depict a canopy over Carleton's chair. See Milton, *The British Delegation*, xxxv. For Gomarus' annoyance, see Arie Theodorus van Deursen, "England and the Synod of Dort," in *The Exchange of Ideas: Religion, Scholarship, and Art in Anglo-Dutch Relations in the Seventeenth Century*, ed. Simon Groenveld and Michael J. Wintle (Zutphen: Walburg Institut, 1994), 37.

[8] Milton, *The British Delegation*, xxxv.

[9] Milton, *The British Delegation*, xxxv.

[10] Milton, *The British Delegation*, xxxv.

[11] Milton, *The British Delegation*, xxxv.

doxy which, in his judgment, Arminius and the Remonstrants undermined. This essay, then, will demonstrate by close examination of Carleton's pertinent works that the bishop thought of *iure divino* episcopacy as ultimately the biblical means of affirming and securing confessional orthodoxy. Before proceeding with Carleton's understanding of the episcopal office, we will first briefly survey his life and career.

2. GEORGE CARLETON'S LIFE AND CAREER[12]

George Carleton was born in 1559 at Northam in Northumberland, the son of Guy Carleton. He received his early education under the tuition of Bernard Gilpin, the "Apostle to the North."[13] In 1576, Carleton matriculated at St. Edmund Hall, Oxford. He graduated with his M. A. degree in 1579, and was elected a fellow at Merton College, Oxford a year later. While at Merton, Carleton distinguished himself in poetry and oratory, as well as in theological disputation. He also studied extensively the writings of the church fathers, and medieval scholastic theologians.

From 1589 to 1605, Carleton was vicar of Mayfield, Sussex. Between 1605 and 1618, Carleton spent much of his time seeking ecclesiastical preferment through the offices of his cousin, Dudley Carleton, who would later serve as James I's ambassador to the Netherlands. The correspondence between the two cousins during this period indicates that George's impediment to higher ecclesiastical office was his lack of governmental experience.[14] However, since he was the chaplain of Prince Charles (the future Charles I), his royal patron helped secure for him the see of Llandaff in 1618.[15] In the same year, James I appointed him along with Joseph Hall (1574–1656), dean of Worcester; John Davenant (1572–1641), master of

---

[12] The source of this information is William Richard Wood Stephens, "Carleton, George (1559–1628)" in *Dictionary of National Biography* (London: Smith, Elder, & Co., 1885–1900), 9:91.

[13] Carleton later wrote a biography of Gilpin, *Vita Bernardi Gilpini, apud Anglos Aquilonares* (London, 1628); *Life of Bernard Gilpin, With the Sermon Preached Before Edward VI in 1552* (London, 1636).

[14] Illustrative of this impediment is the failure of George Carleton's bid for the vacant see of Carlisle in 1616 which he admitted was due to the fact that "I had never yet been in place of government." See Kenneth Fincham, *Prelate as Pastor: The Episcopate of James I* (Oxford: Clarendon Press, 1990), 20.

[15] Fincham, *Prelate as Pastor*, 26.

Queens College, Cambridge; Samuel Ward (1572–1643), master of Sydney Sussex College, Cambridge; Walter Balcanquhall (1548–1616), fellow of Pembroke Hall, Cambridge; and Thomas Goad (1576–1638), chaplain to Archbishop Abbot.[16] It was at the Synod of Dort where Carleton distinguished himself for his vigorous opposition to adoption of Article #31 of the *Belgic Confession*, which affirmed the parity of all ministers.[17] Carleton predicated his case upon a defense of episcopal authority. When the British delegation returned to England in 1619, the Dutch paid the expenses it incurred for the voyage, and presented each member with a gold medal. Later the Dutch sent the king a letter which particularly commended Carleton "as the foremost man of the company and a model of learning and piety."[18] It was indeed his outstanding performance at the Synod that earned Carleton his translation to the see of Chichester in 1619. As bishop of Chichester, Carleton took an active interest in his diocese, especially through his consistory court over which he regularly presided.[19] In May of 1628 George Carleton died, leaving a legacy of faithful service to both his church and his king.

As noted, Carleton's prime contribution to the Synod of Dort was his defense of *iure divino* episcopacy. At this point consideration will now be given to examination of the bishop's doctrine of the episcopal office as explicated in his important ecclesiological work published, eight years before the Synod of Dort, *Jurisdiction Regall, Episcopall, Papall*.

3. CARLETON'S DOCTRINE OF THE EPISCOPAL OFFICE: *JURISDICTION REGALL, EPISCOPALL, PAPALL*

Carleton's most extensive exposition of episcopacy occurs in his treatise, *Jurisdiction Regall, Episcopall, Papall*. Published in 1610, during the controversy

---

[16] Milton, *The British Delegation*, xxviii.

[17] "As for the ministers of God's Word, they have equally the same power and authority wheresoever they are, as they are all ministers of Christ, the only universal Bishop, and the only Head of the Church." See http://www.creeds.net/belgic/.

[18] Stephens, "Carleton, George (1559–1628)," 91.

[19] Fincham, *Prelate as Pastor*, 174–75. Carleton presided over ninety meetings of consistory between 1620 and 1627. See Kenneth Fincham, ed. *The Early Stuart Church, 1603–1642* (Stanford, CA: Stanford University Press, 1993), 74.

surrounding the Oath of Allegiance,[20] this work argues against the Pope's claim to "coactive," or coercive power, from which stems his authority to depose the civil magistrate. In substantiating his thesis, Carleton distinguishes the types of power legitimately possessed by kings and bishops while incisively critiquing that claimed by the Pope. Specifically, Carleton's discusses apostolic succession in chapter IV of the work where he contends that external, coercive power did not exist in the Church during the period in which there were no Christian magistrates. Rather, the only power that the Church possessed was that of spiritual jurisdiction, which did not in any way lead to coercive authority. Even the Church's corrective power of excommunication, Carleton maintains, was not coercive. "Coactive" authority, by divine appointment, has, and always will be the sole property of princes. Carleton describes the nature of ecclesiastical authority thus:

> Concerning the jurisdiction which Christ left to his Church, let all the Scriptures be searched, and there will nothing be found of external jurisdiction consisting in power coactive: but all that Christ left was partly, yea principally, inward and spiritual power, partly external for establishing doctrines of faith and good order in the Church, by Councils, determinations, judicature, spiritual censures, excommunication: deposing and dispatching of the disobedient, so far as the Church could proceed without coactive power. For by this spiritual power without coaction, the Church was called, faith was planted, devils were subdued, the nations were taken out of the power of darkness, the world was reduced to the obedience of Christ; by this

---

[20] In 1606, one year after the Gunpowder Plot, the Oath of Allegiance was required of the subjects of James I. A particularly controversial feature of this oath was the clause denying the papal deposing power: "Also I do swear that notwithstanding any sentence of excommunication or deprivation I will bear allegiance and true faith to his Majesty &c. &c. And I do further swear that I do from my heart abhor, detest, and abjure, as impious and heretical this damnable doctrine and position,– that princes which be excommunicated by the pope may be deposed or murdered by their subjects or by any other whatsoever. And I do believe that the pope has no power to absolve me from this oath. I do swear according to the plain and common sense, and understanding of the same words, &c." See W.B. Patterson, *James VI and I the Reunion of Christendom* (Cambridge: Cambridge University Press, 1997), 79; Milton, *Prelate as Pastor*, 28–29.

power the Church was governed for three hundred years together without any coactive jurisdiction.[21]

According to Scripture, the authority which Christ committed to the Church, both in its inward and external aspects, being mainly spiritual, served to define doctrine and maintain order, both of which are mutually indispensable for the well-being of the Church. The Church exercised this spiritual authority through its external institutions chiefly by means of excommunication and deposition of those whose teachings and lives would undermine the truth which it possessed. By faithful employment of this authority, apart from any coercive element, the Church won much of the world to the rule of Christ. Having established the primarily spiritual nature of the Church's jurisdiction, Carleton then transitions to the subject of apostolic authority.

Carleton commences his discourse on apostolic authority with an explanation of its origins: "The jurisdiction which the Apostles practiced was partly from the commission of Christ, spiritual: partly from the law of Nature, and from the example of that government which was established in the Church of the Jews."[22] Although emphasizing the spiritual nature of this authority as it is from Christ, Carleton alleges the apostles to have derived aspects of it from natural law and the governmental structure of the synagogue with which the apostles would have been quite familiar since they were Jews. Afterwards, Carleton observes apostolic authority to have extended to two areas of ecclesiastical jurisdiction: "the government of the whole ministery," and "that of the whole Church." "Government of the whole ministery," or authority over the clergy, consisted of three powers, the first of which was the power to ordain ministers. The authority to which Carleton appeals in establishing this aspect of apostolic authority is the New Testament, beginning with the Acts of the Apostles. Specifically, he references Acts 14:23 which reports, he observes, that when Paul and Barnabas called upon the churches in Laconia, Lystra, and Derbe, "They ordained Elders in every Church." Carleton understands the elders in this passage to be "pastors" and "preachers" whose purpose was "to preserve the Doctrine

---

[21] George Carleton, *Jurisdiction Regall, Episcopall, Papall* (London, 1610), reprint (Amsterdam & New York: Da Capo Press, 1968), 39.

[22] Carleton, *Jurisdiction*, 40.

continually which the Apostles once planted."[23] Notably in these comments on the passage, Carleton highlights the purpose of the apostles' act of ordination: to preserve the integrity of their doctrine within the Church.

Carleton further maintains that the apostles committed the authority to ordain to "them that succeeded them in the government of the Church." This fact, Carleton contends, occurs in Titus 1:5 which says: "For this cause I left thee in Crete, that thou shouldest redress the things that remain, and ordain elders in every city, as I have appointed thee." Also on the basis of this passage, Carleton asserts that ordination is to occur in the place where the minister is to serve.[24]

"Government of the whole ministery" secondly consisted of the authority to direct ministers to preach and teach the Word accurately and truthfully while conscientiously avoiding error. "The Apostles had also in themselves, and left to their successors, power and jurisdiction to command those Pastors which thus they had ordained, to preach the truth without mixture of false doctrines."[25] Not only did apostolic authority entail ordination for the preservation of true doctrine, but also the power to order those whom they ordain to maintain the same by preaching it correctly, being careful to present God's Word untainted with heresy. Attendant to this power is the responsibility to supervise ministers in their faithful proclamation of the Word. Carleton cites as the biblical warrant for this authority 1 Timothy 1:3, noting that Paul, having power himself by virtue of his apostolic office, confers it upon Timothy: "As I besought thee to abide still in Ephesus, when I departed to Macedonia, soe do, that thou maist command some that they teach no other doctrine."[26] In appealing to this verse, Carleton stresses the fact of an apostle investing this authority in a successor. St. Paul bestows this power on Timothy who will use it in his stead for the preservation of the truth.

The apostolic powers of ordination and command are permanent; therefore, their continued exercise by those appointed by the apostles to preserve true doctrine is also perpetual.

---

[23] Carleton, *Jurisdiction*, 40.

[24] Carleton, *Jurisdiction*, 40.

[25] Carleton, *Jurisdiction*, 40.

[26] Carleton, *Jurisdiction*, 40.

> These were the principal parts of jurisdiction which the
> Apostles left to their successors, to continue in the Church
> for ever. For the end of this government is perpetuall, as
> to ordaine Preachers, and to see that they so ordained,
> should teach the truth without heresy. It followeth certain-
> ly that such governors as the Apostles themselves ordained
> in the Church for these perpetual uses, are to remain per-
> petual governors in the Church.[27]

Since these elements of apostolic authority and the purpose for which they
are ordained are to remain in the Church, it would stand to reason that the
office which the apostles established for continued exercise of these powers
to maintain truth would also endure. "Thus was the government of Bishops
placed by the Apostles, to stand and continue till the end of the world, because the Apostles placed such for the ordination of ministers, and the
preservation of true Doctrines." Most likely anticipating objections by
Presbyterians, Carleton contends that the offices held by Timothy and Titus
were not extraordinary on the basis that the ends that these positions
served, ordination and the protection of the truth from heresy, were "neither extraordinary nor temporary, but ordinary and perpetuall."[28] In other
words, since the need to ordain ministers and preserve the truth would per-
sist within the Church, so the divinely appointed means of meeting them
would also remain.

Again emphasizing the importance of guarding the truth against heresy, Carleton comes to the third power of "government of the whole ministery," which logically flows from the second, to refute heresy. Carleton ex-
tracts this third aspect of ministerial governance from Titus 1:11 in which
St. Paul tells Titus to silence false teachers or "to stoppe their mouthes." He
further accents the need to proactively counter heresy by calling attention to
Revelation 2:20 where Christ sternly rebukes the "Angel of the Church of
Thyatira," which Carleton understands to be the bishop of Thyatira, for
tolerating "a false Prophetesse to teach, and to deceive the people, and to
make them commit fornication, and toe eate meat sacrificed to idols."
Reading these two passages in light each other, Carleton concludes, "If Titus be commanded to put some to silence, and the other reproved for suf-
fering a false teacher to teach; then the governors of the Church have au-

---

[27] Carleton, *Jurisdiction*, 40–41.

[28] Carleton, *Jurisdiction*, 41.

thoritie and jurisdiction in these things."[29] Furthermore, he adds that while conviction by argument can arrest heresy to some extent, only jurisdiction as possessed and exercised by those charged by Christ through the apostles can extirpate it from the Church by means of lawfully constituted ecclesiastical judicatories and councils.

The second aspect of ecclesiastical jurisdiction to which apostolic authority extends is the church as a whole. Carleton observes that the apostles exercised this feature of jurisdiction through councils "for the determination of such controversies as were raised up by them that troubled the doctrines of the truth, and peace of the Church" as was the case with the Jerusalem Council in Acts 15. Again Carleton accents the need to protect truth from heresy, but this time as it pertains to the Church in general. As exemplified by the Jerusalem Council, the general council represents "greatest power or Jurisdiction of the Church"[30] because it involves "the chief parts" of the Church (i.e. bishops) coming together to render judgments on behalf of the whole. This same kind of "external jurisdiction" is exercised by regional and local bodies dealing with issues affecting those localities as a whole by the collective assembly of their chief ecclesiastical persons.

Throughout the remainder of chapter IV, Carleton refers extensively to the history of the early church and writings of the church fathers, most notably Irenaeus, to demonstrate mainly that his interpretation of Scripture regarding government by episcopacy is correct as it was the shared view of this period. Christ, through the work of the apostles, provided the means to perpetuate the ministry, ensure the preservation of the truth through accurate preaching, and refute heresy: the office of bishop. The persistent existence of the needs for an established ministry, and faithful preaching necessitate, on the basis of God's Word, the continuation of the government by bishops. This would be the doctrine of episcopacy Carleton would defend in opposition of Article #31 of the *Belgic Confession* at the Synod of Dort.

---

[29] Carleton, *Jurisdiction*, 41.

[30] Carleton, *Jurisdiction*, 41.

4. CARLETON'S DEFENSE OF *IURE DIVINO* EPISCOPACY AT THE SYNOD OF DORT

Five years after the publication of *Jurisdiction Regall, Episcopall, Papalll*, Carleton published *Directions to Know the True Church*.[31] A distillation of his larger work on the Council of Trent,[32] this short treatise argues that the Roman Catholic Church altered the Rule of Faith with its unwritten traditions.[33] In changing the Rule of Faith in this way, the Roman Church has removed itself from the true Catholic Church. By contrast, the Protestant churches, and particularly the Reformed churches, comprise this Catholic Church by virtue of the fact that they have retained the Rule of Faith in its purity. This preservation of the Rule of Faith places the Reformed churches in the line of succession from the Apostolic Church. This is because the primary mark of the true Church is its possession of the Rule of Faith. "The Church is knowen by the careful keeping of the true faith, that is, the true Church, which from the Apostles in all successions hath held the true faith: the true faith is knowen by the rule of faith: the rule is the same for all ages."[34] This rule of faith is "the Scriptures contained in the Propheticall and Apostolicall writings" as generally interpreted by the early church.[35] All particular churches, then, together make up the one Catholic Church by virtue of this faith which they profess.[36] Proceeding from this premise, Carleton identifies the fourfold unity of the Church: "The Vnitie of the Church is fourfolde: For though others make moe parts, yet all may be comprised in these foure. For the Church is one, first, by Vnitie of the Body; secondly, by the Vnitie of the Head; thirdly, by Vnitie of the Spirit; fourthly, by Vnitie of Faith. All these are necessarily required to prooue a Church holde Vnitie with the Catholicke Church."[37] Interestingly, Carleton omits episcopacy from these criteria for Catholic unity. This does not betray a contradiction on Carleton's part, who as indicated above, explicated a very strong view of *iure*

---

[31] George Carleton, *Directions to Know the True Church* (London: John Bill, 1615).

[32] George Carleton, *Consensus Ecclesiae Catholicae Contra Tridentinos* (Frankfurt: Ruland, 1613).

[33] Carleton, *Directions to Know the True Church*, Preface.

[34] Carleton, *Directions to Know the True Church*, 48–49.

[35] Carleton, *Directions to Know the True Church*, Preface.

[36] Carleton, *Directions to Know the True Church*, 4.

[37] Carleton, *Directions to Know the True Church*, 6–7.

divino episcopacy. Rather it would seem that he is assuming a distinction articulated by divines such as Robert Sanderson (1587–1663), William Twisse (1578–1646), and John Prideaux (1578–1650) during the Sabbatarian controversies in the 1630s. Sanderson particularly distinguished two senses of *iure divino* which he applied both to the Sabbath and episcopacy. The first entails those things that are by divine right as they are enjoined by God's explicit ordinance and command, or deduced from the preponderance of passages on a given subject.[38] The second encompasses matters inferred from the Scriptures by human reason "as a thing most convenient to be observed by all such as desire unfeignedly to order their ways according to God's will."[39] While the things that are *iure divino* in the first sense must be absolutely observed, those things *iure divino* in the second sense are "such as 'every Particular Church, but much more the Universal, hath a power to alter in the case of necessity.'"[40] However, Sanderson continues, "the exercise of that power is so limited to extraordinary cases, that it may not be safe for her at all to exercise it; unless it be for the avoiding of mighty inconveniences, not otherwise to be avoided."[41] When comparing Carleton's exposition of the episcopal office in *Jurisdiction Regall, Episcopall, Papall* to the criteria for Catholic unity given above, it seems likely that Carleton views *jure divino* episcopacy in this second sense. Approaching church government in this manner would a few years later enable Carleton on the one hand justify his as well as the other members of the British delegation's participation in the Synod of Dort, while at the same time strongly defending episcopacy at the Synod, believing that abandoning this biblical institution would be harmful to the continental Reformed churches. Carleton's own statements regarding his stance at the Synod appear to confirm this position.

In his address before the States General at The Hague, Carleton vividly describes the harm false doctrine can cause the Church if tolerated due to improperly managed ecclesiastical affairs:

---

[38] Milton, *Catholic and Reformed: The Roman and Protestant Churches in English Protestant Thought, 1600–1640* (Cambridge: CUP, 2002), 459.

[39] Milton, *Catholic and Reformed*, 459. See also, Robert Sanderson, *The Works of Robert Sanderson*, ed. William Jacobson (Oxford: Oxford University Press, 1854), 5:12.

[40] Milton, *Catholic and Reformed*, 459. See also Sanderson, *Works*, 5:14.

[41] Milton, *Catholic and Reformed*, 459.

That by iarring of Churchmen, the edification of the Church may be hindered, that the consciences of the multitude be troubled, that wavering and unstable soules be carried about with every winde of Doctrine, that the contempt of the Minister bring with it a contempt of his Doctrine; till at length these Cockatrice egs bring forth the Basiliske, even open Impiety and Atheisme. If Church-affaires be ill managed, all sorts of men, the people, the Priest, yea you your selves shall bee accountable unto Christ for it.[42]

In this oration, Carleton highlights a theme which occupies a central place in his *Jurisdiction Regall, Episcopall, Papall*: the necessity of the Church through its judicatory apparatus to remove heresy. He attributes the cause of heresy and its resulting damage to "churchmen," or ministers who are otherwise charged with preaching and teaching the truth. The implication conveyed by this observation coupled with the admonition concerning mismanaged ecclesiastical affairs is apparent: the improper ordering of the continental Reformed polity has encouraged Arminius and the Remonstrants to plague the Church with what he understood as revived Pelagianism.[43]

Throughout 1619, the Synod of Dort dealt with questions regarding polity. To this effect, Bishop Carleton wrote Dudley Carleton concerning the discussion of the Church of England's practice to read the *Homilies* and the Church's consecration of bishops and ministers.[44] Although the *Acta* of the Synod provide some information about the exchanges pertaining to episcopacy in relation to classical or Presbyterian polity, most of our knowledge with respect to Carleton's specific defense of *iure divino* episcopacy comes from the *Joynt Attestation* (Of which Carleton most likely was at

---

[42] George Carleton, *An Oration made at the Hage before the Prince of Orange, and the Assembly of the High and Mighty Lords, the States Generall of the United Provices: By the Reverend Father in God, the Lord Bishop of Landaff, one of the Commissioners send by the Kings most Excellent Majesty to the Synod of Dort* (London: Ralph Roundwaith, 1619), 4; See also Milton, *The British Delegation*, 119.

[43] Carleton emphatically makes this point in his response to Montagu in the *Examination*. See Carleton, *An Examination*, 13, 24, 18, 30, 34–36, 43, 47, 64, 70, 79, 80, 106. Moreover, Carleton adamantly rejected the argument that Arminianism was not Pelagianism, arguing that Pelagius himself was inconsistent (30–31). Furthermore, he contended that the "Arminian heresie" went farther than Pelagius (138). See also, Milton, *Catholic and Reformed*, 417.

[44] See George Carleton's letter to Dudley Carleton dated January 24, 1619 in Milton, *The British Delegation*, 198.

least the principal author) appended to the *Examination* and Carleton's own account given in his *Testimonie*.[45]

The *Joynt Attestation* testifies that when the Synod considered the *Belgic Confession*, the British delegation "gave our approbation of the substance of the doctrinall Articles, with advice touching some incommodious phrases; and withal (contrary to the expectation of the whole Synode) wee added expresse exception against the suppressed Articles, with some touch also of Argument against them." This argument "was principally performed by him [i.e. Carleton], who for prioritie of age, place, and dignitie it best became, and from whose person, and gravitie it might be the better taken by the *Civill Deputees of the States* there present."[46]

The argument that follows, as given by Carleton, maintains that Christ never instituted a parity of ministers, but rather ordained twelve apostles and seventy disciples. Moreover, the "authoritie of the twelve was above the other."[47] The Church thus preserved this order left by the Savior. The office of apostle was extraordinary, and therefore possessed extraordinary authority. However, the apostles possessed ordinary authority which extended to the government of the ministry and the whole Church. When the apostolic office ceased, the ordinary authority (i.e. the authority to maintain order) attendant with it transferred to the bishops whom the apostles appointed. At this point Carleton stresses the purpose of the bishops' apostolic authority in exactly the same manner as in *Jurisdiction Regall, Episcopall, Papall*: to ordaine Ministers, and to see that they who were so ordained should preach no other doctrine."[48] Furthermore, arguing for different orders within the ministry, Carleton contends that present-day ministers are successors of the seventy disciples who, in rank, were inferior to the apostles whose successors are the bishops. Carleton concludes his address by demonstrating the manner in which the early church scrupulously maintained this biblical, apostolic order of church government.

---

[45] George Carleton, *Testimonie Concerning the Presbyterian Discipline in The Low Countries and Episcopall Government Here in England, Wherein is Briefly Discovered the Novelty of the One, and Antiquity of the Other, With a Short Taste of the Inconveniences that Attend the New Platform Where That is Set Up in the Roome of the Old Primitive Government* (London: Nath. Butter, 1642).

[46] Carleton, et al, *Joynt Attestation*, 10, appended to *An Examination*.

[47] Carleton, et al. *Joynt Attestation*, 10.

[48] Carleton, et al. *Joynt Attestation*, 11.

The *Joynt Attestation* concludes the account by reporting what its authors consider the reception of Carleton's argument by the other delegates. "To this our exception and allegations not one word was answered by any of the Synodiques either Strangers or Provincialls."[49] The delegates allegedly respond with astounding silence from which the authors of the *Joynt Attestation* infer their consent or at the least, sympathy with Carleton's protest. Even though it is somewhat a stretch to declare such silence as indicative of consent, yet this interpretation of events seems to have, for a short time perhaps, accomplished the authors' polemical purpose of portraying their own participation in the Synod as the British delegation as a spirited, biblical defense of their Church.

Carleton's *Testimonie Concerning the Presbyterian Discipline in The Low Countries and Episcopall Government Here in England* is his own account of his public dissent before the Synod of Dort regarding the *Belgic Confession*'s assertion of the parity of ministers. Carleton reports, "That whereas in the Confession there was inserted a strange conceit of the parity of Ministers to be instituted by Christ ... I declared our dissent utterly in that point; I shewed that by Christ a Parity was never instituted in the Church.[50] The bishop then proceeds to rehearse his argument for *iure divino* episcopacy as described in the *Joynt Attestation*.

Carleton's *Testimonie* differs from the *Joynt Attestation*, however, in his narrative of the delegates' response to his protest. Although the bishop reports, as did the *Joynt Attestation*, the continental delegates to have reacted with silence, thereby allegedly showing their consent, Carleton then relays his comments to them following this response. He plainly attributed the crisis caused by Arminius and the Remonstrants to the continental church's abandonment of the true, biblical form of church government as the divinely appointed bulwark against heresy. "I told them that the cause of all their troubles was this, that they had no Bishops amongst them, who by their authority might represse turbulent spirits that broached novelties." Carleton then immediately identifies the phenomenon which the absence of episcopal authority has fostered: "Every man had liberty to speak or write what he list, and as long as there were no Ecclesiasticall men in authority to represse and censure such contentious spirits, their Church could never be without

---

[49] Carleton, et al. *Joynt Attestation*, 11.

[50] Carleton, *Testimonie*, 1–2.

trouble."[51] The implication of these remarks regarding the present state of the continental Reformed churches rejecting episcopacy is unambiguous: classical or Presbyterian government, with its parity of all ministers, effectively democratizes the clergy, thus equalizing all theological discourse, and therefore allowing for any doctrine to circulate throughout the Church to its peril. In Carleton's estimation, this state of affairs will continue as long as the churches in the Netherlands remain disorderly in this way.

Yet, although he does not articulate it, Carleton nevertheless appears to be applying the allegedly assumed distinction between two senses of *jure divino*, mostly likely relating the second one to the ecclesiastical situation in the Netherlands. As earlier observed, Carleton, before the Synod, in objection to the parity of ministers, robustly defended a *jure divino* view of episcopacy. However, he grants the churches in the Netherlands liberty to alter this order in the light of their unique circumstances, which, according to the bishop, they related to him. "Their answer was, that they did much honor and reverenced the good order and discipline of the Church of England, and with all their hearts would be glad to have it established amongst them; but could not be hoped for in their State. Their hope was, that seeing they could not do what they desired, God would be mercifull to them if they did what they could."[52] Debatable as it may be, Carleton claims that the other delegates told him that not only did they highly regard the government of the Church of England, but they would prefer it for their church, except that their civil magistrates will not allow it. For this reason, they have to make do with the order that they have. To this answer Carleton responds with sympathy: "I thinke [it] is enough to excuse them, that they doe not openly aime at an Anarchie, and popular confusion. The truth is, they groan under that burden, and would be eased if they could."[53] Extenuating circumstances have compelled the churches in the Netherlands to adopt an order other than that appointed by Christ in his Word. In keeping with the second sense of *jure divino*, they have this liberty, but exercising it in this regard has, and continues to be injurious to them. For where there is no bishop, there is no order; where there is no order, chaos prevails; where chaos reigns, heresy thrives.

---

[51] Carleton, *Testimonie*, 3.

[52] Carleton, *Testmonie*, 3–4.

[53] Carleton, *Testimonie*, 4.

5. CONCLUSION

George Carleton was a Reformed bishop. As such, he held unreservedly to the doctrine of *sola Scriptura* as well as a generally Reformed understanding of grace. For the bishop of Llandaff and Chichester, Scripture provided not only the substance of orthodox doctrine, but also the means of preserving it and preventing its perversion. Christ himself commissioned the apostles to guard the deposit of truth he committed to them, investing them with authority over the ministry that they would appoint and the Church as a whole. To meet what would be the continuous need of preserving the truth within the Church, the apostles conferred their ordinary authority upon their successors, the bishops who would ordain ministers, command those ministers to preach the truth faithfully unmixed with error, and finally, to refute heretics. Carleton believed this order to be the divinely ordained, and hence biblical means of protecting truth from heresy. Therefore, he believed and argued strongly for *iure divino* episcopacy. This concern to protect truth from heresy occupied a central position in Carleton's doctrine of the episcopal office. Repeatedly throughout his works and recorded speeches, he spoke of the necessity of preserving truth by means of proper order, which was government by bishops who received apostolic power to supervise preaching and teaching as ordained by Christ. The absence of this order, even notwithstanding the two senses of *jure divino*, proved injurious to the Church as it allowed for the unrestrained movement of heresy therein. This, for Carleton, was the serious flaw of classical or Presbyterian polity with its insistence on the parity of all ministers as it removed the divinely ordained, and hence, biblical structure of doctrinal authority, thereby allowing for any minister's opinion to sway entire sectors of the Church. This government of episcopacy was what Carleton defended at the Synod of Dort, believing that the neglect of this biblical polity by the Reformed churches of the Netherlands made possible the revival of ancient heresy in the form of Arminius and the Remonstrants. Thus, for this English bishop and his other colleagues who served in the British delegation to Dort, to be biblical meant to be fully apostolic, which in turn meant using the apostles' authority to ensure that the Church was always reforming.

BIBLIOGRAPHY

Bancroft, Richard. *A Survey of the Pretended Discipline*. London, 1593.

Carleton, George. *An Examination of Those Things Wherein the Author of the Late Appeale Holdeth the Doctrines of the Pelagians and Arminians to be the Doctrines of the Church of England, Whereunto Also There is Annexed a Joynt Attestation Avowing that the Discipline of the Church of England Was Not Impugned By the Synod of Dort*. London: Michael Sparkes, 1626.

———. *Consensus Ecclesiae Catholicae Contra Tridentinos*. Frankfurt: Ruland, 1613.

———. *Directions to Know the True Church*. London: John Bill, 1615.

———. *Jurisdiction Regall, Episcopall, Papall*. London, 1610. Reprint, Amsterdam & New York: Da Capo Press, 1968.

———. *An Oration made at the Hage before the Prince of Orange, and the Assembly of the High and Mighty Lords, the States Generall of the United Provices: By the Reverend Father in God, the Lord Bishop of Landaff, one of the Commissioners send by the Kings most Excellent Majesty to the Synod of Dort*. London: Ralph Roundwaith, 1619.

———. *Testimonie Concerning the Presbyterian Discipline in The Low Countries and Episcopall Government Here in England, Wherein is Briefly Discovered the Novelty of the One, and Antiquity of the Other, With a Short Taste of the Inconveniences that Attend the New Platform Where That is Set Up in the Roome of the Old Primitive Government*. London: Nath. Butter, 1642.

———. *Vita Bernardi Gilpini, apud Anglos Aquilonares*. London, 1628. *Life of Bernard Gilpin, With the Sermon Preached Before Edward VI in 1552*. London, 1636.

Collinson, Patrick. *Richard Bancroft and Elizabethan Anti-Puritanism*. Cambridge: Cambrdige University Press, 2013.

Fincham, Kenneth, ed. *The Early Stuart Church, 1603–1642*. Stanford, CA: Stanford University Press, 1993.

————. *Prelate as Pastor: The Episcopate of James I.* Oxford: Clarendon Press, 1990.

Groenveld, Simon, and Michael J. Wintle, eds. *The Exchange of Ideas: Religion, Scholarship, and Art in Anglo-Dutch Relations in the Seventeenth Century.* Zutphen: Walburg Institut, 1994.

Jewel, John. *Apology of the Church of England*, translated by Ann Bacon, and edited by John Booty. New York: Church Publishing, 2002.

Milton, Anthony. *The British Delegation to the Synod of Dort.* Woodbridge, Suffolk, UK: Boydell, 2005.

————. *Catholic and Reformed: The Roman and Protestant Churches in English Protestant Thought, 1600–1640.* Cambridge: CUP, 2002.

Montagu, Richard. *Appello Caesarem.* London: H.L. for Matthew Lownes.

Oberman, Heiko. "*Quo Vadis, Petre?* Tradition from Irenaeus to *Humani Generis.*" In *Dawn of the Reformation: Essays in Late Medieval and Early Reformation Thought*, 269–96. Grand Rapids: Eerdmans, 1992.

Patterson, W.B. *James VI and I the Reunion of Christendom.* Cambridge: Cambridge University Press, 1997.

Sutcliffe, Matthew. *A Treatise of Ecclesiastical Discipline.* London, 1591.

Van Deursen, Arie Theodorus. "England and the Synod of Dort." In *The Exchange of Ideas: Religion, Scholarship, and Art in Anglo-Dutch Relations in the Seventeenth Century*, edited by Simon Groenveld and Michael J. Wintle. Zutphen: Walburg Institut, 1994.

V:

CONFESSIONAL ORTHODOXY
AND HYPOTHETICAL UNIVERSALISM:
ANOTHER LOOK AT THE WESTMINSTER CONFESSION
OF FAITH

Michael Lynch, Calvin Theological Seminary

SCHOLARS and theologians have long disputed the relationship of hypothetical universalism to the Westminster Confession of Faith (hereafter, WCF).[1] As far back as 1658, Richard Baxter, in defense of his own ortho-

---

[1] Those arguing for the inclusion of hypothetical universalism in Westminsterian orthodoxy include: Philip Schaff, *The Creeds of Christendom*, 3 vols. (Grand Rapids: Baker, 1990), 1:770–73; A. F. Mitchell, John Struthers, eds., *Minutes of the Sessions of the Westminster Assembly of Divines* (Edinburgh: William Blackwood and Sons, 1974), lv–lxi; Gatiss, "A Deceptive Clarity? Particular Redemption in the Westminster Standards," *Reformed Theological Review* 69, no. 3 (2010), 180–96; Richard A. Muller, "Diversity in the Reformed Tradition: A Historiographical Introduction," in *Drawn into Controversie: Reformed Theological Diversity and Debates Within Seventeenth-Century British Puritanism*, ed. Mark Jones and Michael A. Haykin (Göttingen: Vandenhoeck & Ruprecht, 2011), 23–25; Jonathan D. Moore, "The Extent of the Atonement: English Hypothetical Universalism versus Particular Redemption," in *Drawn into Controversie*, 148ff.

Those arguing that HU is excluded from Westminsterian orthodoxy include: William Cunningham, *Historical Theology: A Review of the principal doctrinal Discussions in the Christian Church since the Apostolic Age*, 2 vols. (Edinburgh: T & T Clark, 1863), 2:326–31; A. Craig Troxel, "Amyraut 'at' the Assembly: The Westminster Confession of Faith and the Extent of the Atonement," *Presbyterion* 22, no. 1 (1996): 43–55; Robert Letham, *The Westminster Assembly: Reading its Theology in Historical Context* (Phillipsburg, NJ: Presbyterian and Reformed, 2009), 176–82. It should be noted

---

doxy, claimed that WCF 8.5 did not, in fact, preclude his form of hypothetical universalism. He writes: "And I have spoken with an eminent Divine, yet living, that was of the [Westminster] Assembly, who assured me that they purposely avoided determining that Controversie, and some of them profest themselves for the middle way of Universal Redemption."[2] In this paper, I will defend Baxter's claim that the wording adopted by the Westminster Divines did not intend to exclude (at the very least) the form of English hypothetical universalism espoused by those such as Bishop John Davenant and appealed to by the Westminster Divine Edmund Calamy.[3]

This paper will be divided into three parts. First, I will give an exposition of what appears to be the strongest case against my thesis proffered by William Cunningham, the nineteenth century Scottish Presbyterian theologian. Second, a brief overview of Davenantian hypothetical universalism will be in order, especially in light of the misunderstandings which often attend expositions of his hypothetical universalism. In the final section, after having looked at Cunningham's case and given a brief exposition of Davenantian hypothetical universalism, I will give an argument for my own reading of the WCF as it relates to our question: Does the WCF's wording exclude *all* forms of hypothetical universalism, including, particularly, Davenant's version?

1. WILLIAM CUNNINGHAM'S CASE

Simultaneous with the nineteenth century controversies among American Presbyterians and Scottish Presbyterians over the extent of Christ's satisfaction were discussions about what the WCF excludes, and whether it allows for any hypothetical universalist understanding of the atoning work of

---

that Letham seems to have subsequently argued that HU is allowed within Westminsterian language during his testimony at Peter Leithart's trial in the PCA's Presbytery of the Pacific Northwest; Sebastian Rehnman, "A Particular Defense of Particularism," *JRT* 6 (2012): 24–34.

[2] Richard Baxter, *Certain Disputations of Right to Sacraments and the True Nature of Visible Christianity, Defending them against several sorts of Opponents, especially against the second assault by that Pious, Reverend and Dear Brother Mr. Thomas Blake* (London: William DuGard, 1657), B4ᵛ.

[3] Chad Van Dixhoorn, ed., *The Minutes and Papers of the Westminster Assembly 1643–1652*, 5 vols. (Oxford: Oxford University Press, 2012), 3:692: "I am farre from universall Redemption in the Arminian sence, but that that I hould is in the sence of our devines in the sinod of Dort."

Christ.[4] This is not mere coincidence. Those who held to what we might call a nineteenth-century version of hypothetical universalism, such as James Richards in America and John Brown in Scotland, argued that their theological position was consonant with the language of Westminster or Reformed theology more generally.[5] On the other side, certain nineteenth century theologians such as Cunningham and Benjamin Morgan Palmer were resolute in their belief that the confession excluded all forms of universal redemption.[6]

---

[4] On the controversy in Scotland, see: Ian Hamilton, *The Erosion of Calvinist Orthodoxy: Drifting from the Truth in confessional Scottish Churches* (Ross-shire, Scotland: Mentor, 2010), 43–81. While Ian Hamilton's concluding interpretation of the debate in Scotland is dubious, his brief history is helpful. For a more complete survey of the controversy, see Andrew Robertson, *History of the Atonement Controversy, in Connexion with the Secession Church, From its Origin to the Present Time* (Edinburgh: William Oliphant and Sons, 1846). On the New School/Old School debate see George Marsden, *The Evangelical Mind and the New School Presbyterian Experience: A Case Study of Thought and Theology in Nineteenth-Century America* (New Haven: Yale, 1970). Cf. Samuel J. Baird, *A History of the New School, and of the Questions Involved in the Disruption of the Presbyterian Church in 1838* (Philadelphia: Claxton, Remsen & Haffelfinger, 1868); Charles Hodge, *The Reunion of the Old and New- School Presbyterian Churches* (repr.; New York: Charles Scribner & Co., 1867); Lewis Cheeseman, *Differences Between Old and New School Presbyterians* (Rochester: Erastus Darrow, 1848); S. Donald Fortson, *The Presbyterian Creed: A Confessional Tradition in America, 1729–1870* (Milton Keyes: Paternoster, 2008); Leo P. Hirrel, *Children of Wrath: New School Calvinism and Antebellum Reform* (Lexington: The University of Kentucky Press, 1998), esp. 7–89. Fortson, especially, gives a nice theological overview of the period. J. J. Janeway, *Letters on the Atonement: in which a Contrast is Instituted Between the Doctrine of the Old and of the New School; or Between the Definite and Indefinite Scheme, on this Important Subject* (Philadelphia: A. Finlay, 1827) provides an Old School perspective on the theological issues at play.

[5] James Richards, *The Extent of the Atonement* (Philadelphia: Presbyterian Board of Publication, 1838) [republished in James Richards, *Lectures on Mental Philosophy and Theology* (New York: M. W. Dodd, 1846), 302–27]. Cf. Charles Hodge, "Life and Writings of Dr. Richards," *The Biblical Repertory and Princeton Review* 18, no. 4 (1846): 589–600, 596–97; John Brown, *Opinions on Faith, Divine Influence, Human Inability, the Design and Effect of the Death of Christ, Assurance and the Sonship of Christ*, 2d ed. (Edinburgh: William Oliphant and Son, 1841), 31–38, 54–80, esp., 72–75.

[6] B. M. Palmer, "The Proposed Plan of Union Between the General Assembly in the Confederate States of America and the United Synod of the South," *Southern Presbyterian Review* 16 (1866): 264–307, 296–304. Note that R. L. Dabney argued that the Confession of Faith allowed for his view of the atonement which extended the substitution of Christ and the guilt-bearing of sins to the non-elect. See R. L. Dabney, "Dr. Dabney for the Plan of Union," *Southern Presbyterian* (Columbia, SC), 3 December 1863, New Series, Vol. IV, No. 4: Columns 1–6.

Due to space restraints, this essay will not attempt to give a comprehensive survey of the various nineteenth-century arguments garnered by each side; nor will it review all the pertinent twentieth and twenty-first-century literature. Rather, a survey of Cunningham's argument should cover most of the concerns expressed against my thesis, including the more recent arguments offered by scholars such as Craig Troxel and Sebastian Rehnman. By the conclusion of the essay, I hope to have addressed the *major* lines of argument advanced by those who are not sympathetic to my thesis.

Cunningham's case for exclusion begins by noting a few passages of the WCF which, in his judgment, bear directly on the question of the extent of the atonement vis-a-vis the universal redemption position found among Reformed theologians (whom he terms "Calvinists"). The first passage is from WCF 3.6 on God's Eternal Decree which reads:

> Wherefore, they who are elected, being fallen in Adam, are redeemed by Christ, are effectually called unto faith in Christ by His Spirit working in due season, are justified, adopted, sanctified, and kept by His power, through faith, unto salvation. Neither are any other redeemed by Christ, effectually called, justified, adopted, sanctified, and saved, but the elect only.

Cunningham asks two questions of this passage. First, he asks, does the term "redemption" denote only impetration (a term he glosses as "purchase of pardon and reconciliation") or, on the other hand, does "redemption" denote *both* the ideas of impetration and application.[7] If the former is descriptive of impetration only, then he believes that this passage very clearly teaches "definite or limited atonement" comprehending as the objects of impetration only the elect.[8] On the other hand, if the term redemption is to be understood in the latter sense, as including both the idea of impetration and application, then clearly (and rightly in my judgment), he confesses that any advocate of universal redemption, be it an Arminian, an Amyraldian, or a hypothetical universalist, could affirm the statement that only "the elect" are "redeemed" in the sense of having redemption applied to them alone. He concludes that the best reading of this passage, not surprisingly, is to see

---

[7] Cunningham, *Historical Theology*, 2:326.

[8] Cunningham, *Historical Theology*, 2:326.

the word 'redemption' as denoting impetration alone and so he interprets redemption as one of the many benefits of our salvation alongside other benefits such as justification and sanctification. In summary, we might paraphrase his reading of the passage in this way: "They who are elected are not only redeemed or have the saving benefits purchased for them by Christ, but are also effectually called, justified, etc."

The second question Cunningham asks touches on the last sentence of WCF 3.6 which reads: "Neither are any other redeemed by Christ, effectually called, justified, adopted, sanctified, and saved, but the elect only." He observes that there are two ways to read the modifying phrase, "but the elect only."[9] That phrase can either modify every benefit singly and separately, or it can modify the whole of the sentence whereby the various saving benefits would be taken as a totality. The first reading would then be something like this: "Neither are any other redeemed by Christ but the elect; neither are any other effectually called but the elect, etc." The other way one could read the sentence is to simply claim that only the elect are those who have *all* of the aforementioned benefits, *viz.* being redeemed, called, justified, adopted, sanctified and saved." He, again, not surprisingly, rejects the latter reading and opts for the former reading which once again limits redemption (already argued as denoting impetration alone) to the elect.

Cunningham's case concludes with an argument from two other places in the WCF which, he thinks, bear directly on the exclusion of hypothetical universalism. First, WCF 8.5, which says: "The Lord Jesus, by His perfect obedience, and sacrifice of Himself, which He through the eternal Spirit, once offered up unto God, has fully satisfied the justice of His Father; and purchased, not only reconciliation, but an everlasting inheritance in the kingdom of heaven, for those whom the Father has given unto Him." The second text comes from 8.8: "To all those for whom Christ has purchased redemption, He does certainly and effectually apply and communicate the same; making intercession for them, and revealing unto them, in and by the word, the mysteries of salvation." It is in this second text especially that he believes the state of the question is contained and "was intended to contain."[10] To get at how it is that he concludes that WCF 8.8 directly addresses the state of the question in the controversy among those

---

[9] Cunningham, *Historical Theology*, 2:327.

[10] Cunningham, *Historical Theology*, 2:328.

advocates of universal redemption and those arguing for what he calls definite atonement, we need to make a couple observations.

First, Cunningham does not seem to think that the Reformed versions of universal redemption substantially differ from the Arminian versions.[11] Cunningham claims:

> [The state of the question] is to be explained by a reference to the mode of conducting this controversy, between the Calvinists and Arminians, about the time of the Synod of Dort, and also to the mode of conducting the controversy excited in France by Cameron, and afterwards carried on by Amyraldus in France and Holland, and by Baxter in England. The fundamental position of all who had advocated the doctrine of atonement against the Socinians, but had also maintained that it was universal or unlimited, was—that Christ, by His sufferings and death, purchased pardon and reconciliation for all men, without distinction or exception; but that these blessings are applied or communicated to, and, of course, are actually enjoyed by, those only who came, from whatever cause, to repent and believe.[12]

According to Cunningham, there is common ground among all advocates of universal redemption—whether they be Calvinistic or Arminian—and this common ground is found in the belief that "Christ ... purchased pardon and reconciliation for all men, without distinction or exception." He consistently represents all the advocates of universal redemption as teaching that the death of Christ "[purchased] for all men the pardon of their sins and reconciliation with God" and "that these blessings are impetrated for many to whom they are never applied." Put in scholastic language, according to Cunningham, all advocates of universal redemption not only distinguish between impetration and application, but also deny the co-extensiveness of the two ideas.[13] In his exposition of all forms of universal

---

[11] Note, e.g., the curious citation of Davenant in Cunningham, *Historical Theology*, 2:321. Cf. William Cunningham, *The Reformers and the Theology of the Reformation*, 2d ed. (Edinburgh: T. and T. Clark, 1866), 205.

[12] Cunningham, *Historical Theology*, 2:328.

[13] This is in marked contrast to my reading of English hypothetical universalism, along with Gatiss and Fesko's reading of English hypothetical universalism.

redemption, God, in Christ, impetrated *for all* remission of sins and reconciliation, on the one hand; while, on the other hand, God applies the death of Christ to the elect (or those who believe) alone. Cunningham sees such theology as directly contrary to the WCF which maintains that impetration and application are co-extensive. Again, note the language of WCF 8.8: "To all those for whom Christ has purchased redemption, He does certainly and effectually apply and communicate the same." Thus, we can summarize his basic reading of the WCF thus: redemption in these two chapters of the WCF refers particularly to the impetration of the saving benefits of redemption, especially remission of sins and reconciliation; and these saving benefits are impetrated, purchased, or merited for the elect alone. This reading of the WCF is a sound interpretation. What is not sound is his exposition of all forms of universal redemption. While Davenant does hold to a form of universal redemption, he unambiguously denies that Christ obtained or impetrated remission or reconciliation for any sinners except the elect. It is Davenant's form of universal redemption to which we now turn.

2. JOHN DAVENANT'S HYPOTHETICAL UNIVERSALISM

Having given our attention to Cunningham, we are now in a position to explore John Davenant's hypothetical universalism, insofar as his exposition impacts the questions raised by Cunningham. For example, does Davenant affirm or deny a universal impetration of sins and reconciliation? Further, does he affirm or deny that Christ purchased any to-be-applied saving benefits for the non-elect? Finally, would he, on Cunningham's reading of the WCF, affirm or deny the various propositions found in the WCF concerning redemption? Does his theology agree with Cunningham's interpretation of the WCF in making impetration and application coextensive? In other words, does he affirm that Christ purchased redemption (in the sense Cunningham understands it) for the elect alone? It is my contention that, yes, he would affirm such language.

It may be best to begin noting some key distinctions undergirding Davenant's hypothetical universalism. The most important distinction for his hypothetical universalism regards God's twofold intention or will with regard to what Christ would accomplish in his work of redemption. Put simply, he believes there are two ends in the accomplishment of redemption—a general end and a special end.[14] God's general end in Christ's death is to provide and ordain the blood of his Son to be a universal remedy applicable on the condition of faith and repentance for all human beings. The special end in Christ's death is the obtaining of an infallible salvation to be applied to the elect alone. Making up these two ends, we can, further highlight three critical theses or elements of his hypothetical universalism.

First, there is the element of a universal remedy.[15] Most, though not all, Reformed theologians affirmed that there was an internal sufficiency in the death of Christ such that the work of Christ would have been able to redeem a thousand worlds of infidels had God so willed.[16] Yet, many of these same theologians denied that Christ was actually offered up as a substitute or mediator for any but the elect.[17] This would be the position famously held by John Owen.[18] While the death of Christ could have been ordained to be a remedy for the sins of all, in truth, the death of Christ was only ordained to be a remedy for the sins of the elect.[19] For Davenant, this theory is untenable given both the testimony of Scripture (John 3:16; 1 John 2:2, etc.) and the logic of the gospel offer ("universal covenant"). The logic goes something like this: The gospel offer, which ministers are called to proclaim, must indiscriminately include this proposition: *God is, according to his divine justice and on account of the person and work of Jesus Christ, able to forgive any person of their sins.* For this proposition to be true, it then must be the case that God in Christ made a remedy for every person such that God is able to fulfill the antecedent condition proclaimed in the gospel—*viz.*, God is able to forgive the sins of any person. In order to claim that God in Christ made a remedy sufficient for every person, we must affirm that God

---

[14] Cf. John Davenant, A *Dissertation on the Death of Christ, as to its Extent and Special Benefits*, in *An Exposition of the Epistle of St. Paul to the Colossians*, 2 vols., trans. Josiah Allport (London: Hamilton, Adams, and Co., 1832), II:396. Cf. II:369–70.

[15] This corresponds to proposition 1 (II:340ff.) and 2 (II:401ff.) in Davenant's *Dissertation on the Death of Christ*.

[16] Cf. Canons of Dort, 2.iii.

[17] So, e.g., Johann Piscator, *Ad Conradi Vorstii, S. Theol. D. Parasceuen Responsio apologetica Johan. Piscatoris* (Herborn: 1613), I.7 [93–104]; Piscator, *Ad Conradi Vorstii, S. Theol. D. Amicam Collationem, etc.* (Herborn: 1613), LXXXVII [145–47].

[18] John Owen, *Salus Electorum, Sanguis Iesu: Or The Death of Death in the Death of Christ [...]* (London: W. W., 1648).

[19] Owen, *Death of Death*, 4.I [173].

intended that Christ make a remedy for every person. Davenant summarizes this first element:

> We therefore call Christ the Redeemer of the world, and teach that he made satisfaction for the sins not of some, but of the whole world, not because that on account of the payment of this price for the sins of the human race, all mankind individually are to be immediately delivered from captivity and death, but because by virtue of the payment of this price, all men individually may and ought to be delivered from death, and, in fact, are to be delivered according to the tenor of the evangelical covenant, that is, if they repent and believe in this Redeemer.[20]

The second element of Davenant's hypothetical universalism is his affirmation that actual remission of sins and reconciliation with God is obtained only when a sinner exercises faith and repentance.[21] He expressly denies any form of eternal justification or justification at the cross. Consequently, against certain Remonstrants, Lutherans (especially Samuel Huber), and even some Reformed theologians who apparently argued for an actual reconciliation with human beings at the cross or in eternity, he denies that the death of Christ places any *adult* in a state of grace before such a person believes and repents.[22] To be sure, he does affirm that in consideration of the death of Christ, "God is ready to grant pardon and life to all individually who humble themselves before him and believe in the Mediator," yet, *actual* reconciliation with God and *actual* remission of sins is not obtained by human beings until they believe.[23]

---

[20] Davenant, *Dissertation on the Death of Christ*, II:375.

[21] This element corresponds to proposition 3 (II:440ff.) in Davenant's *Dissertation*.

[22] On the Lutheran side of the debate, including Huber, see esp. Pareus, *Brevis Repetitio ex Verbo Dei Doctrinae Catholicae Ecclesiarum Palatinatus [...]* (Heidelberg, 1593), A3v–B1r. Cf. my lecture "Hypothetical Universalism Meets Arminianism: David Pareus's Response to the Second Remonstrant Article," ETS Annual Meeting (Atlanta, GA), 2015. Concerning the Reformed, Davenant writes (*Dissertation on the Death of Christ*, II:448): "Now as to the latter opinion [eternal justification], I do not remember to have read of any one of our people who expressly defends it. But our Thomson in his Diatribe (cap. 24, p. 92 and 99) mentions some persons who endeavour to prove that through the dignity and efficacy of the merits of Christ, the sins of the elect were pardoned from eternity."

[23] Davenant, *Dissertation on the Death of Christ*, II:442.

Davenant's denial of an actual reconciliation and remission of sins at the cross has direct bearing on the Remonstrant language of universal impetration. The Remonstrants, in the second of their five articles, explicitly affirmed "that Christ by his death has impetrated for all human beings reconciliation and remission of sin."[24] It was this particular theological affirmation in the Remonstrants' second article that Reformed theologians criticized the most regarding the extent of Christ's satisfaction. Further, some of the strongest criticism of universal impetration language can be found among some hypothetical universalists.[25] For example, the British delegation at Dort (which included Davenant) specifically renounced such language. According the British delegation's Suffrage, the third erroneous opinion of the Remonstrants was "[t]hat Christs death hath obtained [Latin: *impetrasse*] for all men, restitution into the state of grace and salvation."[26] Davenant himself in his treatise on the death of Christ takes on the universal impetration position of the Remonstrants: "[W]e do not undertake the cause of those who declare that Christ by his death obtained [Latin: *impetravisse*] remission of sins, reconciliation with God, and a state of salvation for each and every man."[27]

Finally, consider Ussher's attempt to avoid confusion regarding his hypothetical universalism. Ussher begins his second letter on universal redemption (written in response to some negative feedback he received in his first letter) stating unambiguously:

> For that Christ hath so died for all men (as [the Remonstrants] lay down in the conference of Hague) ["so that he has impetrated for each individual reconciliation with God and remission of sins,"] I hold to be untrue, being well assured, that our Saviour hath obtained at the hands of his

---

[24] Petrus Bertius, *Scripta Adversaria Collationis Hagiensis [...] De Divina Praedestione et Capitibus ei adnexis* (Brittenburg: Johannes Patius, 1615), 123: *ut per mortem crucis impetraverit reconciliationem et remissionem peccatorum omnibus hominibus.*

[25] Cf. David Pareus, "Sententia Doctoris Paraei de quinque Remonst. Articulis," in *Acta Synodi Nationalis [...]* (Leiden, 1620), part 1, 212–18.

[26] *The Collegiat Suffrage of the Divines of Great Britaine, Concerning the Five Articles Controverted in the Low Countries [...]* (London: Robert Milbourne, 1629), 61. Latin: *Suffragium Collegiale Theologorum [...]* (London: R. Young, n.d.), 37.

[27] Davenant, *Dissertation on the Death of Christ*, II:366. Latin: *illud praemonendum est, nos haud agere illorum causam qui statuunt Christum morte sua omnibus et singulis hominibus impetravisse remissionem peccatorum, reconciliationem cum Deo, et statum salutis.*

> father reconciliation, and forgiveness of sins, not for the reprobate, but elect only, and not for them neither, before they be truly regenerated, and implanted into himself.... I agree therefore thus far with Mr. Ames ... that application and impetation, in this matter we have in hand, are of equal extent.[28]

It is this final affirmation by Ussher, that application and impetration are of equal extent, wherein it seems that Davenantian hypothetical universalism is most often misunderstood. In fact, this misunderstanding is evident in Cunningham who does not give any indication that certain Reformed advocates of universal redemption deny universal impetration, nor does Cunningham note that at least some forms of hypothetical universalism, just as in his own theology, limit both impetration and application to the elect (or believers) alone.

Before looking at Davenant's third element, a brief summary of what we have covered will be helpful. The first element in his hypothetical universalism is the notion of universal redemption wherein God willed Christ to make a universal remedy for all human beings applicable for reconciliation and remission of sins on the condition of faith and repentance. This first element regards redemption *accomplished*. God in Christ accomplished this in Christ's person and work. His second element teaches that, in regard to the *application* of redemption, only believers (i.e., those who fulfill the conditions of the covenant of grace) actually receive remission of sins and reconciliation with God. We also briefly noted the caveat that according to him, this holds true only with regard to adults.

We are now in a position to look at the third element in Davenant's hypothetical universalism. Scholarship usually ignores this final element, but it plays a pivotal role in his theology and this essay's thesis.[29] As one surveys popular expositions of hypothetical universalism, one usually finds the first two elements of his hypothetical universalism—namely, universal redemption accomplished on behalf of all; and a limitation of the application of

[28] Ussher, "An Answer to Some Exceptions," in *Works*, 17 vols. (Dublin: Hodges, Smith, and Co., 1864), 12:563–64.

[29] There are exceptions, however, to this popular account of hypothetical universalism. For example, note the discussion of Davenant and English hypothetical universalism by Donald Macleod, *Christ Crucified: Understanding the Atonement* (Downers Grove, IL: IVP, 2014), 124–27, esp. 123–26.

redemption to the elect, or, more properly, to those who have believed and will believe. These elements are arguably present in Cunningham's exposition when he summarizes all forms of universal redemption (he specifically names Baxter and Amyraut among others): "that Christ, by His sufferings and death, purchased pardon and reconciliation for all men, without distinction or exception; but that these blessings are applied or communicated to, and, of course, are actually enjoyed by, those only who came, from whatever cause, to repent and believe."[30]

Although we have already seen that Davenant would most certainly reject the language of having purchased pardon and reconciliation for all human beings, the basic notions of a universal redemption and a limited application are, in fact, in him. In other words, he does believe that Christ has obtained a universal remedy for all human beings which makes all human beings forgivable or reconcilable. And he clearly limits the application of the blessings of forgiveness and reconciliation to believers. Therefore, while he would take strong exception with Cunningham's impetration language, Cunningham does seem to identify two of the basic elements one finds in Davenant's theology. Yet, what Cunningham (along with other popular expositions of hypothetical universalism) fails to include is the third element of Davenant's hypothetical universalism—the very element which I suggest is the element actually taught in the aforementioned passages of the WCF and the element which distinguished Ussher and Davenant from the Remonstrants when it came to the extent of Christ's death.

Davenant's proposition for his final chapter entitled "Of the death of Christ, as it regards the Predestinated alone" found in his *De Morte Christi* asserts that:

> [t]he death of Christ, from the special design of God the Father, who from eternity ordained and accepted that sacrifice; and of Christ, who offered it in the fulness of time to God the Father; was destined for some certain persons, whom the Scripture calls the elect, and for them alone, so as to be effectually and infallibly applied to the obtaining of eternal life.[31]

---

[30] Cunningham, *Historical Theology*, 2:328.

[31] Davenant, *Dissertation on the Death of Christ*, II:516.

Now without all subordinate clauses: "The death of Christ…was destined for some certain persons…and for them alone, so as to be effectually and infallibly applied to the obtaining of eternal life."

A few observations are worth making. First, and most fundamentally, Davenant clearly affirms a sense in which Christ died for the elect alone. He says that it is "the elect alone; whose special prerogative it is that according to the absolute will of God the Father and of Christ the Mediator, they are decreed and caused to be infallibly saved through the death of Christ."[32] Put simply, to crib the Dominican Domingo Banez, whom he goes on to quote, Christ's merit does not have *equal* regard to the predestined and reprobate.[33] Christ purchased a to-be-applied[34] redemption for the elect alone.

Second, note that for Davenant this redemption purchased for the elect alone is an affirmation with regard to redemption *accomplished*, not redemption applied. He distinguishes between an application destined and an application made.[35] Both truths are founded upon the death of Christ, though the former has as its object the elect *qua* unbelieving, while the latter is on behalf of the elect *qua* believing. Put a different way, application destined refers to his third element, while application made corresponds to his second element.

To illustrate Davenant's third element more clearly, it may be beneficial to briefly observe the language of the British Suffrage written for the Synod of Dort. The first two theses presented by the British delegation to Dort are as follows:

> Out of an especiall love and intention both of God the Father, and of Christ himselfe, Christ dyed for the Elect, that hee might effectually obtaine for them, and infallibly bestow on them both remission of sinnes, and salvation.

> Out of the selfe same love by and for the merit and intercession of Christ, faith, and perseverance, are given to the

---

[32] Davenant, *Dissertation on the Death of Christ*, II:517.

[33] Domingo Banez, *Scholastica Commentaria in Primam Partem Angelici Doctoris S. Thomae Usque ad LXIIII. Quaestionem, Tomus Primus* (Douai: Petrus Borremans, 1614), 296–97.

[34] This is my own way of putting it, in distinction to a "may-be-applied" redemption, i.e., an applicable redemption.

[35] Davenant, *Dissertation on the Death of Christ*, II:516–17.

same Elect, yea and all other things, by which the condition of the covenant is fulfilled, and the promised benefit, namely, eternall life is obtained.[36]

The British delegation is clear that there is an intention in the death of Christ to obtain a to-be-applied remission of sins and reconciliation for the elect alone. Further, note how the delegation terms this act as "effectual redemption":

> This position sheweth, that out of the death and intercession of Christ, those gifts of grace doe flow to the Elect, by which they are effectually brought to life eternall. Rom. 8. 32. 33. 39. *Hee that spared not his owne Sonne, how shall he not even with him give us all things?* Heb. 8. 10. *I will give my lawes into their mindes, and in their hearts I will write them.* For that grace, which is given unto the Elect for the death of Christ, is the grace of effectuall reemption. Now wee understand by the grace of redemption, not such a grace, by which men may bee redeemed, if they will, [p. 46] but by which they are in event mercifully redeemed, because God so willeth.[37]

The grace which is infallibly given to the elect alone is termed "the grace of effectual redemption." It is in this notion of "effectual redemption" wherein we find Davenant's hypothetical universalism most clearly distinguished from the Remonstrant position. The Remonstrants, along with Cunningham's characterization of hypothetical universalism, held that the death of Christ merely opened the door for the redemption of all humanity.[38] As the Remonstrant Grevinchovius put it: "I acknowledge in God

---

[36] *The Collegiat Suffrage of the Divines of Great Britaine*, 43–44, 45. On the background to the British delegation's role at Dort, see Anthony Milton, ed., *The British Delegation and the Synod of Dort (1618–1619)* (Woodbridge: The Boydell Press, 2005).

[37] *The Collegiat Suffrage of the Divines of Great Britaine*, 45–46.

[38] It seems rather obvious that Davenant's form of universal redemption cannot fit within the picture painted by Cunningham, *Historical Theology*, II:329: "The advocates of this doctrine [i.e., universal redemption] accordingly say, that He impetrated or purchased these blessings for all men ; and as many are never actually pardoned and reconciled, they are under the necessity, as I formerly explained, *because they hold a universal atonement*, both of explaining away pardon and reconciliation as meaning merely the removing of legal obstacles, or the opening up of a door, for

indeed a constant and perpetual desire of applying to all men individually the good obtained; but I deny that the application itself was destined by the certain counsel and will of God for any man but him that believeth."[39] Or again, Grevinchovius:

> That there was not any absolute promise or will of God concerning the effectual redemption of any individual persons, but that God willed or did not will the application of the death of Christ to all men individually not absolutely but conditionally; He willed it to all if they had faith; he did not will it if they disbelieved and therefore, although Christ laid down his life, it was possible nevertheless that his death might not be applied to any that is, it was possible that he might be defrauded of his promised seed, on account of the unbelief of all men intervening.[40]

In contrast to Grevinchovius, Davenant's third element makes it impossible that the death of Christ not be applied to certain persons, because in the death of Christ God purchased a to-be-applied effectual redemption for the elect alone. The nineteenth century Scotsman, George Smeaton, who was on the faculty at the New College in Edinburgh with Cunningham for a short time, recognized just this element in Davenant. Smeaton argues that it is this element in Davenant (and he also mentions Baxter), namely the notion of an effectual redemption accomplished on behalf of the elect, which, using his words, "draws a wide line of demarcation between the theology of Davenant, or of the Church of England, and that of Amyraldus, which insisted on a view of the atonement which, on the one hand, did not contain the element of its own application, and, on the other, continued to hold that Christ's death was equally for all."[41] To use Smeaton's language,

---

God's bestowing these blessings, and of maintaining that these blessings are impetrated for many to whom they are never applied."

[39] Nicolaas Grevinchovius, *Dissertatio Theologica De Duabus Quaestionibus Hoc Tempore Controversis, Quarum Prima Est De Reconciliatione Per Mortem Christi Impetrata Omnibus ac Singulis Hominibus [...]* (Rotterdam: Mathias Sebastian, 1615), 7. Quoted in Davenant, *Dissertation on the Death of Christ*, II:516.

[40] Nicolaas Grevinchovius, *Dissertatio Theologica De Duabus Quaestionibus*, 8, 14. Quoted in Davenant, *Dissertation on the Death of Christ*, II:524–25.

[41] George Smeaton, *The Apostles' Doctrine of the Atonement* (1870; reprint, Grand Rapids: Zondervan, 1957), 540–543, 542.

Davenant's hypothetical universalism does contain in the atoning work of Christ an element of its own application, and he clearly does not affirm that Christ died equally for all.

So what then are we to make of the WCF and its limiting of redemption to the elect? Does it not *ipso facto* exclude all forms of universal redemption? There is good reason to believe that this is not the case. First, we should recognize that many Reformed theologians, not just the hypothetical universalists, argued that redemption is in some sense universal. E.g., in a chapter written against the Remonstrant version of universal redemption, William Lyford, a non-conformist theologian chosen to be a Westminster Divine who did not affirm hypothetical universalism, explicitly affirmed three ways that redemption is universal.[42] Further, it was well known that the term redemption had "sundry acceptions," as the Scottish Divine David Dickson observed.[43] Dickson notes four different uses of the term! Most tellingly, however, might be what Thomas Aquinas himself says about the word "redemption" in his commentary on Revelation:

> Concerning the redemption accomplished by the passion of God we speak in two ways: either according to its sufficiency, and so his passion redeemed all, because as far as it concerns himself, he delivered all; for it is sufficient to redeem and save all as well as if there were infinite worlds ... or according to the efficacy, and so he did not redeem all by his passion because not all adhere to the redeemer and therefore not all have the efficacy of redemption.[44]

Distinguishing between various "redemptions" had a theological pedigree well before the WCF.

There are then at least a few options available to interpreters of the WCF redemption language, two of which were noted by Cunningham. Re-

---

[42] William Lyford, *The Plain Mans Senses Excercised [...]* (London: Richard Royston, 1655), 260–62.

[43] David Dickson, *Therapeutica Sacra [...]* (Edinburgh: Evan Tyler, 1664), 1.4.2 [23].

[44] Thomas Aquinas, *Opera Omnia*, 34 vols. (Paris: Ludovicus Vives, 1871), 32:168: *de redemptione facta per passionem Dei est loqui dupliciter: Aut secundum sufficientiam: et sic passio redemit omnes, quia quantum est de se omnes liberavit: omnibus enim redimendis et salvandis sufficiens est, etiam si essent infiniti mundi, ut dicit Anselmus II libro Cur Deus Homo, cap. 14: Aut secundum efficientiam: et sic non omnes redemit per passionem, quia non omnes adhaerent redemptori; et ideo non omnes habent efficaciam redemptionis.*

demption in the relevant passages of the WCF could simply denote applied redemption; but as he and others point out, this hardly works. There does appear to be a progression from redemption to effectual calling, justification, sanctification, glorification, etc. Redemption does appear to be the first step in the process, not the process of application itself. Second, redemption could denote what Davenant calls a remedy or satisfaction or the sufficiency of redemption. Now had they used redemption in this second sense, then hypothetical universalism would be clearly excluded. But it is very likely that redemption means something more than "made a remedy or satisfied for sins." It is doubtful that the Westminster Divines are trying to argue that redemption was *sufficient* for the elect alone! Further, if Westminster's language was intending to limit the satisfaction of sin to the elect alone, then one does wonder why such language would not have been used. Baxter seems to agree with my reading saying that he understands the term "redemption" in the noted passages of the WCF to denote "not...the meer bearing the punishment of mans sins, and satisfying Gods justice."[45]

What then would it mean to purchase redemption for the elect alone? I think it would cover precisely what Davenant affirms in his third element—namely, a purchased to-be-applied application destined for the elect. The logic of WCF 8.8 appears to lean in that direction: "To all those for whom Christ hath purchased Redemption, he doth certainly, and effectually apply, and communicate the same." The logic infallibly connects the purchased redemption (including all the benefits of redemption, such as effectual calling) with its application. It is hardly surprising that Baxter, when contemplating whether this text allows for his view of the extent of redemption, understands the WCF's use of the term as referring to "that special Redemption proper to the Elect, which was accompanied with an intention of actual application of the saving benefits in time."[46] Baxter admits that the WCF speaks against some forms of universal redemption, but it is precisely the Remonstrant form it intends to exclude. With the affirmation that Christ purchased a to-be-applied redemption for the elect alone, all Remonstrant theology (at least as exemplified in the likes of Grevinchovius and the Remonstrant Articles) along with the various Lutherans, including Huber and Pucci, is excluded from Westminsterian orthodoxy. Additionally, one cannot affirm that Christ died equally for all (as Amyraut did in 1634)

---

[45] Richard Baxter, *Rich: Baxter's Confession of his Faith [...]* (London: R.W., 1655), 21.

[46] Baxter, *Rich: Baxter's Confession*, 21.

and affirm the language of Westminster. In his death, according to the WCF, Christ purchased a to-be-applied redemption for the elect alone.

It is my contention, then, that the WCF affirms that God obtained or impetrated in the person and work of Jesus Christ for the elect, and the elect alone, all the benefits of redemption to be applied to them in time. But this does not exclude the belief that God *also* ordained that in Christ a sufficient remedy was made for both elect and non-elect. While the WCF makes room for the latter belief—the distinctive element in Davenant's hypothetical universalism—it explicitly affirms the former impetration of Christ's work vis-a-vis the elect alone. Thus, the WCF's theological claim stands in perfect harmony with his own theology including his version of hypothetical universalism. While other versions of hypothetical universalism may be excluded by the WCF at this point, there is good reason to believe the anonymous Westminster Divine who, in conversation with Richard Baxter, claimed that the WCF did not determine the controversy among the various Westminster advocates of universal redemption such as Edmund Calamy (following the British Delegation at Dort) and those who denied universal redemption. Instead, the WCF was written in such a way as would allow both sides of the debate to wholeheartedly affirm it.

BIBLIOGRAPHY

Aquinas, Thomas. *Opera Omnia*. 34 vols. Paris: Ludovicus Vives, 1871.

Baird, Samuel J. *A History of the New School, and of the Questions Involved in the Disruption of the Presbyterian Church in 1838*. Philadelphia: Claxton, Remsen & Haffelfinger, 1868.

Banez, Domingo. *Scholastica Commentaria in Primam Partem Angelici Doctoris S. Thomae Usque ad LXIIII. Quaestionem, Tomus Primus*. Douai: Petrus Borremans, 1614.

Baxter, Richard. *Certain Disputations of Right to Sacraments and the True Nature of Visible Christianity, Defending them against several sorts of Opponents, especially against the second assault by that Pious, Reverend and Dear Brother Mr. Thomas Blake*. London: William DuGard, 1657.

_____. *Rich: Baxter's Confession of his Faith [...]*. London: R.W., 1655.

Bertius, Petrus. *Scripta Adversaria Collationis Hagiensis [...] De Divina Praedestione et Capitibus ei adnexis*. Brittenburg: Johannes Patius, 1615.

Brown, John. *Opinions on Faith, Divine Influence, Human Inability, the Design and Effect of the Death of Christ, Assurance and the Sonship of Christ*. 2nd ed. Edinburgh: William Oliphant and Son, 1841.

Cheeseman, Lewis. *Differences Between Old and New School Presbyterians*. Rochester: Erastus Darrow, 1848.

The Collegiat Suffrage of the Divines of Great Britaine, Concerning the Five Articles Controverted in the Low Countries [...]. London: Robert Milbourne, 1629.

Cunningham, William. *Historical Theology: A Review of the principal doctrinal Discussions in the Christian Church since the Apostolic Age*. 2 vols. Edinburgh: T & T Clark, 1863.

_____. *The Reformers and the Theology of the Reformation*. 2nd ed. Edinburgh: T. and T. Clark, 1866.

Dabney, R. L. "Dr. Dabney for the Plan of Union." *Southern Presbyterian* (Columbia, SC), 3 December 1863, n.s., vol. 4, no. 4: Columns 1–6.

Davenant, John. A *Dissertation on the Death of Christ, as to its Extent and Special Benefits*, in *An Exposition of the Epistle of St. Paul to the Colossians*, translated by Josiah Allport. 2 vols. London: Hamilton, Adams, and Co., 1832.

Dickson, David. *Therapeutica Sacra [...]*. Edinburgh: Evan Tyler, 1664.

Fortson, S. Donald. *The Presbyterian Creed: A Confessional Tradition in America, 1729-1870*. Milton Keyes: Paternoster, 2008.

Gatiss, Lee. "A Deceptive Clarity? Particular Redemption in the Westminster Standards." *Reformed Theological Review* 69, no. 3 (2010): 180–96.

Grevinchovius, Nicolaas. *Dissertatio Theologica De Duabus Quaestionibus Hoc Tempore Controversis, Quarum Prima Est De Reconciliatione Per Mortem Christi Impetrata Omnibus ac Singulis Hominibus [...]*. Rotterdam: Mathias Sebastian, 1615.

Hamilton, Ian. *The Erosion of Calvinist Orthodoxy: Drifting from the Truth in confessional Scottish Churches*. Ross-shire, Scotland: Mentor, 2010.

Hirrel, Leo P. *Children of Wrath: New School Calvinism and Antebellum Reform*. Lexington: The University of Kentucky Press, 1998.

Hodge, Charles. "Life and Writings of Dr. Richards." *The Biblical Repertory and Princeton Review* 18, no. 4 (1846): 589–600.

_____. *The Reunion of the Old and New- School Presbyterian Churches*. New York: Charles Scribner & Co., 1867.

Jons, Mark, and Michael A. Haykin, eds. *Drawn into Controversie: Reformed Theological Diversity and Debates Within Seventeenth-Century British Puritanism*. Göttingen: Vandenhoeck & Ruprecht, 2011.

Janeway, J. J. *Letters on the Atonement: in which a Contrast is Instituted Between the Doctrine of the Old and of the New School; or Between the Definite and Indefinite Scheme, on this Important Subject*. Philadelphia: A. Finlay, 1827.

Letham, Robert. *The Westminster Assembly: Reading its Theology in Historical Context*. Phillipsburg, NJ: Presbyterian and Reformed, 2009.

Lyford, William. *The Plain Mans Senses Excercised [...]*. London: Richard Royston, 1655.

Macleod, Donald. *Christ Crucified: Understanding the Atonement.* Downers Grove, IL: IVP, 2014.

Marsden, George. *The Evangelical Mind and the New School Presbyterian Experience: A Case Study of Thought and Theology in Nineteenth-Century America.* New Haven: Yale, 1970.

Milton, Anthony, ed. *The British Delegation and the Synod of Dort (1618–1619).* Woodbridge: The Boydell Press, 2005.

Mitchell, A.F. and John Struthers, eds. *Minutes of the Sessions of the Westminster Assembly of Divines.* Edinburgh: William Blackwood and Sons, 1974.

Moore, Jonathan D. "The Extent of the Atonement: English Hypothetical Universalism versus Particular Redemption." In *Drawn into Controversie: Reformed Theological Diversity and Debates Within Seventeenth-Century British Puritanism,* edited by Mark Jones and Michael A. Haykin, 124–61. Göttingen: Vandenhoeck & Ruprecht, 2011.

Muller, Richard A. "Diversity in the Reformed Tradition: A Historiographical Introduction." In *Drawn into Controversie,* 11–30. Göttingen: Vandenhoeck & Ruprecht, 2011.

Owen, John. *Salus Electorum, Sanguis Iesu: Or The Death of Death in the Death of Christ [...].* London: W. W., 1648.

Pareus, David. *Brevis Repetitio ex Verbo Dei Doctrinae Catholicae Ecclesiarum Palatinatus [...].* Heidelberg, 1593.

_____. "Sententia Doctoris Paraei de quinque Remonst. Articulis." In *Acta Synodi Nationalis [...].* Leiden, 1620.

Piscator, Johann. *Ad Conradi Vorstii, S. Theol. D. Parasceuen Responsio apologetica Johan. Piscatoris.* Herborn: 1613.

_____. *Ad Conradi Vorstii, S. Theol. D. Amicam Collationem, etc.* Herborn, 1613.

Rehnman, Sebastian. "A Particular Defense of Particularism." *Journal of Reformed Theology* 6 (2012): 24–34.

Richards, James. *The Extent of the Atonement.* Philadelphia: Presbyterian Board of Publication, 1838.

Robertson, Andrew. *History of the Atonement Controversy, in Connexion with the Secession Church, From its Origin to the Present Time.* Edinburgh: William Oliphant and Sons, 1846.

Schaff, Philip. *The Creeds of Christendom.* 3 vols. Grand Rapids: Baker, 1990.

Smeaton, George. *The Apostles' Doctrine of the Atonement.* 1870. Reprint, Grand Rapids: Zondervan, 1957.

Palmer, B. M. "The Proposed Plan of Union Between the General Assembly in the Confederate States of America and the United Synod of the South." *Southern Presbyterian Review* 16 (1866): 264–307.

Troxel, A. Craig. "Amyraut 'at' the Assembly: The Westminster Confession of Faith and the Extent of the Atonement." *Presbyterion* 22, no. 1 (1996): 43–55.

Ussher, James. "An Answer to Some Exceptions." In *Works,* edited by Charles Richard Elrington, and James Henthorn Todd. 17 vols. Dublin: Hodges, Smith, and Co., 1864.

Van Dixhoorn, Chad, ed. *The Minutes and Papers of the Westminster Assembly 1643–1652.* 5 vols. Oxford: Oxford University Press, 2012.

VI:

PAGAN CIVIL VIRTUE IN THE THOUGHT OF FRANCIS TURRETIN

Stephen Wolfe, Louisiana State University

CAN A totally depraved man be good apart from redemptive grace? Today, in both popular Calvinist circles and academic scholarship outside theology (and sometimes within it), the answer is an unqualified, "no." The question, however, is imprecisely stated, for the answer is, according to a broad witness in the Reformed tradition, both "yes" and "no," depending on what we mean by "good." Is it civil and earthly good or spiritual and heavenly good? Is it external good before man or internal good before God? Is it ultimate and meritorious good? Scholars in several academic disciplines have succumbed to a tradition of simplistic analysis, tainting their work with imprecise and erroneous premises about Reformed theology on this issue and others. Errors have risen to the level of common knowledge and are sometimes asserted with little argument or evidence—they are merely assumed.[1]

Recently, however, scholars have revealed the shaky foundations of these and other assumptions, showing that certain theological positions,

---

[1] For a critique of these assumptions as they affect scholarship on the American founding, see my essay "Reformed Natural Law and the American Founding: A Critique of Recent Scholarship," in *For Law and For Liberty: Essays on the Trans-Atlantic Legacy of Protestant Political Thought*, ed. by W. Bradford Littlejohn (Moscow, ID: The Davenant Trust, 2016), 21–60. For an expanded critique, see my essay "The American Founding and the Harmony of Reason and Revelation: A Rediscovery of Calvinist Sources," in *History of Political Thought* (forthcoming).

despite being popular within Reformed circles from the 20th century to our day, are inconsistent with Reformed orthodoxy. The most important development for our purposes is the rediscovery of the importance of *natural law* in Reformed theology, [2] especially its *positive* function in civil ethics. Scholars have not, however, sufficiently delineated how this is theologically possible and coherent, given the fundamental tenets Reformed theology, nor have they brought this positive role of natural law to bear upon Reformed political theology.[3]

The conclusions of post-Reformation Reformed theologians on the possibility of virtuous pagans might surprise us. Johannes Althusius (1563–1638), for example, a Dutch Reformed political theorist, wrote, "In political life even an infidel may be called just, innocent, and upright because of [their external and civil life of words, deeds and works]," since they have "natural knowledge of and inclination towards the Decalogue."[4] How can Reformed theology, a theology in which moral depravity affects the whole being of man, accommodate such a position? Althusius's positive view of the moral potential of unbelievers cannot be consistent with a theological system in which natural law functions only negatively, *viz.*, a law that leaves men inexcusable before God. There must be something remaining in post-lapsarian and unbelieving man inclining him towards the natural law and civil duty.

The purpose of this essay is to systematically show how Reformed Christians, given their theological tradition, can recognize and even expect civil virtue from unbelievers and how this expectation might affect Reformed political theology. To do this, I rely primarily on Francis Turretin's (1623–1687) work, *The Institutes of Elenctic Theology* (*IET*), which some con-

---

[2] See Stephen Grabill, *Rediscovering the Natural law in Reformed Theological Ethics* (Grand Rapids: Eerdmans Publishing Company, 2006); David VanDrunen, *Natural Law and the Two Kingdoms: A Study in the Development of Reformed Social Thought* (Grand Rapids: Eerdmans, 2010).

[3] Kirk Nolan in *Reformed Virtue after Barth: Developing Moral Virtue Ethics in the Reformed Tradition* (Louisville: Westminster John Knox Press, 2014) does not address in detail the possibility of virtuous pagans in Reformed theology.

[4] Johannes Althusius, *Politica*, trans. Frederick S. Carney (Indianapolis: Liberty Fund, 1995), 147.

sider the "apex" of Reformed theological development in the post-Reformation era.[5]

1. SOURCES OF MISUNDERSTANDING

The widespread misunderstanding of the Calvinist tradition with regard to natural law, philosophy, the use of pagan sources, and pagan virtue is due in part to a few works of the 20th century whose popularity have endured. Analyzing one of these works and its influence is helpful to see how the affirmation or rejection of the possibility of virtuous pagans in Reformed theology affects both theology and how humans relate to creation and to each other.

Michael Walzer has continued to influence the scholarship of both Christian and non-Christians on Calvinism with his book *The Revolution of the Saints*. He argues that for Calvinism the Fall of Adam was not merely a "religious fall" but a political one that ushered in a meaningless universe, a world that would be similar to the one of Thomas Hobbes (on his reading of Hobbes) were it not for the divine commands found in Scripture. The world is one of radical divine voluntarism: the will of God for man is *exclusively* found in Scripture and has no essential correspondence with any natural law. Walzer writes, "In fact, social order, command, and obedience were created by God for his own inscrutable reasons and were only incidentally useful to humanity."[6] Divine commands are not the same in substance as any natural law, and as non-natural, the power to implement them is likewise non-natural and arbitrary vis-à-vis nature. Power is a pure instrument to bring about the political order prescribed in Scripture.

Since the world is devoid of inherent meaning and purpose—being nothing but pure disconnected and pattern-less events and brute facts—the Calvinists adopted, as Charles Taylor said, whom Walzer influenced, an "instrumental stance towards the world," treating "things of creation merely as instruments and not as ends valuable in themselves."[7] Following Walzer,

---

[5] Richard A. Muller, "Scholasticism Protestant and Catholic: Francis Turretin on the Object and Principles of Theology," *Church History* 55, no. 2 (June 1986): 195.

[6] Michael Walzer, *Revolution of the Saints: A Study in the Origins of Radical Politics* (London: Harvard University Press, 1965), 36.

[7] Charles Taylor, *Sources of the Self: The Making of the Modern Identity* (Cambridge: Harvard University Press, 1989), 232.

Ralph Hancock writes, "For the factual [in Calvinism] is not an eternal and stable reality but a field of change."[8] In other words, since there is no built-in order and meaning in the cosmos and since no event is part of some inherent cosmic pattern (as in medieval thought),[9] all events or occurrences are simply brute facts whose patterns can change at God's seemingly arbitrary will. Walzer's Calvinist is one who sees in the natural world only opportunities for radical change; and, having been empowered by special grace and the Word, the Calvinist is to "to put this right, to clean up the human mess."[10] The regenerate exclusively possess this claim to virtue, since as Taylor says of Calvinism, the "human will is so depraved by the Fall that humans require grace even to make a decent attempt at and perhaps even properly to discern the natural good."[11] The regenerate have exclusive access to virtue and are commanded to implement it in the world—to put creation into an order not dictated by it, but dictated by the adventitious revelation contained in the Bible.

Post-lapsarian man, in Walzer's understanding of Calvinism, is now an "asocial" and "solitary" man, one who is under the reign of command and obedience, not authority and reverence. The medieval view of human society as a graduated order with the lower naturally bound to serve the higher with reverence is rejected as mere opinion and fiction. The rightful ruler rather is simply one who can successfully bring about what he commands, and the obedience due to him is not based on his occupancy of the seat of natural civil authority, but because he, like the God of Calvinism, can issue commands that demand obedience for the sheer fact that they were commanded by him. Man's relationship to the original, pre-lapsarian natural order and his capacity for knowledge of proper natural ends has been obliterated, and he has only a *dis*inclination towards the moral order, making only "brutal forms" of power sufficient for political order. The

---

[8] Ralph C. Hancock, *Calvin and the Foundations of Modern Politics* (Ithaca: Cornell University Press, 1989), 76.

[9] See Walzer, *Revolution of the Saints*, 155–56. "In any case, men were known to be unequal and their equality was most often described in direct analogy to the cosmic hierarchy. Within the great chain there were discovered a whole series of lesser chains."

[10] Taylor, *Sources of the Self*, 228.

[11] Taylor, *Sources of the Self*, 246.

"Word," Walzer argues, had to be "brutally and firmly authoritative in the world."[12]

The natural recognition of authority and reverence toward leaders, clear in certain strains of medieval thought is no longer possible. Only an instrumental use of power remains, enforcing order through command and fearful obedience. Hancock, along these lines, writes, "Thus the authority of political rulers, according to Calvin, is not grounded in the good they are supposed to know and to represent but is a sheer right to command."[13] The natural law, then, has no positive function in civil society, for "political order [is not] an end accessible to man."[14] As Walzer writes, "Society and the state were not natural associations."[15] Therefore, "fallen Adam was politically helpless," for nature could not provide any criteria by which one could frame political judgment. Hence, man "submitted only to force, to the facts of power." Humankind, being a "terrified animal" is "incapable even of the consolations of human association." Due to the Fall, man is no longer a social animal, cannot cherish society, does not have an innate sense of civil order and honesty, and is devoid of the light of reason.

Whatever civil virtues one could find among the pagans, they "need not [for Calvinists] be ascribed to human nature at all," but be attributed to adventitious gifts of God. These gifts are not restorative of human nature, enabling conformity to the natural law. They simply cause right action despite and against human nature. Natural law, even if it exists, does not and cannot have a positive role in ordering human civil life. "The first nature [i.e., Adam's original righteousness]," writes Walzer, "was so nearly dead that its existence had virtually no political significance." Human life is now "nasty, brutish, and short." Knowledge of natural duty and the capability to properly order one's life in accordance with this knowledge is lost. The virtuous pagan then is an oxymoron.

The impossibility of virtuous pagans is due to the obliteration of man's connection with the original created order. Man is now solitary *vis-à-vis* fellowman and creation itself. The universe has an "order of divinely ordained facts" of arbitrary divine providence. There is no enduring moral

---

[12] Walzer, *Revolution of the Saints*, 26.

[13] Hancock, *Calvin*, 68.

[14] Hancock, *Calvin*, 68.

[15] Walzer, *Revolution of the Saints*, 32. For the quotes in the next few paragraphs, see pages 32–37.

order corresponding with an eternal law manifesting God's justice and holiness. Nature is red in tooth and claw. The regenerate then must look upon the outward actions of unregenerate man with more than suspicion. They must utterly reject them as fundamentally tainted with sin. The fallen world is not only opposed to the proper worship of God, the acknowledgement of the kingship of Christ, and the Gospel, but opposed to proper civil order, peace, and tranquility; modesty and decorum; and affection for neighbor. It is a war of all against all, and only the power of a seemingly arbitrary authority can bring order. Everything in the political realm is either a set of arbitrary power relations or an enforced divine order.

Though Calvin is not always consistent, clear, and systematic in his treatment of natural law and post-lapsarian capabilities of man—making Walzer's account of Calvin and the tradition that bears his name seemingly plausible—there is much to criticize in Walzer's account and it ought to be largely rejected. The evidence shows that, as Grabill successfully argues, for Calvin "the nonsaving, natural knowledge of God still functions competently in the earthly sphere of law, society, politics, economics, and ethics" and, for this reason, we can say that Calvin does not "deny the formal possibility of developing subsidiary doctrines of...natural law on the basis of God's reliable but obfuscated natural revelation within creation, design of the human body, and conscience."[16] Moreover, Walzer and those who follow him fail to cite any later continental Reformed theologians who developed the Reformed view of natural law, such as Zacharias Ursinus (1534–1583),[17] Franciscus Junius (1545–1602),[18] Althusius, and Francis Turretin, theologians who provided clarity and precision with regard to man's capabilities. The Reformed theological development of the 17th century identified the moral works of unbelievers as civilly virtuous without inconsistency both to Calvin and the broader Reformed tradition. They believed in an enduring moral order accessible to fallen man. On the whole, the Calvinist tradition rejects the universe that Walzer and his followers attribute to it.

---

[16] Grabill, *Rediscovering*, 84, 96.

[17] Zacharias Ursinus, *The Commentary of Dr. Zacharias Ursinus on the Heidelberg Catechism*, trans. G. W. Williard (The Synod of the Reformed Church in the United States, 2004), Q. 91 & 92 (845–83).

[18] Franciscus Junius, *The Mosaic Polity*, trans. Todd M. Rester (Grand Rapids: CLP Academic, 2015), ch. 2.

Walzer's account is important however not for its accuracy, but because it shows the logical result of the rejection of a positive role of natural law in post-laparian human society. If natural law could not order society, then what could? Only an arbitrary authority—brute political power—could bring order. The individual, as asocial, is an isolated subject against other subjects, struggling for recognition or for some social alliance. As Hobbes argued, man has "a perpetual and restless desire for power after power, that ceaseth only in death."[19] Prior to imposed order, as Hobbes stated, "nothing can be unjust. The notions of right and wrong, justice and injustice, have there no place."[20] There is no civil *summum bonum* understood by all. The pre-sanctified civil realm is held together by a system of power relations. Social order does not arise naturally, but by arbitrary force; and any claims to some natural social or political order serve only to mask power. The work of the saints is to tear down the false system—to become revolutionaries and impose the will of God deposited in Scripture.

Calvinism as "World-Formative"

Many Christians, after affirming this chaotic state of the post-lapsarian world, hear a call for radical action. Philosopher Nicholas Wolsterstorff, who relies on the work of Walzer in his book *Until Justice and Peace Embrace*, promotes Calvinism as a "world-formative" rather than an "avertive religion."[21] The chief duty of Christian social action, according to Wolsterstorff, is to bring *shalom* to creation and thereby bring the kingdom of God to earth. And though he sees this as a "human calling," it is fundamentally part of the Christian redemptive narrative. [22] Wolterstorff is largely in agreement with Walzer on the state of the post-lapsarian Calvinist world and Calvinist social duty. Since the Christian *qua* Christian exclusively possesses the principles of just civil order and since the world is utterly disor-

---

[19] Thomas Hobbes, *Leviathan*, edited by Edwin Curley (Cambridge: Hackett Publishing Company, 1994), 58.

[20] Hobbes, *Leviathan*, 78.

[21] Nicholas Wolterstorff, *Until Justice and Peace Embrace* (Grand Rapids: Eerdmans Publishing Company, 1983), 5.

[22] Nathan D. Shannon discusses Wolterstorff's position on natural reason in *Shalom and the Ethics of Belief: Nicholas Wolterstorff's Theology of Situated Rationality* (Eugene: Pickwick Publishin, 2015), 116–18.

dered with regard to those principles, it is the Christian duty, as servants of the kingdom of God, to implement those principles, which happen to be, for Wolterstorff, liberal democracy, religious tolerance, and human rights. The saints are in charge of setting things right—to bring shalom to earth. When Calvinist piety meets a disordered world, Calvinism becomes a world-formative religion. The Gospel is at its core a social project.

For Wolterstorff, the Reformation was a political reformation in addition to being a religious one. The medieval world believed that "society in all its hierarchical differentiation is…something natural, brought about by God."[23] The justification for social hierarchy was the cosmic hierarchy—the social order was "both part and mirror" of the cosmic order. The status quo of authority, which was hierarchical, was maintained by notions of a graduated cosmic order, which effectively reduced the set of legitimate social actions and reforms for the faithful. This made medieval Christianity a "world-avertive" Christianity. The Reformation however ushered in a new and correct way of seeing the world. After citing Walzer, he writes,

> The saints are responsible for the structure of the social world in which they find themselves. That structure is not simply part of the order of nature; to the contrary, it is the result of human decision, and by concerted effort it can be altered. Indeed, it *should* be altered, for it is a fallen structure, in need of reform. The responsibility of the saints to struggle for the reform of the social order in which they find themselves is one facet of the discipleship to which their Lord Jesus Christ has called them. It is not an addition to their religion; it is there among the very motions of Christian spirituality.[24]

This is packed with Walzer's conclusions. There is no natural social order. Social order arises only from human decision, and if it arose apart from the work of the regenerate, it is a fallen social order in need of reform. Only arbitrary power can hold such fallen social systems together, and any claim to natural order only masks the underlying reality of power. One basic duty of Calvinist piety was, unlike Roman Catholicism and Lutherans, to reform this disorder and bring proper order to society through the applications of

---

[23] Wolterstorff, *Until Justice and Peace Embrace*, 8.

[24] Wolterstorff, *Until Justice and Peace Embrace*, 3.

biblical social ethics. They sought the "[t]he reformation of society according to the Word of God: this was the Calvinist goal."[25]

While acknowledging that natural law still communicates God's will, Wolterstorff insists that it would be "folly" to use our "faltering apprehension" of natural law and the "voice of reason" to critique the social order. The Bible is a "comprehensive guide" for our social activities. We ought to use, he argues, "a word *from outside*—a word from God."[26] This indicates that since natural law and reason are weak guides for principles of social action for Christians apart from Scripture, natural law and reason have limited roles in the moral life of unbelievers. Their role would be primarily negative—useful only for just condemnation, not for civil order, social affections, and right actions. This precludes the legitimacy of "consent of the nations" arguments used throughout the Christian tradition to justify proper civil action and arrangements (which we see below in Turretin), since the Fall was a political fall. Hence, the collective witness of the nations shows only what is corrupt and fallen, not what is proper. The natural order only condemns; it is not a positive force for human social ordering and individual conduct. Only the saints, empowered by grace, committed to action, and entrusted with the divine commands deposited in the Bible, could bring order to human society.

Wolterstorff's account of the Christian political action is essentially a social gospel: the Gospel institutes a world-formative religious project, whose principal task is not to accomplish something otherworldly, but radically this-worldly. Christians are the redemptive agents struggling "to establish a holy commonwealth here on earth."[27] Society can be and must be redeemed, and this redemption is not simply the implementation of the proper worship of God, correcting some social errors, or even the adorning of society with Christian culture. It is the reformation and overthrow of all pre-Gospel social structures.

The early reformers and the post-reformation theologians did not share Wolterstorff's understanding of the extent of redemptive activity, as we shall see in my discussion below. For them, the task of the Christian political leader *qua* Christian is the establishment of the proper worship of God and the protection of the Church. The implementation of civil justice

---

[25] Wolterstorff, *Until Jesus and Peace Embrace*, 18.

[26] Wolterstorff, *Until Jesus and Peace Embrace*, 18.

[27] Wolterstorff, *Until Jesus and Peace Embrace*, 19.

is, of course, part of the Christian prince's duty, but his duty *as a Christian* concerned religious piety, not justice. Natural justice is a *human* matter, not an exclusively Christian one.[28] The differences between the Reformers' and the Wolterstorff's (and many 20th and 21st-century Reformed Christian) positions on redemptive activity stem from a differing conception of the fall. If the unbeliever could be virtuous, if they could implement just civil laws apart from special revelation, then what they lacked was not knowledge of the principles and the practice of justice, but proper piety, namely, the worship of the true God. The effects of the fall on this account were mainly religious, not political, making the reformation a matter of proper worship and supernatural doctrine. But if their social and political systems were corrupted (as Wolterstorff asserts), then the fall separated man from the natural law and Christian duty is to fundamentally transform these systems in accordance with special revelation.

2. EXPOSITION OF TURRETIN

Unbelievers can, however, be externally and civilly virtuous, according to Reformed orthodoxy. To show how this is possible, I discuss the thought of Francis Turretin.

Original Righteousness

The composition of Adam's original righteousness was hotly debated in the 17th century. Roman Catholic, Remonstrant, Socinian, Lutheran, and the Reformed theologians all had different answers. The Roman Catholics, for example, considered original righteousness to be a supernatural, superadded gift on top of the already constituted native gifts. This is a type of nature/grace dualism: grace is a substance added on top of nature. Man in a state of pure nature, one in which man does not have the addition of grace, was necessarily in conflict between his flesh and spirit—between sin and a sort of neutral state—and the supernatural addition was a "golden bridle,"

---

[28] For a discussion the qua human/Christian distinction see Junius, *The Mosaic Polity*, 38 and 104–105.

according to Roman Catholic theologian Bellarmine,[29] that secured Adam's integrity. Put differently, the grace held at bay the natural tendency for nature to fall. The consequence of the Fall was the removal of this grace, leaving Adam in the natural flesh/spirit conflict, giving free reign to concupiscence, which, though not sinful itself, "wrought disorder in the body, obscured the mind, and weakened the power of the will."[30] The Fall, then, did not directly or in itself corrupt habits (it is not "sin formally...[but] it sprang from sin and incites to sin");[31] it simply removed that supernatural element necessary to control the drift of human nature away from proper thought and action.

The Reformed theologians rejected this nature/grace dualism and instead posited that Adam was created with natural integrity apart from the addition of anything adventitious to nature. Nature was in no need of a stabilizer. Turretin insists that God could not have created man as so-called "pure nature"—as neither righteous, nor unrighteous, as Roman Catholics assert. That is, God could not create man without the spiritual habits necessary for a heavenly orientation that glorifies God. Man had to be "made to glorify and worship God, duties he could not perform unless endowed with the necessary gifts (viz. wisdom and holiness)" (5.9.5). For this reason, there cannot "be a man who is not either righteous or a sinner" (5.9.6). Man *by nature*, Turretin argues, has original righteousness, since it is impossible for God to create man in a state lacking the features necessary for the complete worship of God—a necessary requirement of righteousness. Otherwise, man would be *un*righteous, and God cannot create unrighteousness. Hence, no superadded, adventitious element was necessary for pre-lapsarian man's moral integrity, since the state of "pure nature" is an impossibility.

Still, though Adam's original righteousness is natural, Turretin admits that such righteousness is not natural in every sense of the word, following a long tradition, going back at least to Lombard, in distinguishing the "earthly" and the "heavenly" features of man's being. Turretin does not go into detail on the content of each, so I will use Calvin. Calvin in his *Institutes*

---

[29] See Francis Turretin, *Institutes of Elenctic Theology*, trans. George Musgrave Giger (Phillipsburg: P&R Publishing, 1994), 1:471 [5.11.5]. This work is cited parenthetically throughout this essay.

[30] NewAdvent.org, Accessed through: http://www.newadvent.org/cathen/04208a.htm, (May 17, 2016).

[31] NewAdvent.org.

distinguishes Adam's native gifts as "natural" and "supernatural" gifts, each pointing to and necessary for earthly ("the present life") and heavenly ends ("future blessedness") respectively.[32] The latter consists in "the light of faith and righteousness," and "mysteries of the heavenly kingdom," all of which was "sufficient for the attainment of heavenly life and everlasting felicity." The natural gifts (the "earthly things") consisted of "soundness of mind and integrity of heart" and "matters of policy and economy, all mechanical arts, and liberal studies." Each is a set of capabilities with a common orientation: one to earth and one to heaven. Together their final end is the glorification of God.

Turretin at times calls the heavenly oriented gifts "supernatural" but prefers "spiritual" to avoid confusion (5.10.2, 16), and he uses the term "heavenly things" as well (10.4.13). These spiritual gifts, which crowns man with original righteousness, is, along with man's earthly gifts, natural, though there is a crucial difference: the spiritual is natural as *adorning and perfecting* of man's essential, constitutive nature and therefore removable from man without destroying his essence. That is, original righteousness is non-essential to man as man. The spiritual gifts are necessary for righteousness, but not necessary to constitute man as man (i.e., not an essential property of man as man). This "dual" aspect of man's original state (i.e., essence and perfecting) might seem to be in tension with what we have just said, but we must look more carefully into the different uses of "nature." Turretin lists four ways one can use the term (5.11.2):

> Natural is taken in four ways: (1) originally and subjective-
> ly, drawn from nature and concreated or born together
> with it and most deeply implanted in it (which is opposed
> to the adventitious); (2) constitutively and consecutively,
> constituting the nature of the thing or following and flow-
> ing from the principles of nature (as such as are the essen-
> tial part or properties of a thing which is opposed to the
> accidental); (3) perfectively, agreeing with the nature and
> adorning and perfecting it (opposed to that which is
> against nature); (4) transitively, which ought to be propa-
> gated with nature.

---

[32] John Calvin, *Institutes of the Christian Religion*, trans. Henry Beveridge (Grand Rapids: Eerdmans Publishing, 1989), 234 [2.2.13].

The spiritual gifts are not natural constitutively or consecutively, because they are not essential to man as man. But they are natural *originally* and *perfectively*. That which perfects a thing need not be an essential property of the thing it perfects. Nor are these gifts adventitious (*contra* Bellarmine); they are concreated with and deeply implanted in nature itself and necessary. They are *perfecting* qualities, adorning nature itself unto completion. Again, these perfecting qualities are essential for man to be *righteous* and *holy* before God, but not necessary to constitute man as *man*. That which constitutes man as *man* is not sufficient to constitute man as *righteous*. Turrretin writes, "Thus it [original righteousness] is so necessary to the perfection of innocent man that without it he could not have been such" (5.11.6). For as Turretin writes (5.11.11),

> It is one thing to speak of the essence of man; another of his integrity and perfection. At the taking away of a part or of some essential property, there follow in truth the destruction of the thing, but not forthwith at the privation of that which contributes to the integrity and perfecting of nature (as such as original righteousness was). The nature indeed remains mutilated and depraved (since it has lost what perfected it), but is not destroyed as to essence.

These distinctions allow Turretin to affirm that the spiritual gifts of man are necessary for perfection and moral integrity—and therefore native in pre-lapsarian man—while also allowing him to say that these qualities are not superadded to some neutral "pure nature." They are part of creation, embedded in creation itself, and God had to create man with such gifts. Without the spiritual/heavenly gifts, man is not innocent. Their removal does not leave man in a state of neutrality or pure nature. That which constitutes the nature of man is not sufficient for man to be righteous and holy. Such a man is unrighteous, since he lacks the qualities necessary for man's perfection. Further, their removal, while leaving man "mutilated and depraved," does not destroy the essence of man as man.

Turretin insists that one can distinguish between the native gifts of man in his pre-lapsarian state as essential properties and perfecting qualities without any need to talk of superadded grace and "pure nature;" and, most important for our purposes, he can claim that the loss of original righteousness—man's perfecting qualities or spiritual gifts—is itself sufficient to declare man unrighteous before God regardless man's uprightness vis-à-vis earthly duties. In other words, even if man after losing these spiritual gifts remains in conformity with earthly duties, man is still justly condemned because he fails to fully glorify God in heart and in worship. To summarize the argument, since man in a state of righteousness must exercise properly both sets of his native gifts (earthly and heavenly) in order to remain righteous, the loss or failure to exercise just one of those sets of gifts is sufficient for man to be unrighteous and worthy of divine judgment. The loss of the heavenly features of man does not leave man in a state of pure nature or innocence, but in a state of unrighteousness.

Turretin emphasizes that the principal effect of the Fall was the loss of this original righteousness. The "holiness and wisdom" (9.8.3) of original righteousness, which is "truly life," was lost by the "dissolution of union with God and the privation of holiness" (10.4.11). The Fall was a loss of "all spiritual sense and motion," and "what little remains of spiritual life" cannot "kindle spiritual life" (10.4.12). In the fall man lost those qualities sufficient to perceive and perform for the coming heavenly blessings that transcend earthly matters. The "spiritual," or the perfecting, qualities are gone, but the natural, or essential properties, remain. He writes (5.10.16),

> Adam after his fall had the image [of God] still (as also his posterity even now have), since they are said to be made after the image of God. Yet this must be understood only relatively (as to certain natural remains of that image) and not absolutely (as to spiritual and supernatural qualities which are evidently lost and must be restored to us by the grace of regeneration.)

The heaven-oriented qualities of man are lost, but there remains an earthly orientation (and indeed a disordered orientation to earthly concerns). The image of God in man, then, is not fully extinguished; it remains not absolutely, since the spiritual qualities of man are necessary to complete any image of God, who is spirit; but the image of God remains relatively on account of the natural gifts. The fall did not destroy "whatever gifts upright man received from God," because "certain remains of it [remain] in the mind and heart of man after the fall" (9.8.3). What is essentially man remains, even free will, "which can never be taken away from man in whatever state he may be" (10.3.11). And these remaining gifts serve as a "bond of discipline in political society" (9.8.7).

The loss of the spiritual gifts, however, had the secondary effect of producing "contrary habits." For original sin is not merely a privation, but also a "positive quality," being "highly active and efficacious" (9.11.16).[33] It does not destroy the essence of man, but it damages his rectitude without "extinguishing its internal principles of action," like a disease in the body (9.11.16). Put differently, original sin is not merely the removal of original righteousness; it is a powerful effect that strikes through man. Original sin cannot corrupt the very essence of the soul, for "every substance was created by God and in this sense is good" (9.11.3).[34] Men are still, however, "full of unrighteousness" and "inclined to evil" due to "vicious" qualities. Human nature does not itself become sinful, but it has sin. It is like a rotten apple: though rotten, its rottenness does not make it any less an apple as to essence. So the Fall affected more than man's orientation to heavenly things.

Still, "reason may be a small light…in things civil and natural," says Turretin (1.8.22). Since man as man is essentially a being with reason, one who still knows, despite the Fall, the "principles of nature…true and sure," the errors and falsehoods of human reason are the *conclusions* from the principles, which come from an abuse of "natural light." Though the principles are "known of themselves," the conclusions are "often erroneous and fallible" (1.8.21; cf. 1.9.5). Turretin writes (11.1.20),

> Although various practical notions have been obscured after sin and for a time even obliterated, it does not follow either that they were entirely extinguished or that they never existed at all. For the commonest principle (that good should be done and evil avoided) is unshaken in all, although in the particular conclusions and in the determination of it good men may often err because vice deceives us under the appearance and shadow of virtue.

He later states that the giving of the Law of Moses "confirmed" and "corrected," not replaced, the natural law.[35] Indeed, though "wicked laws" can

---

[33] This is consistent with Thomas Aquinas in *Summa Theologica* (*ST*) I–II.82.1. See also Turretin, *IET*, 1:638 [9.11.13].

[34] Similarly, Calvin wrote, "The natural gifts which remained were corrupted after the fall. Not that they can be polluted in themselves insofar as they proceed from God, but that they have ceased to be pure to polluted man." *Institutes*, 237 [2.2.16].

[35] Cf. Aquinas, *ST* I–II.94.5.

"suppress" the natural law as to the proper conclusions flowing from it, they cannot cause its "extinction and destruction as to…the first principle" (11.1.18).[36] Knowledge of the principles of duty, as with intelligence and reason, are inextinguishable, since "there is no mortal who cannot feel its [i.e., the natural law's] force either more or less" (11.1.7). For these reasons, the Fall did not and could not destroy the possibility that unregenerate man could be, civilly and externally speaking, virtuous.

Moreover, the principal effect of regeneration is the adventitious restoration of the spiritual and supernatural qualities, *not* the natural qualities.[37] Though there are "natural remains of the image [of God]," the "spiritual and supernatural qualities…must be restored to us by the grace of regeneration" (5.10.16). This righteousness is, properly speaking, adventitious since it is not original to nature, as Adam's pre-lapsarian righteousness was. The "renewed" image of God is "the spiritual image (as to supernatural gifts)" (5.10.2). By competing and restoring man there is the secondary effect of strengthening one's rectitude with regard to earthly matters, but the main effect is the fundamental transformation of one's spiritual and internal disposition towards God and his heavenly kingdom, *not* his activity in the earthly kingdom.[38]

Turretin repeatedly emphasizes that the loss of original righteousness itself, the chief mark of the image of God in man, leaves man in unspeakable depravity, quite apart from their performance on earthly matters. The negativity toward man's fallen state, easy to find in Reformed theological writings and sermons, is, though not always acknowledged, primarily in ref-

---

[36] Cf. Aquinas, *ST* I–II.94.6.

[37] Calvin says that fallen "human nature possesses none of the gifts which the elect receive from their heavenly father through the Spirit of regeneration." *Institutes*, 239 [2.2.20].

[38] For Calvin, the Gospel diverts the believer from his obsession with earthly concerns, directing him to heaven. He writes, "we creep on the earth; nay, we find that our flesh ever draws us downward: except then the truth from above becomes to us as it were wings, or a ladder, or a vehicle, we cannot rise up one foot; but, on the contrary, we shall seek refuges on the earth rather than ascend into heaven. But let the word of God become our ladder, or our vehicle, or our wings, and, however difficult the ascent may be, we shall yet be able to fly upward, provided God's word be allowed to have its own authority." *Commentary on the Twelve Minor Prophets: Habakkuk, Zephaniah, Haggai*, trans. John Owen (Grand Rapids: Baker Books, 2005), 59 (comment on Habakkuk 2.1). The primary purpose of the Gospel is to restore that "ladder" to heaven—to escape the fleeting and insecure refuges of earth.

erence to man's refusal to acknowledge and properly worship God (both in heart and publicly), not his failure to live up to civil ethics. For, as Calvin writes, the "chief object of life is to acknowledge and worship God, (which alone is our principal distinction from the brutes)…to direct to him all our prayers, and, in a word, all the thoughts of our heart."[39] If worship is the chief end of man, then failing to worship is worse before God than failing in any lesser end.[40] The civil uprightness of a pagan does no harm to the claims of the Law and Gospel, namely, that all have fallen short of the glory of God and need some supernatural means of salvation. Righteousness *coram hominibus* is nowhere near sufficient for righteousness *coram deo*, and unrighteous in the latter is far worse than unrighteousness in the former.

In summary, the key to understanding the effects of the Fall on the man is to distinguish between what constitutes man as to essence and what perfects him. Man in his original state is essentially an earthly creature, perfected by qualities that orient him to God and heaven. The Fall almost obliterated the perfecting properties, leaving a corrupted man who, though retaining his essential properties, is given over to evil. Still, this leaves open the possibility of a relatively well-regulated political society, since man's evil is primarily in his failure to acknowledge and properly worship God publicly and from the heart (i.e., internally). Regeneration restores man to completion by the supernatural and adventitious bestowal of Christ's righteousness to the believer, the same righteousness as to substance as Adam's prior to the fall, though not in the same mode of possession (*viz.* not *original* righteousness). This righteousness restores man unto God and his heavenly, spiritual, and to-be-revealed kingdom; and though this restoration strengthens one's ability to fulfill civil duty, it does not completely re-orient or fundamentally transform this ability.

---

[39] Calvin, *Commentary on the Prophet Isaiah*, vol. 2, trans. William Pringle (Grand Rapids: Baker Books, 2005), 368–69 (comments on Isaiah 44:9).

[40] Calvin affirms this explicitly: "As the name of God is more excellent than any thing in the whole world, so the worship of him ought to be regarded as of more importance than all those duties by which we prove our love towards men." *Commentary on the Twelve Minor Prophets: Jonah, Micah, Nahum*, trans. John Owen (Grand Rapids: Baker Books, 2005), 343–44 (comments on Micah 6:8).

Knowledge of God's Law in Civil Law

In the next two sections, we discuss both the knowledge of natural law among pagans and their ability to perform it. We have seen that unregenerate man, though evil for his failure to acknowledge God and worship him correctly, still retains the natural gifts that constitute him as man. One would expect some knowledge of the natural law with regard to civil duty and the ability to externally perform it.

Turretin argues that the natural law corresponds "with the eternal and archetypal law of in God, since it is its copy and shadow, in which he has manifested his justice and holiness" (11.2.16). As such, it is "immutable and perpetual." And though sin affects man's reasoning subjectively and concretely, it does not change the Law "in the abstract and objectively." The natural law was not abrogated or subjected to any objective change due to the fall of man, and it continues to be the standard for "all nations in every age" (11.2.17). The law, "the pattern of God's image in man" (11.2.16) contains nothing inaccessible by sound reason.[41] When reasoning properly, therefore, one produces correct conclusions and determinations from universally known principles. Since reason is an essential feature of man,[42] the ability to reason, however corrupted, remains in fallen man, making it at least possible for unregenerate man to reason and perform properly. The natural law is after all "founded upon the rational nature [and] is impressed upon man by nature" (11.2.17).

Pagan political communities, according to Turretin, generally gravitate towards the implementation of just civil laws. Due to the force of the natural law on the conscience, "sharp-sighted" unregenerate public leaders implement just laws (11.1.21). Just laws are so ubiquitous in human societies that Turretin appeals to the "consent of the nations" to bolster his claim to the existence of natural law. He writes, for example (11.1.13),

> [T]he consent of the nations [is evidence of the natural law], among whom (even the most savage) some law of the primitive nations obtains, from which even without a teacher they have learned that God should be worshipped,

---

[41] Cf. Aquinas, *ST* I–II.93.5.

[42] Calvin likewise states that "one of the essential properties of our nature is reason." *Institutes*, 237 [2.2.17].

166

parents honored, a virtuous life be led and from which as a fountain have flowed so many laws concerning equity and virtue enacted by heathen legislatures, drawn from nature itself. And if certain laws are found among some repugnant to these principles, they were even with reluctance received and observed by a few, at length abrogated by contrary laws, and have fallen into desuetude.

From the knowledge of the natural law flows, even among the unregenerate, "so many" just and virtuous laws, and unjust laws are eventually replaced or ignored and tyrants are resisted and restrained.[43] Just laws naturally arise in nations almost completely dark with regard to the heavenly kingdom and apart from special revelation. And civil wickedness arises only from an abuse of the light of nature through "leisure ill employed." The suppression of the principles of natural law requires "struggling against and striving with all their might to extinguish it" (11.1.19).[44] Turretin even states that men have "by nature in them an earnest desire" for the "good of socie-

---

[43] Calvin suggests this in the following. "This also is the dictate of nature; that is, that an end will some time be to unjust plunders…. [T]yrants and their cruelty cannot be endured without great weariness and sorrow; for indignity on account of evil deeds kindles within the breasts of all, so that they become wearied when they see that wicked men are not soon restrained. Hence almost the whole world sound forth these words, How long, how long? When any one disturbs the whole world by his ambition and avarice, or everywhere commits plunders, or oppresses miserable nations,—when he distresses the innocent, all cry out, How long? And this cry, proceeding as it does from the feeling of nature and the dictate of justice, is at length heard by the Lord. For how comes it that all, being touched with weariness, cry out, How long? except that they know that this confusion of order and justice is not to be endured?" *Commentary on the Twelve Minor Prophets: Habakkuk, Zephaniah, Haggai,* 93 (comments on Habakkuk 2:6). In his *Institutes,* Calvin identifies the resistance to *real* injustice and *true* tyrants as one of the few defects of the pagan civil life. The other defect is the "depraved desires" that "the mind can quietly indulge." Hence, the common defects of pagan civil life are outward resistance to injustice and tyranny and the quiet, inward indulgence of desire. External order resists the "grosser forms" of vice. See *Institutes,* 243 [2.2.24].

[44] Full quote: "If various wicked laws obtained among the heathen, repugnant to the natural law (such as those sanctioning idolatry, human sacrifices, permitting theft, rapine, homicide, incest), they do not prove that no light of reason granted to men by nature…. Rather they prove only that men with leisure ill employed have wickedly abused the conceded light and, by struggling against the striving with all their might to extinguish it, were given over to a reprobate mind" (*IET,* 2:6 [11.1.19]).

ty" (11.1.16). Since there is universal desire for "honesty and order in human society," there must be a natural law. For, he writes, "This moral right and government of God [i.e., natural law] being taken away, all the foundations of right will be removed...[along with] all the laws of men which could have flowed from no other source." The result is that the "world [would] be turned into mere confusion and villainy" (11.1.16). But because it is not villainous—since "the commonest principle (that good should be done and evil avoided) is unshaken in all" (11.1.20)—there is a natural law and its force on human conscience and society remains.[45]

Turretin suggests here that the natural law, as it pertains to earthly duty, is a force suppressed only through active and aggressive resistance with deliberate intention to prevent its proper application to the political community. Eventually, however, political communities, seeking the good of society, recognize and enact just laws (though imperfectly). This should surprise us, not because it contradicts anything we have discussed so far, but because it runs so counter to popular opinion on the Calvinist theology of depravity and sin. Unregenerate pagan communities that do not struggle against and strive to extinguish the natural law naturally conform, albeit incompletely, to the natural law.[46]

Turretin's account of the natural law directly contradicts the Hobbesian view of the origins civil morality: The Reformed orthodox "affirm that there is a natural law, not arising from a voluntary contract or law of society, but from a divine obligation being impressed by God upon the conscience of man in his very creation" (11.1.7). It should be obvious by now that Reformed theology, according to Turretin, does not predict the world of Walzer's Hobbesian Calvinist. It is important to recognize, however, that Turretin's account shows Walzer's Calvinist to have a theoretically coherent view of fallen man. At the destruction of the natural law, says Turretin, "all government, honesty and order in human society will perish and the world be turned in mere confusion and villainy." Further, he writes, "all things

---

[45] Calvin states, "As to the precepts of the Second Table, there is considerably more knowledge of them, inasmuch as they are more closely connected with the preservation of civil society" (*Institutes*, 243 [2.2.24]).

[46] To be sure, the first-table precepts of the Decalogue, which dictate proper worship, are part of the natural law. With few exceptions, such as the laws of the early Roman leader Numa (see Plutarch's *Lives* "Numa" 8.7), pagan communities did not conform to natural principles of worship, mainly due to worship being a heaven-directed activity. See Calvin's *Institutes*, 243 [2.2.24].

would be equally lawful: to hate God as well as to love him; to kill parents as well as to honor them, and each one's own will would be to him for a reason and a law, so that he might do whatever he pleased" (11.1.16). It is a Hobbesian world, and it is a world Turretin rejects precisely because there remains an active and universal moral order even in a post-lapsarian world.

Pagan Moral Action

The remaining capabilities of fallen man that prove so useful for the implementation of just laws in a political community are not limited to the political elite. The average person, or non-elites, also earnestly desire the good of society and seek to perform right actions and abstain from unjust actions.[47] In his discussion on free will, Turretin states (10.4.3):

> We do not deny that some strength still remains in man after the fall as to those external and civil good works, so that he can exercise justice and temperance, put forth acts of mercy and charity, abstain from theft and homicide, and exhibit the operations of similar virtues, with the antecedent concourse and general help of God, to which the virtues of the heathen belong.

The unregenerate can be just and temperate, exercise mercy and charity, avoid criminal activity, and exhibit civil virtues. They can achieve an astonishing degree of civil uprightness. Not only can the elite know and legislate law conforming to the natural law, the non-elites know and act in accordance with civil duty.

---

[47] Althusius writes, "There is a knowledge and natural inclination for this law [i.e., the natural law] in the human heart. Because of it, a person knows what is just and is urged by the hidden impulse of nature to do what is just and to not do what is unjust." However, knowledge of and tendency towards the natural law differs from person to person and nation to nation. He writes, "Moreover, although those principles of nature are one and the same to all nations, still they differ in the level and means of their inscribing and urging. In fact, these principles are not equally inscribed on the hearts of all; in some, they are inscribed more eloquently, abundantly, and effectively, while in others not eloquently, but sparingly, according to God's will for inscribing and teaching." *On Law and Power*, trans. Jeffrey J. Veenstra. (Grand Rapids: CLP Academic, 2013), 9, 10–11. Turretin agrees (*IET*, 2:6–7 [11.1.21]).

Ultimately these works, however, are not meritorious or good before God. Free will remains in man with regard to earthly objects, because free will "can never be taken away from man in whatever state he may be" (10.3.11). But man, having lost the spiritual gifts that orient one towards heavenly objects, does not have free will with regard to the true God and spiritual realities. "Man has no strength for heavenly things either in his intellect or will from which faculties the free will arises" (10.4.13). And since what constitutes righteousness is exercising both man's essential properties and the perfecting qualities, the loss of the latter makes man's externally good works nothing but, as Augustine said (and quoted by Turretin), "splendid sins." Still, they are *civilly* good works and conducive to the proper ordering of society.

The distinction between civil good and ultimate good permits us to say that though *before God* all unregenerate actions are regarded by God as sinful, *before man* their works can be celebrated and, to repeat Althusius, can be "just, innocent, and upright." For this reason, Turretin can claim (1.4.17):

> Although some of the heathen (comparatively considered and in relation to each other) may have been better than others; although their works civilly and morally speaking may be called virtues, and so followed by the double reward of a well-regulated life, both positive (as productive of some temporal good and peace of conscience in this world) and negative (as making their punishment more tolerable), nevertheless (theologically speaking and relatively to God) their works best in form were nothing than more splendid sins and in the sight of God worthy of no reward.

The heathen can have "civilly and morally" virtuous works, achieve a well-regulated life (which produces temporal good and peace of conscience), and even reduce divine punishment. Turretin is not conceding too much here. Man is either righteous or unrighteous, and since righteousness is having and exercising those essential properties and perfecting qualities necessary for righteousness, exercising only the former is unrighteousness before God and unworthy of a heavenly reward, *even if* the action deserves a civil parade in honor and praise of it. The consequence is that the Calvinist, according to Turretin, can praise excellent actions while never conceding that the work is ultimately meritorious.

What precisely makes a moral action good and acceptable before God? To answer this we should first look at Turretin's view of sin (9.13.4). Sin occurs in two ways: by the act itself or some accidental defect of the act. An act itself is sinful when the substance of the act is contrary or prohibited by the law of God or commanded by the law and not fulfilled. An act is accidentally sinful when an action that is "otherwise good is performed badly" i.e., when the substance of the act is good but some necessary quality is missing (e.g., a good intention). The actions good in substance are bad with regard to "internal rectitude of heart and intention of the end" (10.5.2).[48] A work ultimately acceptable to God is an external action that conforms to God's law and is performed with internal conformity to the proper principle, form or mode, and end. The principle is that which "proceeds from a heart purified by faith" (10.5.4). The form or mode is an action "exercised sincerely and honestly" and from "spiritual obedience" in accordance with the "spiritual law of God" (9.13.4; 10.5.4). The end is performing the action to the glory of God. The unregenerate cannot satisfy these internal conditions.[49] Turretin writes, (10.5.4):

> For in reference to the principle, they could not proceed from faith or a clean heart (of which they were destitute); so as to the mode, they had no internal and spiritual obedience; and as to the end, no direction to the glory of God.... Now a good work is from an entire cause, but an evil work from even a single defect.

---

[48] Calvin likewise stated, "No work, however praised and applauded by the world, is valued before God's tribunal, except it proceeds from a pure heart." *Commentary on the Twelve Minor Prophets: Habakkuk, Zephaniah, Haggai*, 371 (comments on Haggai 2:1–10). Althusius wrote, "If the external and civil life of words, deeds and works is accompanied by faith—together with holiness of thought and desire, and with right purpose, namely, the glory of God—then it becomes theological. So therefore, when the works of the Decalogue are performed by the Christian to the glory of God because of true faith, they are pleasing to God" (*Politica*, 147).

[49] Calvin similar wrote, "When they speak of works morally good, they refer only to the outward deeds; they regard not the fountain or motive, nor even the end. When the heart of man is impure, unquestionably the work which thense flows is also ever impure, and is an abomination before God....[T]he deed, however splendid it may appear, is filth in the presence of God." *Commentary on the Twelve Minor Prophets: Jonah, Micah, Nahum*, 67 (comments on Jonah 1:16).

A good work before God is one that is both in substance good and performed in accordance with the necessary perfecting accidental qualities. These accidental qualities can accompany an act good in substance only when the actor has the requisite capabilities, namely, the spiritual/supernatural gifts. Regeneration restores these gifts, which were once native, but now adventitious and supernatural (5.10.16, 21; 5.11.2, 3). The unregenerate, of course, does not have these supernatural gifts.

With the distinction between act and mode, which corresponds with substance and accident, Turretin could say that "the moral actions of the heathen are not sins per se…but by accident" (10.5.6).[50] They do not meet the "essential conditions," because they do not perform the action with internal rectitude. The fact that any action is only accidentally sinful does not reduce the severity of the sin. For just as the spiritual qualities, native and original to man, though lost, perfect man, these internal qualities of good actions perfect works. And just as the loss of the perfecting qualities makes man unworthy of heavenly life, the lack of the perfecting qualities of works good in substance makes the works unworthy of heavenly reward.

The achievement of Turretin is a theological system that consistently affirms, however inconsistent it might seem at first, the possibility that one can be simultaneously both unrighteousness before God and righteous before man. One can be externally innocent, yet guilty before God. One can be an upright citizen of the earthly city and yet lack citizenship in heaven.

Walzer's account of Calvinism is already undermined and does not require extensive examination. The Reformed theological tradition affirms a positive role for natural role in the ordering of human society, contrary to many of its interpreters and popular opinion. Walzer's account is false, at least with regard to the tradition that culminated in the work of Turretin. The Fall did not extinguish natural law and image of God in man. Reason and free will, though corrupted, remained, since these properties are essential to man *qua* man. Man is even drawn to the natural law, which is a "force" upon man's conscience, and must actively struggle against it. Con-

---

[50] As Ursinus stated, "the difference which exists between the works of the righteous and the wicked, goes to prove that the moral works of the wicked are sins, but yet not such sins as those which are in their own nature opposed to the law of God: for these are sins in themselves, and according to their very nature, while the moral works of the wicked are sins merely by an accident; viz., on account of some defect, either because they do not proceed from a true faith, or are not done to the glory of God" *Commentary*, 849. See also his "Table of Good Works," 850.

trary to Walzer, Taylor, and Hancock, the Reformed theological tradition, through at least the 17th century, while retaining its distinctives, is manifestly consonant with the broader Christian natural law tradition.

3. CONCLUSION

Having completed our exposition of Turretin, the following is an attempt to apply some of the conclusions from this exposition to Reformed political theology.

Regeneration, while fundamentally reorienting the individual to ultimate good and restoring the individual both to God and man's original eschatological destination, does not necessarily radically change one's outward behavior, nor the principles from which one behaved prior to conversion. Other than one's religious observance, it is possible that a convert will not change as to the substance of one's civil acts much at all, since his civil life, though full of sin due to a failure to meet the internal conditions of good works, could have been externally good. This is *possible*, though not probable. In most cases, a convert, while not radically changing outward, civil behavior, will change in important and noticeable ways. The point, however, is simply that the restoration of one's heavenly orientation (i.e., spiritual gifts) is *always* radical and is the chief object of redemption, completing man and therefore strengthening his whole being. But this restoration is *not* fundamentally (though secondarily) for the restoration of civil morals.

Moreover, if past unregenerate societies had "laws concerning equity and virtue enacted by heathen legislatures, drawn from nature itself" (11.1.13) and that all societies tend toward the establishment of civil order and the fulfillment of civil duty (and even requires a "struggle" by the elite not to), then civil justice is a secondary effect of the Gospel, not its direct object. There is no Social Gospel, if by the term we refer to the implementation of some radical social system that is impossible to enact apart from special revelation and regeneration. The Gospel might restore civil order and natural justice in some cases and correct it in others, but it does not restore an order at odds with the natural order. Nor is human society a blank slate, moldable to some adventitious design and subject to pure "human decision." The Gospel *corrects*, in individuals and societies, defects in conformity to natural justice and civil order; it does not fundamentally transform societies. The Gospel is radical, not in earthly matters, but in heavenly ones. Furthermore, if the natural law continues to be a force for conformity in human society, we ought not to look at past unregenerate societies and their similarities with profound suspicion. Turretin's repeated appeal to the consent of the nations suggests the opposite, namely, that similarities we find in human societies of all times indicate the will of nature's God. Calvin himself called the "consent of all nations" on "principles of equity and justice" the "voice of God."[51]

This calls into question Wolterstorff's claim that the Reformation inaugurated a social project to transform the world's "fallen social systems," a claim that relies on, among other things, the natural law having no positive role in properly ordering the social systems of unregenerate communities. If the natural law has a post-lapsarian positive function in the political community, then the social order produced by the nations of history is a reliable indicator of the *natural* order ordained by God. And, indeed, the consent of the nations suggests that the natural order for human society is hierarchical, the same set of social systems that Wolterstorff calls for the saints to dismantle. Calvin himself states that "natural reason itself dictates" the need for a "distinction of ranks" in society.[52] It is a "natural order."[53] And those in the higher ranks possess greater political responsibility than the average person, for "the nearer they have been brought to God, the more sacredly are they bound to proclaim his goodness."[54] Further, according to Calvin, internal spiritual equality in Christ has no relevance to outward, civil order, for "Christ did not come to mix up nature." He writes,

---

[51] Full quote: "But as some principles of equity and justice remain in the hearts of men, the consent of all nations is as it were the voice of nature, or the testimony of that equity which is engraven on the hearts of men, and which they can never obliterate." *Commentary*, 93 (comments on Habakkuk 2:6).

[52] Calvin, *Commentaries on the Four Last Books of Moses: A Harmony*, vol. II, trans. Charles William Bingham. (Grand Rapids: Baker Books, 2005), 221 (comments on Numbers 3:5). See also *Institutes*. 3.10.6 and comments in his commentaries on Genesis 6:4; Psalms 87:6, 148.11; Isaiah 1:13, 14:3, 24:2; Daniel 4:13–16; Lecture 26 on Hosea; Luke 1:52; Cor. 11:3, 15:24 and Eph. 6:5–9. Calvin does, however, reject hereditary political regimes. See his comments on Micah 5:5.

[53] John Calvin, *Men, Women and Order in the Church: Three Sermons by John Calvin*, trans. Seth Skolnitsky (Dallas: Presbyterian Heritage Publications, 1992), 49.

[54] Calvin, *Commentary on the Books of Psalms*, vol. 5, trans. James Anderson (Grand Rapids: Bakers Books, 2005), 308 (comments on Psalm 148:11).

> Regarding the kingdom of God (which is spiritual) there is
> no distinction or difference between man and woman,
> servant and master, poor and rich, great and small. Never-
> theless, there does have to be some order among us, and
> *Jesus Christ did not mean to eliminate it.*[55]

The evidence supports a reading of Calvin as a consistent adherent of natural social hierarchy. Turretin also affirms that social distinction is neces-sary for the existence of human society (11.2.18, 19). Many others in the Christian tradition embraced social hierarchy as well.[56] The social realm is not then a realm of "human decision," but one of *conformity* to the natural order. The Reformed tradition is far more consistent with the medieval no-tions of hierarchy than the modern one of equality. Further, pagan society is not necessarily, nor should we expect it to be, a thoroughly "fallen struc-ture, in need of reform." Christianity is less "world-forming" than it is "world-perfecting": the restoration not of civil ethics, but of adorning indi-viduals and political societies with the proper worship of God.

There are many more implications for political theology that must be drawn out elsewhere. It is important to recognize here, even if the reader does not agree with the application above, that the one's view of the possi-bility of pagan virtue affects not only one's political theology, but also his view of the principal restorative effects of the Gospel, theological anthro-pology, the nature of sin, the natural law, and more. Indeed, accounts of Reformed theology such as Walzer's would have significant effects throughout one's theology. The possibility of the civilly virtuous pagan is a *consequence* of the Reformed theological system, not an idea forced into it. Walzer's take would wreak havoc in Reformed theology, possibility under-mining it.

The greatest and most unexpected implication of this exposition on Turretin and pagan virtue is not about virtuous pagans. It is that the Gospel is the achievement and declaration of salvation with the chief purpose of

---

[55] Calvin, *Men, Women*, 19–20. Emphasis mine. See also Perez Zagorin *Rebels and Rulers, 1500–1600*, vol. 1 (Cambridge: Cambridge University Press, 1982), 155.

[56] See Aquinas *Summa Theologica* I.96.4; *Summa Contra Gentiles* III.97; Richard Hook-er, *Of the Laws of Ecclesiastical Polity*, Book 8, Section 2; John Winthrop, "A Model of Christian Charity" (first couple paragraphs of the sermon); Robert L. Dabney, *Sys-tematic Theology* (St. Louis: Presbyterian Publishing, 1878), 868–69. For "Anglican" views of hierarchy, see Walzer, *Revolution of the Saints*, 155–58.

restoring the *true worship of God*—the reverence and awe directed at another world. Such worship declares the true end of the Gospel and reminds us of the world as the *metaxy*, the time 'in-between,' and the not-yet. The second coming of Christ, not the first, inaugurates the fundamental transformation of the cosmic order (a new order based on *spiritual*, not civil merit). And this revolution is His; it is not the revolution of the saints.

BIBLIOGRAPHY

Althusius, Johannes. *On Law and Power*. Translated by Jeffrey J. Veenstra. Grand Rapids: CLP Academic, 2013.

_____. *Politica*, edited and translated by Frederick S. Carney. Indianapolis: Liberty Fund, 1995.

Calvin, John. *Commentaries on the Four Last Books of Moses*. Vol. 2, translated by Charles William Bingham. Grand Rapids: Baker Books, 2005.

_____. *Commentary on the Books of Psalms*. Vol. 5, translated by James Anderson. Grand Rapids: Bakers Books, 2005.

_____. *Commentary on the Prophet Isaiah*. Vol. 2, translated by William Pringle. Grand Rapids: Baker Books, 2005.

_____. *Commentary on the Twelve Minor Prophets: Habakkuk, Zephaniah, Haggai*, translated by John Owen. Grand Rapids: Baker Books, 2005.

_____. *Commentary on the Twelve Minor Prophets: Jonah, Micah, Nahum*, translated by John Owen. Grand Rapids: Baker Books, 2005.

_____. *Institutes of the Christian Religion*, translated by Henry Beveridge. Grand Rapids: Eerdmans Publishing, 1989.

_____. *Men, Women and Order in the Church: Three Sermons by John Calvin*, translated by Seth Skolnitsky. Dallas: Presbyterian Heritage Publications, 1992.

Dabney, Robert L. *Systematic Theology*. St. Louis: Presbyterian Publishing, 1878.

Hobbes, Thomas. *Leviathan*, edited by Edwin Curley. Cambridge: Hackett Publishing Company, 1994.

Grabill, Stephen. *Rediscovering the Natural law in Reformed Theological Ethics*. Grand Rapids: Eerdmans Publishing Company, 2006.

Hancock, Ralph C. *Calvin and the Foundations of Modern Politics*. Ithaca: Cornell University Press, 1989.

Junius, Franciscus. The Mosaic Polity. Translated by Todd M. Rester. Grand Rapids: CLP Academic, 2015.

Muller, Richard A. "Scholasticism Protestant and Catholic: Francis Turretin on the Object and Principles of Theology." *Church History* 55, no. 2 (June 1986): 193–205.

Nolan, Kirk. *Reformed Virtue after Barth: Developing Moral Virtue Ethics in the Reformed Tradition.* Louisville: Westminster John Knox Press, 2014.

Shannon, Nathan D. *Shalom and the Ethics of Belief: Nicholas Wolterstorff's Theology of Situated Rationality.* Eugene: Pickwick Publishing, 2015.

Taylor, Charles. *Sources of the Self: The Making of the Modern Identity.* Cambridge: Harvard University Press, 1989.

Turretin, Francis. *Institutes of Elenctic Theology.* 3 Volumes, translated by George Musgrave Giger. Phillipsburg: P&R Publishing, 1994.

Ursinus, Zacharias. *The Commentary of Dr. Zacharias Ursinus on the Heidelberg Catechism*, translated by G. W. Williard. The Synod of the Reformed Church in the United States, 2004.

VanDrunen, David. *Natural Law and the Two Kingdoms: A Study in the Development of Reformed Social Thought.* Grand Rapids: Eerdmans, 2010.

Walzer, Michael. *Revolution of the Saints: A Study in the Origins of Radical Politics.* London: Harvard University Press, 1965.

Wolfe, Stephen. "Reformed Natural Law and the American Founding: A Critique of Recent Scholarship." In *For Law and For Liberty: Essays on the Trans-Atlantic Legacy of Protestant Political Thought*, edited by W. Bradford Littlejohn, 21–60. Moscow, ID: The Davenant Trust, 2016.

_____. "The American Founding and the Harmony of Reason and Revelation: A Rediscovery of Calvinist Sources." In *History of Political Thought.* 2017, forthcoming.

Wolterstorff, Nicholas. *Until Justice and Peace Embrace.* Grand Rapids: Eerdmans Publishing Company, 1983.

ABOUT THE DAVENANT TRUST

The Davenant Trust supports the renewal of Christian wisdom for the con-temporary church. It seeks to sponsor historical scholarship at the intersec-tion of the church and academy, build networks of friendship and collabo-ration within the Reformed and evangelical world, and equip the saints with time-tested resources for faithful public witness.

We are a nonprofit organization supported by your tax-deductible gifts. Learn more about us, and donate, at www.davenanttrust.org.

Made in the USA
Monee, IL
19 April 2023

32089441R00108